D1400679

Primer for Treating Substance Abusers

∞

LIBRARY OF SUBSTANCE ABUSE AND ADDICTION TREATMENT

A Series of Books Edited By
Jerome David Levin, Ph.D.

Substance abuse and addiction are the third most common cause of mortality in the United States. They are among the most prevalent mental illnesses, not only in the United States, but throughout the world. They are also notoriously difficult to treat. Mental health professionals see few patients whose lives or illnesses have not been profoundly affected by their own use or that of their families or peers. Addiction is not peripheral but central to the human condition and research into it is illuminating our understanding of self.

The *Library of Substance Abuse and Addiction Treatment* is dedicated to providing mental health professionals with the tools they need to treat these scourges—tools ranging from scientific knowledge to clinical technique. Nonideological, it is equally open to behavioral, cognitive, disease model, psychodynamic, and least harm perspectives. An overdetermined disorder affecting millions of people requires multiple viewpoints if it is to be successfully treated. The *Library* provides those multiple perspectives for clinicians, students, and laypeople as articulated by the most insightful workers in the field. Practical, utilitarian, scholarly, and state-of-the-art, these books are addressed to all who wish to deepen their understanding of and increase their clinical efficacy in treating addiction.

Primer for Treating Substance Abusers
Jerome D. Levin

Treatment of Alcoholism and Other Addictions: *A Self-Psychology Approach*
Jerome D. Levin

Recovery from Alcoholism:
Beyond Your Wildest Dreams
Jerome D. Levin

Couple and Family Therapy of Addiction
Jerome D. Levin

The Dynamics and Treatment of Alcoholism: *Essential Papers*
Jerome D. Levin and Ronna Weiss, Editors

Gender and Addictions:
Men and Women in Treatment
S. Lala Ashenberg Straussner
and Elizabeth Zelvin, Editors

Psychodynamics of Drug Dependence
Jack D. Blaine and
Demetrios A. Julius, Editors

The Hidden Dimension:
Psychodynamics in Compulsive Drug Use
Leon Wurmser

Substance Abusing High Achievers:
Addiction as an Equal Opportunity Destroyer
Abraham J. Twerski

Creating the Capacity for Attachment:
Treating Addictions and the Alienated Self
Karen B. Walant

Psychotherapy of Cocaine Addiction:
Entering the Interpersonal World of the Cocaine Addict
David Mark and Jeffrey Faude

Drug Dependence:
The Disturbances in Personality Functioning that Create the Need for Drugs
Henry Krystal and Herbert A. Raskin

Treating Addiction as a Human Process
Edward J. Khantzian

∞

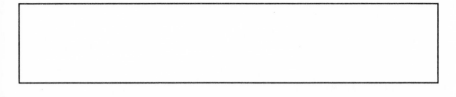

Primer for Treating Substance Abusers

Jerome David Levin, Ph.D.

JASON ARONSON INC.
Northvale, New Jersey
London

The author gratefully acknowledges permission to reprint material from the following sources: "Smoke Gets In Your Eyes," written by Jerome Kern and Otto Harbach, copyright © 1933 PolyGram International Publishing, Inc. Copyright renewed. Used by permission. All rights reserved. "Renascence," by Edna St. Vincent Millay. Used by permission of Elizabeth Barnett.

This book was set in 11 pt. Times Roman by Alpha Graphics of Pittsfield, NH and printed and bound by Book-mart Press, Inc. of North Bergen, NJ.

Library of Congress Cataloging-in-Publication Data

Levin, Jerome D. (Jerome David)
    Primer for treating substance abusers / Jerome David Levin.
      p. cm.
    Includes bibliographical references and index.
    ISBN 0-7657-0078-6
    1. Substance abuse—Treatment. I. Title.
RC564.L4825   1998
616.86'06—dc21   98-6397

Printed in the United States of America on acid-free paper. Jason Aronson offers books and cassettes. For information and catalog write to Jason Aronson Inc., 230 Livingston Street, Northvale, New Jersey 07647-1726. Or visit our website: http://www.aronson.com

Since I was

"in unity defective, which requires
collateral love, and dearest amity,"

I found them in my wife, Ginny,
to whom this book is dedicated

It is good for me to bear with their ignorance . . .

and not put impatient knowledge in the stead of loving wisdom.

George Eliot, *Daniel Deronda*

It is the Ego which is the arch-enemy of sobriety. . . .

The object of therapy is permanently to reduce the Ego and its activity.

Harry Tiebout

Contents

Acknowledgments

I would like to thank the usual suspects, as well as my publisher, Jason Aronson, at whose suggestion this book came into being.

I also wish to acknowledge my debts to Judy Cronin who turned roughly dictated cassettes into a manuscript with great skill; and to Judy Cohen, production editor, and the rest of the staff at Jason Aronson who made this book a reality.

As always, my patients proved to be my best teachers and supervisors.

I

Defining and Diagnosing Substance Abuse and Addiction

Introduction

Substance abuse treatment is both the same as, and different from, other psychotherapies. The fact that substances have powerful pharmacological effects and distort bodily functioning, cognition, affect, and interpersonal relations must be taken into consideration in the treatment of the substance abuser. The medical complications of substance abuse as well as the psychiatric complications sometimes make crisis intervention necessary. However, all substance abuse treatment is not a matter of crisis intervention. There are many kinds of learning that go on in substance abuse treatment. Modifications of attitudes, inculcation of knowledge, and the working through of emotional conflict all occur in the course of substance abuse treatment. One purpose of this primer is to put into perspective the use of various modalities, ranging from the cognitive to the psychodynamic, in the treatment of substance abuse and addiction. In speaking of substance abuse, I have in mind primarily addiction to chemicals of various sorts; however, other addictions such as compulsive gambling, compulsive sexuality, and some forms of what Karen Horney (1942, 1945) many years ago called morbid dependency, more currently known as codependency, are strikingly similar to substance abuse in their dynamics if not entirely in their phenomenology since the pharmacological complications are missing. Although this book focuses on chemicals and their abuse, essentially the same principles apply in working with such disorders as compulsive gambling.

There is more discussion of alcoholism than any other addiction in this primer simply because we know far more about alcoholism than we know about the other chemical addictions. Therefore, I use alcoholism as a paradigm. These days, most patients abuse more than one substance so that the distinctions in the dynamics of the use of the various drugs become more and more blurred; nevertheless, the drug of choice is significant and says something about the cultural situation, developmental level, and emotional needs of the user. I use the terms *substance abuse* and *addiction* interchangeably, although addiction has the broader meaning encompassing various nonchemical compulsions.

Substance abuse is a radically overdetermined condition. Its etiology is extremely complex, involving pharmacological, sociological, cultural, cognitive, familial, interpersonal, and intrapsychic components. Accordingly, the only approach that does justice to such a complex phenomenon is a biopsychosocial approach. Although this primer is not formally organized around the biopsychosocial dimensions, I repeatedly return to each of these three dimensions of substance abuse. Accordingly, treatment must be multimodal. Perhaps "must" is too strong a way of putting it, but multimodal approaches are certainly preferable and have the highest success rate. They should address all aspects of this complex disorder. Among the modalities employed in substance abuse treatment are detoxification, a medical procedure; inpatient rehabilitation programs of various sorts; therapeutic communities; cognitive and behavioral treatments; self-help support groups; family therapy; and psychodynamic therapy.

A word about how to use this primer. It can be profitably read either straight through or as a reference text in which the reader turns to the topic that is currently of interest and puts the book aside until the next occasion for consulting it arises. For this reason, some material and some case illustrations appear in more than one place, in each of which they have relevance. This should not seriously hinder the cover-to-cover reader, as the very complexity of the material makes some redundancy desirable. It is my hope that the catechism-like structure of questions and answers of this primer does not preclude its presenting an integrated picture of a complex phenomenon.

What is substance abuse?

Substance abuse, addiction, and alcoholism have all been defined in maddeningly and bewilderingly disparate ways. This makes it extraordinarily difficult to read and interpret the research literature, which is often talking about different phenomena while purporting to speak of the same phenomenon. More saliently for our purposes, our clinical course is not clear until we know what we are treating, and the bewildering and indeed contradictory definitions of substance abuse, alcoholism, and addiction make diagnosis extraordinarily difficult. The *Diagnostic and Statistical Manual* of the American Psychiatric Association, fourth edition (*DSM-IV*) has Axis I diagnoses of substance abuse and substance dependence, which differ in their severity. Substance abuse involves the ongoing use of substances in such a way as to damage the user in one or another vital life area. Substance dependence, although it does not imply physiological dependence as it did in the *DSM-III-R*, does entail the compulsive use of the substance because the cessation of that use would lead to serious and painful adverse consequences, which range from potentially fatal medical complications of withdrawal to intense psychological pain. These are not mutually incompatible; one can be physiologically *and* psychologically dependent on the substance of abuse.

The *DSM-IV* also has an Axis I category of substance-induced disorders. For the most part these are transient and are seen mostly in early sobriety; however, unfortunately, some of them are highly persistent. For example, there is the phenomenon of postcocaine anxiety disorder. This is found mostly in people who freebased or injected cocaine for extended periods of time and have now altered their neurochemistry in such a way as to make them extraordinarily vulnerable to anxiety. It is a difficult condition to treat psychopharmacologically or psychotherapeutically. In fact, some sufferers of this disorder simply have to accommodate to living with high anxiety states, perhaps forever. Another example of a post–

substance use disorder would be flashbacks following the extensive use of hallucinogenics.

I would define substance abuse rather simply. If the use of the drug is hurting the user in a major life area such as health, interpersonal relations, or educational or vocational achievement, then it is a case of substance abuse. The severity of that abuse varies and is partly gauged by the amount the person uses but even more importantly by what it is doing to the user. The salient question is how much damage it is doing.

When I had my appendix removed many years ago, my roommate was in the hospital for his tenth or twentieth—I don't quite recall—amputation. These amputations were necessitated by his compulsive smoking. (He suffered from Buerger's disease, which constricts the capillaries.) Nevertheless, he was driving the nurses to distraction, sneaking cigarettes around the oxygen lines. My roommate was an extremely clear case of substance abuse.

There are other situations in which the diagnosis is much less clear. Generally speaking, severity makes the diagnosis manifest. If someone has a history of delirium tremens (DTs), has been fired from several jobs for drinking, and has a cirrhotic liver, clearly that person is alcoholic. But how about the surgeon who has a few martinis before dinner, wine with dinner, and sometimes takes a Valium in the morning to make sure his hands are steady during surgery? Is that addiction? Is that substance abuse? It is not all that clear. The diagnosis of addiction or substance abuse is partly subjective. In different times and places different degrees of substance abuse have been normative. Among the Camba, a Mestizo tribe in Bolivia, drunkenness is the norm and no one considers it abnormal or pathological, with the possible exception of American anthropologists. But even there, the anthropologist (Heath 1958) who did most of the work studying this tribe did not really define such culturally syntonic drinking as pathological. In the '90s, Americans drink less, there is less tolerance of drunkenness, and there is a "war" on drugs. Thus, what is socially acceptable and normative has clearly changed. The clinician is caught in a dilemma between underdiagnosing—an easy thing to do since many patients never mention their substance use, minimize it, don't see it because of psychodynamic unconscious denial, or consciously dissemble, so that we miss the essence of the problem—and overdiagnosing by going to the opposite extreme and seeing addiction in every sip of wine. Overzealousness is as wrongheaded as taking denial at face value; as Sir Toby says in *Twelfth Night* (II, 3, 117–8): "Dost thou think, because thou art virtuous, there shall be no more cakes and ale?"

> *What are the* DSM-IV *criteria for substance abuse and dependence?*

The *DSM-IV* presents us with a shopping list of symptoms for each of its disease entities. A certain number of these symptoms must be present for the diagnosis to be made. In the case of substance abuse, one of these four must be present: recurrent substance use resulting in major problems at home, school, or work; recurrent substance use in situations where it is dangerous; substance-related legal problems; or continued substance use in spite of having had problems. The symptom must have occurred during the past year and constitute a maladaptive pattern of substance use. This is circular reasoning and really doesn't tell us much. Nevertheless, these are the criteria by which substance abuse is diagnosed.

The criterion for substance dependence is the same maladaptive pattern of substance abuse also characterized by three or more of the following: tolerance (that is, needing more of the drug to get the same effect); withdrawal (that is, having some sort of symptoms once one stops using the drug); taking more than intended, or needing larger amounts; multiple unsuccessful efforts to cut down or control use; investing a great deal of energy in obtaining the substance; the giving up of other activities; or continuing to use in spite of serious physical or psychological problems secondary to the substance use. In addition, according to the *DSM-IV* schema one can specify with or without physiological dependence. This is not bad; the list is helpful. However, it doesn't add an awful lot to common sense. What it amounts to is that we simply have to be alert to how much the drug use is hurting the person and how central it is to the complex of problems he or she presents in the treatment.

What are the major categories of drugs of abuse?

The sorts of substances people abuse generally fall into one of five categories: central nervous system depressants, central nervous system stimulants, marijuana and hashish, opiates (narcotics), and hallucinogenics (psychedelics).

What are central nervous system depressants?

Central nervous system (CNS) depressants are drugs that reduce the activity of the central nervous system, slowing synaptic transmission and differentially depressing brain circuits. They are the most commonly used class of drugs of abuse. Among the central nervous system depressants commonly encountered are alcohol, the so-called minor tranquilizers including Valium, Librium, Xanax, Miltown, Atavan, and Halcyon. The minor tranquilizers are properly known as anxiolytics or antianxiety drugs. There are a host of other less frequently encountered anxiolytics. Also included in the category of CNS depressants are the barbiturates, including pentobarbital (Nembutal), secobarbital (Seconal), amobarbital (Amytal), phenobarbital (Luminal), and thiopental (Pentothal). General anesthetics and methaqualone (Quaaludes) are also central nervous system depressants. Although we seldom see addiction to anesthetics in the general population, among medical personnel—doctors, nurses, veterinarians, and pharmacists—addiction to inhalation anesthetics is not uncommon.

What are central nervous system stimulants?

Central nervous system stimulants, also known as uppers, are the third most popular drugs of abuse. The central nervous system stimulants increase the activity of the central nervous system, including the rate of synaptic transmission. Drugs in this category include cocaine, amphetamines, and crack. Methamphetamine is currently enjoying a vogue. Crack is cocaine that has been cooked with an alkali and is ready to smoke. Cooking cocaine with an alkali and smoking it is known as "freebasing." Uppers can be smoked, orally ingested as the amphetamines usually are, inhaled ("taking a line"), and injected or mainlined.

What are opiates?

Opiates are also called narcotics and they are characterized by having both depressant and analgesic effects. They are among the oldest drugs known to mankind and have been popular in many different times and places. They are highly addictive in the sense that one may need hundreds of times the initial dose to get the equivalent effect once tolerance has been established. They are also characterized by painful withdrawal. Among the opiates are opium, which is usually smoked; morphine, which is extracted from the opium poppy; heroin, a form of synthetic morphine originally developed to treat morphine addiction; methadone, developed during World War II as a painkiller; and codeine, which is a milder opiate also derived from the poppy plant. These drugs can be inhaled, usually called "snorting"; skin-popped, that is, worked under the skin for subcutaneous absorption; or mainlined, that is, injected into a vein.

What are marijuana and hashish?

Marijuana and hashish are extremely popular "recreational" drugs and are frequent drugs of abuse. Although there is some controversy about the matter, they do not appear to be physiologically addicting, but may be highly psychologically habituating. Hashish is much more potent than marijuana, but both drugs depend on tetrahydrocannabinal (THC) for their pharmacological effect. Marijuana and hashish are usually smoked; however, they can be baked into cookies and various other foodstuffs, a much slower and less efficient route of administration.

What are hallucinogenics?

Hallucinogenics, also known as psychedelics, are drugs that radically alter perception. Their use often leads to experiences of depersonalization and derealization. Among the most popular of them are LSD, mescaline, magic mushrooms, peyote, and psilocybin. People rarely become addicted to hallucinogenics, although they may develop psychological dependence on them.

Is alcoholism (addiction) a disease?

The disease concept of alcoholism has been promulgated and popularized by the self-help organization Alcoholics Anonymous (AA), but it has a long history. As early as the American Revolution, Benjamin Rush (1785), Surgeon General of the Revolutionary Army, adumbrated an anticipation of the modern concept of addiction as a disease. In his famous essay on inebriety, Rush stated that alcoholism is a disease, detailing many of the somatic complications of alcoholism, while also showing a fine awareness of the psychogenic aspects of the disease and of the psychological consequences of drinking.

In 1804, Thomas Trotter, a British physician, wrote a dissertation on alcoholism for his medical degree at Edinburgh in which he also advanced a disease model (Jellinek 1943). Trotter believed that alcoholism was caused by "premature weaning" and heredity—that is, by early trauma interacting with constitutional predisposition.

In modern times, William Silkworth, an internist in charge of Knickerbocker Hospital, an expensive drying-out tank in Manhattan in the '30s and '40s, described alcoholism as an obsession of the mind and an allergy of the body. Although this is more metaphorical than scientific, it is probably not far off. Bill Wilson, the cofounder of AA, knew Dr. Silkworth, having been detoxified many times in his hospital, and incorporated his particular form of the disease concept into the AA literature. It was, however, Emil Jellinek

(1960), in his ground-breaking book, *The Disease Concept of Alcoholism*, who made the disease concept scientifically respectable.

In that book, Jellinek looked at the many different possible meanings of alcoholism as a disease. He also looked at different drinking patterns and came to the conclusion that some were wisely described as diseases and some not. It was a form of alcoholism he called gamma alcoholism that seemed to him to be most clearly a disease. He thought it was a disease because it had two characteristics: (1) loss of control and (2) progression. By loss of control Jellinek meant that those who have crossed what AA calls the "invisible line" and who cannot predict what will happen if they pick up a drink have effectively lost the ability to regulate their consumption once they start drinking. This does not mean that they will always drink to unconsciousness, but that may very well happen even though it is not their intention. Loss of control essentially means loss of predictability. The progression part comes from a famous survey that Jellinek did of early AA groups in which he asked members to rank order their symptoms. He found there was a fairly invariant progression as their drinking proceeded, which either ended in abstinence and recovery or in madness, physical decline, or death. Jellinek's analysis of varying types of alcoholism is discussed in more detail on pages 23–25.

Jellinek's concept has been much criticized. His critics hold that later research has shown that the progression is by no means invariant, that problems associated with drinking come and go, and that the so-called loss of control is essentially tautological. Drinking to oblivion demonstrates loss of control according to disease model advocates, starting with Jellinek, while the critics say this may very well be a choice and have nothing to do with a disease process. I think Jellinek's critics have been unfair to him; his analysis is actually an extremely subtle one. He is well aware that there are many different patterns of drinking, not all of which are reasonably described as diseases, and he is also aware that there are forms of drinking in which something like loss of control does indeed occur and in which there is a definite progression in the sense that if the user continues to use, things get worse in the way that Jellinek predicted they would, even if not exactly in his order. Thus, it makes a good deal of sense to regard as diseases those patterns of drinking that lead to loss of control and demonstrate progression, patterns Jellinek called gamma alcoholism.

Supporting Jellinek and the disease concept from another perspective, there is currently a good deal of empirical research concerning predisposition to addiction, a predisposition increasingly understood in terms of levels of neurotransmitters, these levels being genetically controlled. Another way of saying this is that if you come into the world with one neurochemistry rather than another, you are more likely to become addicted.

There is also a body of evidence (Schuckit and Gold 1988) concerning the reaction of children of alcoholics to alcohol that is strikingly different, on the average, than the reaction of children of nonalcoholics, this being particularly true for sons of alcoholic fathers.

Definitions are decisions—they are prescriptive as well as descriptive. To regard alcoholism as a disease is a political, no less than a scientific, decision. Given the evidence of scientific research and Jellinek's conceptual analysis, it is reasonable to conclude that some forms of addiction are rightly described as diseases, however diseases not so much understood in terms of a model of an infectious disease such as pneumonia, but much more modeled on one such as hypertension, in which self-care and lifestyle are extremely potent determinants of the outcome of the disease. This is indeed the case with alcoholism.

The evidence for the appropriateness of the disease concept for other drugs of abuse is much weaker and is mostly based on analogy to alcoholism. It is my own view that much as in physics we have the law of complementarity in which electromagnetic phenomena are sometimes best explained as waves and sometimes as particles, in addiction we can best account for the data by viewing the addiction sometimes as a disease and sometimes as a symptom of some underlying disorder. Jellinek and the other apostles of the disease concept are very careful to distinguish between the diseases caused by the addiction, whether they be medical or psychiatric, and the disease of addiction itself. This is a crucial distinction that is sometimes lost.

What is problem drinking or drugging?

Problem drinking or drugging usually involves the reactive use of a substance to deal with a life crisis, a use leading to some sort of problem.

But it doesn't have to be that. The crisis may develop as a result of the pattern of using, a pattern that falls short of addiction and doesn't quite qualify as substance abuse. Nevertheless, the patient has a driving while intoxicated (DWI) citation, or a health problem, or some economic or interpersonal negative consequence of using that brings the patient to treatment. Problem drinkers and druggers may or may not go on to full-blown addiction, to alcoholism, or drug abuse. The survey literature tends to show that problems associated with use come and go, and don't necessarily progress according to Jellinek's (1960) model. However, such demographic and epidemiological research using questionnaires cross-sectionally has its own methodological problems, and these studies of problem drinking may underestimate the degree to which problem drinking progresses into something else. The distinction, however, between problem drinking and addiction is an important one. Someone who is truly addicted has, in my experience, little or no chance to return to the level of social use, while the problem drinker may be able to. The differential diagnosis is not a clear one or an easy one, and requires a very careful look at what effect the use is having on the patient's life, how persistent that use has been, how many problems have accompanied it, and the degree of resiliency and flexibility in both the patient's ego and the pattern of use. The more problems, the less likely the patient will be a candidate for control rather than abstinence.

As we have seen, Jellinek's version of the disease concept of alcoholism did not consider all forms of pathological drinking to be diseases. Almost all other observers agree with this. Generally speaking, the notion that alcoholism and drug addiction are diseases is restricted to the more malign and advanced cases. There are many instances of reactive substance abuse and reactive addiction. For example, someone has difficulty dealing with a severe loss and turns to alcohol to self-medicate the pain of mourning. This is an extremely common dynamic. It may or may not lead to alcoholism, although it will if the drinking continues long enough, but in itself it is better described as problem drinking. Had that same person turned to amphetamines to self-medicate his or her depression, then we would speak of problem drugging. Once again, continued use could lead to full-blown abuse or addiction, but the reactive type of use is not best so described. There is also much evidence from epidemiological studies that the symptoms and difficulties secondary to substance use tend to come and go, leading epidemiologists to conclude that problem drinking and drugging may be episodic rather than progressive. Jellinek casts some light on this; he has a category he calls *epsilon alcoholism* in distinction to the *gamma alcoholism* already discussed. Epsilons are periodics who go on "benders" separated by extended intervals of sobriety. Jellinek has various other categories (discussed in detail below) that do not fit the disease model. For example, *alpha alcoholism* is characterized by psychological, but not physiological, dependence, and is best seen as an emotional problem; *beta alcoholism* is culturally syntonic heavy drinking in which the person continues to drink, in spite of serious medical consequences, because it is normative and expected in the person's milieu. Problem drugging or drinking is somewhat parallel to the *DSM-IV*'s substance abuse category but does not precisely overlap with it, and *addiction* as I use the term is closer to the *DSM-IV* substance dependence category.

What is lifestyle substance use?

Lifestyle substance use is the martini before, and wine with, dinner as part of one's daily routine, which involves considerable consumption of alcohol, but is culturally and ego syntonic for many people. In some forms of lifestyle consumption, the alcohol and the rituals around it are, mutatis mutandis, the smoking of the joint after work. Lifestyle use may be a very important part of life, and like any other time-consuming ritual has a powerful effect on those who live it. This effect is pervasive, impacting on relationship to self and to others, on values and on perception of reality, and on the body. There is a downside to lifestyle drinking, but that is true of all lifestyles. I would not consider this kind of lifestyle drinking or drugging pathological per se, but if I were taking an analytic stance in treating a patient, I would be very interested in the meaning of, and reasons for, "choosing" to drink in this way, just as I would be interested in the meaning of any other highly emotionally invested behavior.

Lifestyle drinking or drugging can also be viewed like culturally syntonic heavy and frequent use of alcohol or other drugs that seems to lead to few emotional, interpersonal, or physical problems. It is a style one may consider unwise—a value judgment—but it is certainly not a disease. Lifestyle drinkers and druggers sometimes become problematic drinkers and druggers, and after becoming problematic may progress into abuse or dependence. But other lifestylers are very stable and have their three martinis every day for sixty years, and no doubt somewhat blunt their emotions and do various other things to themselves, but do not have serious difficulties because of their martini drinking. In our obsessively work-driven culture, where work spills into everything, and efficiency and productivity are becoming our highest values, one can make an argument for the revival of the cocktail hour as a necessary punctuation between the workday and the cessation of work, clearly separating work from the realm of the personal and recreational. But then demarcations other than martinis are also possible.

What are the main etiological factors in the development of substance abuse and substance dependence?

Four factors contribute to any addiction: the pharmacology of the drug, the personality of the user, the environment of the user, and the constitutional predisposition or absence of it. Pharmacology, personality, environment, and heredity interact to drive an addiction. In each individual there will be a different mix of the four, usually with one predominating.

Mary was a saleswoman with no alcoholism in her family who traveled a great deal, entertained a great deal, was often alone, and gradually went from lifestyle drinking to problem drinking to abusive drinking. She seemed to have little genetic predisposition. She was not a woman with serious emotional conflicts, and the two factors that were most prominent in her addiction were (1) the pharmacology of alcohol, which builds tolerance and necessitates using more and more to get the same effect, as well as the toxic effects of alcohol (and it is a highly toxic drug); and (2) the environment, the subculture of the salesperson being an extremely potent factor in the development of Mary's alcoholism.

Joe, on the other hand, has much alcoholism in his family, a father who died in the DTs, and a grandfather who died of a cirrhotic liver, and he reacted strongly and pathologically to alcohol from the first drink. In his case, genetic predisposition was by far the most powerful factor.

Larry, a behaviorally heterosexual but strongly homosexually inclined man, turned to alcohol to mediate an intense internal conflict between id and superego. He became a psychodynamic alcoholic, in which the use of alcohol to lessen his internal psychological tension, combined with the addictive quality of alcohol, its pharmacology, led Larry down the slippery path to progression and eventually dependence.

Sam discovered cocaine when he flunked out of college. It instantly raised his self-esteem and enabled him to escape the deep depression his failure had induced in him. Here again, the psychological factor was by far the most powerful.

> *Could you give an example of an addiction with a strong constitutional predisposition?*

Hank is preprogrammed to self-destruct when he drinks. He knows this, but he can't stop trying to drink like everyone else. He isn't having much success in that endeavor. He is musing about his drinking.

What happened last night? I took the crew out for drinks and that's as far as I can take it. How did I get this black eye? The first time I got high, way back in tenth grade, it was a disaster. Wrecked Jim's house and his parents went bananas. I'm not a kid anymore. I can't get away with this shit. Why? Why can't I drink like other people? I'm general manager on a million-dollar construction project and I act like a drunken sailor. Nothing like this ever happens when I don't drink. I like my life. I'm good at what I do. You can't work construction without drinking. Especially if you're the boss. The men expect you to set them up. But they don't expect you to brawl. That's for kids. It's outrageous. Everybody can drink but me. Car accidents, fights, in jail twice, lost a couple of jobs and I don't know how many girls. I didn't have a drink for two months and then last night I did it again. Am I nuts? I can just see this crew if they thought I was seeing a shrink.

Dad had the same problem, but he stopped when he was young. I hardly remember him drinking. But he was in the clothing business. Who cares if a shopkeeper drinks or not? Nobody. It's not like that for me. My crew expects it. What the hell am I supposed to do, put soda pop in my beer bottle? . . . I wonder who I hit? This can't go on. I guess I don't have to drink until the Christmas party. That gives me six weeks to cool out. No reason I can't nurse a beer all night. Nobody will notice. Figured it out, didn't I? No different from a problem on the site, all I have to do is think it out. Hell-raising makes sense for a kid; it doesn't for a 35-year-old. It's not fun anymore. I wonder if it ever was. Sometimes I wonder if I go crazy because I'm a pussycat sober. Some pussycat. I can put a guy through the wall cold sober, so that's not it. . . . I'm smarter than I thought. I doped it out. All I have to do is nurse the same drink all night. I can't wait for that Christmas party. I'll show them that I can drink like a gentleman.

Hank drinks too much because he has the type of alcoholism that is most preprogrammed. He is wired to self-destruct if he drinks, and yet drinking is irresistibly attractive to him. He reacts to alcohol differently from other people. It does strange things to him. Hank's problem lies in his genes. He handles alcohol differently from normal drinkers and problem drinkers whose problem drinking is not biologically based. He suffers from male-limited susceptibility to alcoholism. (See discussion of Cloninger's research on page 27.) There is something about his liver or his nervous system or both that does something different with alcohol. Most male-limited susceptibles are in much worse shape than Hank. They quickly get into serious difficulty, often with the law, and have a hard time getting out of it. Their prognosis is not good. Hank's way of reacting to alcohol used to be called pathological intoxication, which is an accurate description of what happens to him when he drinks.

> *Could you give an example of an addiction where*
> *personality is the major etiological factor?*

Rose is schizoid and depressed. She is self-deluded. Her despair is bottomless, and yet she denies it, just as she denies that she drinks too much. She ponders her drinking in her journal.

Why is it that in moments of quiet contemplation my thoughts turn with a certain inevitability to the consumption of spirits either in the contemplation of the not-to-be-long-delayed consumption thereof, or to obsessional rumination over the frequency and quantity of that consumption and its effects on my productivity and sense of well-being? There can be no real question but that which has been fermented inspires and vivifies me. It adds a certain excitement to my life and what, after all, can be the harm in an afternoon glass of what my colleagues and I have taken to denoting "faculty sherry"? The English department practically runs on sherry. After all, what is poetry other than intoxication? Intoxication of the spirit—chills running down my back as Blake's lines run though my head. A sip or so of wine intensifies that. There can be no question of Dionysian abandon in my case. In fact, the penultimate occurrence of a somewhat excessive consumption was on the occasion of my presentation of my paper, "Covert Eroticism in *Beowulf* with Particular Reference to the Relation between Grendel and His Mother." Odd that I should have been nervous at that meeting. I am, after all, a professional orator. I usually drink only wine at the Language Association meetings; however, at this the most recent occurrence of, perhaps I do have to so admit, overdrinking, martinis played their role. Ah, martinis—divine magic, so slightly green-reflected clarity, penetrating the gleaming stemware. Yet, at the same time so much more scintillating than sherry or claret, or the dry, dry Mosel I so covet—covet? Yes, I must admit covet—during languorous summer afternoons. In winter there is the martini at lunch in the Faculty Club, the afternoon sherry, the martini before dinner, the red or white with dinner, and the brandy postprandially. I have to concede a certain constancy in my consumption, but in total it is not so very much. Is not so much too much? I do not believe so. Paper after paper written in the warm afterglow of sips and scents and through an almost subliminal fascination with glass and ice, tray and shaker. It is part of my lifestyle, which is, after all, sedate, academic, productive, satisfying. Lonely, though. There have been a few, but never one; but love is an experience that I have not really needed, and so, except in moments of slightly tipsy melancholy, I have not regretted not having it.

I must concede that things have changed. My productivity wanes, my moments of melancholy intensify and deliquesce through my already damp soul and, in short, I am no longer happy. Do I drink a bit more to recover my former state of inner peace? Or do I drink in an attempt to transcend known states and discover an as yet undiscovered bliss? Or is my increased consumption an attempt to compensate for a diminution in the intensity of my life? I do not know. Perhaps happiness is over for me. Whichever of these contingencies, if any, is in fact the case, dinner without wine is not civilized and I am, whatever else I may be, civilized. So I pour another sherry and turn my thoughts outward to my lecture on the influence of Anglo-Saxon poetry on the romantics.

Rose is a bullshit artist. Her self-deception is so total that it endangers her life. Her life is a secret from herself. She drinks around the clock, has long since ceased to be productive, and is increasingly melancholy—depressed. She can rationalize anything in service of her denial. "Faculty sherry," which she seems to think is in some miraculous way different from ordinary sherry, is certainly harmless. Martinis could be part of the problem, but they are practically works of art, so there can't be anything wrong there, the English department runs on alcohol, and it isn't civilized to have dinner without wine.

Rose truly believes that her drinking starting at lunch and ending with her passing out after dinner is not heavy, although she does have some instantly repudiated doubts. People who drink far too much commonly deny it and assume that everybody drinks more or less as they do. They need to believe this.

Rose is a schizoid personality. She copes with this in two ways, one adaptive and one self-destructive. Her relationship to literature, which in her early years was imaginative and insightful, is the adaptive one, and her relationship to alcohol is the self-destructive one.

Rose is tragic—a brilliant woman who has become vain, pretentious, and empty, with the progressive inner impoverishment that inevitably occurs as an alcoholic career progresses. She has no meaningful human relationships; she must drink to give papers, whose quality is far below what she is capable of; her teaching, once enlivened by her passion for literature, now limps along; and she is sitting on the edge of despair. Rose is the kind of person who is found dead one day, to the shocked amazement of colleagues, who say, "How could she have done it? I never knew she was so unhappy. The last few years she drank too much, but nobody thought too much about it—she was so witty and creative. I guess nobody was close to her, but everybody liked her. There will be a lot of tears at the memorial service."

Could you give an example of an addiction in which the environment is a major etiological factor?

Peggy is on the fast track. She's young, bright, well educated, and in the right place at the right time. Opportunity knocks, yet she is miserable. Alcohol and drugs play an all-too-important role in her life. She is thinking about last night.

> Who's this guy? Jesus, it's the third time this has happened. Well, they do it pretty much the same way so what difference does it make? I feel awful. Went to Smith for this? Shit, I'll have to do something to change my life. I'm really out of it. Never got that smashed before. Have to stop using grass when I drink, or maybe it's the coke—coke sucks. I'll stick to margaritas and this won't happen. He's really out. Jesus, he isn't even circumcised. Never had one of those before. I wonder what it felt like. Probably real primitive, I must have loved it. Maybe he'll wake up and we'll go around again. Not with this headache. I think I'm going to puke. One more night like this one and I think I might pack it in. Oh hell, I'm too young to check out. Maybe some coke will straighten me out. No, I'm not doing any more of that. Just clean up and get dressed, kid. There's some beer in the fridge. I'll have a bottle—just like a Hemingway character. Beer in the morn-

ing; death in the afternoon. Stop this melodrama. So you slept with some hunk in a blackout. Who hasn't? I'll douche when I get home. Just get the hell out of here, okay?

Jesus, I'm scared. I don't like what's happening to me. I have a great opportunity at Wallace Publishing and I act like a slut. Only when I drink, though. Sex isn't all that great, especially if you don't even remember it. Could screw up my job, too. Feeling better now. That beer really helped. Well, I am having a hell of a good time. I'll cut the coke and either drink or smoke but not both. A little lipstick sure makes a difference. "Oh, hello there, I was just leaving." Nothing like being young and carefree. Why don't I stop for a margarita on the way home? Never hate myself after a few of them. Stop this doom and gloom guilt shit. It's still the weekend, isn't it? Weekends are to have fun. No coke or grass today, though. Everything will be all right. I know it. Maybe I should lay off the booze, too. Naw, leave that for Mother Theresa. "So long, fellow. I'll be down at Tony's if you want to join me later. I like the margaritas there."

Peggy drinks for many reasons. One of the most powerful is peer pressure. Adults tend to think of peer pressure as something that influences teenagers. The kid got into drugs because he got into the wrong crowd. It has nothing to do with adults. That is plainly untrue. We are all deeply influenced by our fellows. Peers profoundly affect behavior. They are models and to a greater or lesser degree we want their approval. To some extent people choose the people whose approval is important to them, but not entirely. Circumstances and unconscious needs determine much more of choice of associates than is generally believed.

Peggy runs with a crowd that drinks and drugs one hell of a lot. It is a lifestyle that works for some people; it is not working for Peggy. Peggy had fallen in with a literary bohemian crowd in college. Typically they were ambitious, convinced that they would write great novels and profound poetry. Some of them may, but for the most part they were dreaming the dreams of youth. They tended to be arrogant, unconventional, and contemptuous of ordinary folks. They spent a lot of time telling each other how great they were. Peggy desperately wanted to be one of them. She identified with their values and with their lifestyle. They drank a great deal of wine, and not a little bit of the hard stuff. Peggy joined right in. She loved drinking and what it did for and to her from the first sip. It was love at first taste. It took away her insecurity and brought her acceptance in the aspiring-poets clique. Her new friends served as models for heavy drinking. They gave her permission to drink as much as she wished and rewarded her for doing so. Since Peggy liked to drink anyway, she took full advantage of that permission. The feeling of belonging, of being part of an elite club, which went with her drinking, strongly reinforced it. Pot smoking was just as much a badge of membership as was wine drinking in her literary circle. Although she didn't like it as much, Peggy was soon drawing on a joint with as much relish as the single published member of the clique. Drinking and drugging were romanticized by Peggy's friends. She came to share in this romanticization. As she says, she's "just like a Hemingway character." She forgets, or unconsciously identifies with, Hemingway's suicide, a suicide intimately connected with his alcoholism.

Of course Peggy selected her friends, chose a peer group that drank heavily. But that's not the whole story. She went to college at a time when pot smoking was virtually a graduation requirement, and shortly afterward entered a viciously competitive profession just as coke came in. Almost all of the young people she was thrown in with drank and drugged. So once again her peers expected her to act in a way she wanted to anyway. But Peggy would never have found cocaine on her own. By now she was often depressed. Coke took care of that and it was the "in" thing to do. She did it, early and often, as Tammany Hall is said to have recommended to its voters on election day. Environment played a crucial role in Peggy's early entry into the fast lane. Everybody she associated with was into alcohol and drugs. For all her bravado, Peggy badly needed approval. Outwardly brash, inwardly she was jelly. Taking a drink or smoking a joint was an easy way to get that approval.

Peggy also drinks to assuage guilt. She is a "closet puritan." She talks like a streetwalker, but the truth is that she is very uncomfortable with her sexuality. She has never had sex cold sober. I have had many patients who had never had sex sober, and who were unaware that they needed to drink to go to bed until I drew their attention to it. They were closet puritans without knowing it. Peggy drank in order to have sex and she didn't know it, at least not consciously. She had gotten high in order to lose her virginity and she continued to have a drink or smoke pot to go to bed with her college boyfriend. There were other relationships, all tinged with fear, and then she found anonymous sex. Leaving college and moving into the adult world was overwhelming for Peggy. The real literary world, the publishing game, was not like her college literary crowd. It was faster, tougher, smarter. If she barely felt safe in college, she now felt terrified. Again, she didn't let herself know it. Instead, she drank and drugged and before long started taking men home with her. Her conquests were reassuring. They were more about being with somebody and being wanted than about sensual pleasure. In the short run they shored up her tenuous self-esteem, but she was never really comfortable with any of it. Her guilt became unmanageable and she picked up a drink, a joint, or a line of coke to escape that guilt. Before she came down, more likely than not she was in bed with someone else, only to awake even more guilt-ridden. What could she do at that point? Drink, of course, and the merry-go-round would start again. Driving ambition; deep-seated insecurity, masked and denied; relentless, repressed feelings of guilt; and a peer group that's heavy into the sauce and other stuff—what else did she need to get hooked?

Could you summarize classifications of drug use?

There have been a number of ways, some of which have been discussed earlier in this primer, to classify substance users. Most of these nosological schemata are ways of classifying alcoholics, but, mutatis mutandis, they almost certainly apply to other substance users. Major classificatory schemata, which have considerable overlap, have been developed by Jellinek, Knight, Blane, Winokur, Cloninger, Babor, and Zuckerman. Additionally, drug use can be looked at as lifestyle use, problem use, and addictive use. And, the *DSM-IV*, as we have seen, makes a distinction between substance abuse and substance dependency.

By far the most famous classificatory schema was offered by Jellinek in 1960. His classificatory system, which he called a typology, is based on survey research he did on early AA groups. He concluded that useful distinctions could be made among five types of pathological drinking, all of which involve damage to the user, but only one of which he regarded as a disease. Jellinek made his distinctions both for clinical and conceptual research reasons. His first type, *alpha alcoholism*, is characterized by psychological dependency, which can be either specific—for example, a drinker who has to drink in order to speak in public, or to have sex, or (as several patients have told me) to drive a car (crazy as that may sound)—or general—a drinker who is emotionally dependent on alcohol, yet whose drinking pattern is stable and does not progress. In alpha alcoholism there is no physical dependence and there is no social deterioration; nevertheless, it must be regarded as pathological because of the restriction that it imposes on the drinker's ability to function without the aid of the drug.

Beta alcoholism is a condition that Jellinek thought was characteristic of male blue collar workers (and usually restricted to that group) in which the drinking is generally heavy beer drinking and in which physical symptoms develop, most commonly liver or heart problems. Yet the beta alcoholic continues to drink in spite of threats to health and life. Beta alcoholism does not progress in the sense of increased quantity consumed or social deterioration of the drinker, but his health continues to fail if his drinking continues.

Jellinek's most famous subtype is *gamma alcoholism*, which is characterized by progression that Jellinek believed to be fairly invariant in terms of the rank ordering of symptoms, and by loss of control, meaning that the drinker cannot predict what will happen when he or she drinks. Unlike the social drinker, who may occasionally choose to get drunk, but more or less knows what the outcome is going to be, the gamma intends to have one beer and winds up in a blackout after her tenth—or at least that may happen anytime she has that first drink. As they say in AA, "It's the first drink that gets you (assumed to be a gamma) drunk." Jellinek regarded gamma alcoholism as a true disease because it looks very much like an organic disease in terms of having a predictable outcome and course and a definite etiology, even if it is biopsychosocial and not well understood.

Delta alcoholism is a socially and culturally syntonic form of alcoholism found in viticultural countries such as Italy, France, and Spain (Jellinek having Spain, in particular, in mind) in which there is very heavy drinking. There are often physical problems associated with delta alcoholism, but no guilt and no hangovers (no doubt partly because deltas just continue to drink, so they drink over the hangover). The drinking is often judged as pathological by those outside of the culture, but viewed by members of the culture as perfectly normal. Deltas have withdrawal symptoms if they abruptly stop drinking.

Epsilon alcoholism is episodic drunkenness, also known as periodic alcoholism. In the nineteenth-century psychiatric literature this was called dipsomania. This is the pattern of the person who has long periods of sobriety and then goes on sudden benders in which, usually, he drinks to collapse, and requires care and nursing. The epsilon drinker is usually counterdependent, denying his need for others until he regresses to infantile dependency.

Many epsilons are stable in their drinking behavior and may repeat their patterns of sobriety followed by binge for many years. In other cases, the periods between the binges decrease and epsilon alcoholism collapses into gamma alcoholism. In my experience, epsilon alcoholism is extremely difficult to treat, which is also the case for its analogue with other substance abuse. This is so because the epsilon drinker is not very treatable in the middle of the binge (except by detoxification), and usually has an impenetrable blanket denial between drinking episodes, claiming that he has no problems whatsoever and no desire to drink. He doesn't know what the therapist is talking about and tells her so. The best prognosis for epsilons is for those who progress into gammas and reach a state of collapse, which can lead to hitting bottom and recovery.

Jellinek's typology has been criticized by those who believe that a significant number of apparent alpha and beta drinkers are really early gammas.

Robert Knight (1937) distinguished between *essential alcoholics* and *reactive alcoholics* in his work at the Menninger Clinic. The essentials were never able to drink safely and had little in the way of developmental achievements; the reactives had as often as not done well in life until they hit a situation in which they could no longer cope, and what had previously been a form of social or lifestyle drinking became compulsive and they wound up in the Menninger Clinic. Many researchers have seen essentially the same distinction as Knight did between essentials and reactives, although they called it different names. It is a distinction that can be understood in many ways. Perhaps, in psychodynamic terms, it is a distinction between borderline and narcissistic drinkers.

Biologically oriented researchers look at the essential–reactive distinction more in terms of genetic loading and vulnerability, and it may be the case that essential alcoholics are those who simply cannot process alcohol normally because of neurochemical vulnerability.

Winokur and colleagues (1971) made a very important distinction between *primary alcoholism* and *secondary alcoholism*. Unfortunately, these words are not used consistently in the literature and mean different things in different contexts, so the reader has to be careful. But, as most commonly used, the terms *primary substance abuse, primary addiction,* and *primary alcoholism* mean that the substance use is the primary problem, which is exactly what the term says, and such other conditions as depression, anxiety disorder, and paranoia are secondary to the substance use. Psychiatric disorders secondary to substance use generally remit with sobriety and recovery. On the other hand, secondary addictions are secondary to a major mental illness—in Winokur's view usually major depression for women (and sometimes for men), and antisocial personality disorder for men. In the case of secondary alcoholism, the drinking is either an attempt at self-cure or a manifestation of the underlying psychopathology. The primary-secondary distinction is vital clinically. If a therapist is treating a secondary addiction but fails to treat the primary problem—psychotherapeutically, psychopharmacologically, or rehabilitatively—there is no way the patient is going to establish any kind of stable sobriety.

The contrary is also true, that if the therapist is treating a patient for an anxiety disorder and the anxiety is being caused by cocaine use, the therapist will fail unless the primary problem—cocaine use—is addressed. Although most cases of substance abuse are either essentially primary or essentially secondary, human beings are complex, and not infrequently the therapist has to deal with a complex dialectical interplay between primary and secondary factors. The only hope of cure is if both are addressed.

Howard Blane (1968) believed that dependency conflict was the central dynamic in male alcoholism and was, in fact, etiological. Blane described three ways of handling dependency. *Open dependency* is illustrated by the patient who says, "I'm here for my welfare check, would you sign the slip please and not bother me." Most often the dependents will package their motive for seeing the therapist rather better than this, but the latent content of their communications is the same. Blane thought open dependents had a very poor prognosis. *Counterdependency* is illustrated by the patient who says, "I don't need anyone," although his dependence on substances is all too clear. Blane thought that counterdependents also had a poor prognosis.

The drinker or drugger with the best prognosis Blane gave the awkward name of *dependent-counterdependent.* Dependent-counterdependent alcoholics are those in which the conflict about how to meet dependency needs is most active and alive, and since it has not yet been resolved by a regression to open dependence or a reaction formation to counterdependency, Blane thought it could be worked through in the transference where it would manifest itself, and that therapy with dependent-counterdependents had the best chance of success.

Blane believed that the central dynamic in female addiction involved self-esteem and that women drank to raise their self-esteem. He saw the self-esteem of female alcoholics as very fragile. There's an overlap between Blane's low self-esteem female drinkers and Winokur's depressive female secondary alcoholics, but Blane means to say something about female alcoholism in general which Winokur does not.

C. Robert Cloninger (1983, 1987) described two types of alcoholism (and by extension of substance abuse in general) based on his analysis of the Swedish adopted-out study discussed elsewhere in this primer. He saw a *male-limited* (type 2) alcoholism characterized by antisocial behavior, absence of guilt, low treatability, early onset, and severity. Cloninger believed that this type of alcoholism, or substance abuse, was largely genetically determined with environmental factors playing little or no role. He has been criticized for having described antisocial personality disorder and not alcoholism.

Cloninger's *milieu-limited* (type 1) alcoholism is characterized by late onset; less severity, guilt, and anxiety; high treatability, and requiring environmental provocation in addition to genetic predisposition. It is found in both men and women. The necessary environmental provocation is heavy drinking in the home and/or social surround. Cloninger distinguished between two ways of experiencing anxiety: *somatic anxiety*, which he found in male-limited alcoholics, was characterized by body rigidity, but not by worry or conscious fear or guilt; and *cognitive anxiety*, which he found in the milieu-limited alcoholics, was characterized as an obsessional, worrying, guilty kind of rumination that is very uncomfortable and very often self-medicated with alcohol.

Babor and colleagues (1992a,b), who did work on a longitudinal study looking for genetic factors in alcohol addiction and who did not have the kind of neurochemical and hereditability scaffolding that Cloninger did, have described more phenomenologically almost exactly the same distinction between two groups as Cloninger. Babor calls his two groups *alpha alcoholics* and *beta alcoholics.* The alphas and betas are both men and women, and in that way his typology differs from Cloninger's, but he makes the same distinction between the antisocial, early-onset, severely treatment-resistant alcoholism, and a more gradual, later-onset, more treatable type of alcoholism characterized by emotional torment.

MacAndrew (1965) developed a scale, based on Minnesota Multiphasic Personality Inventory (MMPI) items, that identifies 85 percent of male alcoholics. It can discriminate between alcoholic and nonalcoholic patients and accurately make the diagnosis of alcoholism. The items he picked are those that characterize externalizing defenses, acting out, mildly antisocial behavior, and the use of denial, projection, and splitting. He also identified a group he called secondary alcoholics (using *primary* and *secondary* somewhat differently than Winokur). The secondary alcoholics were characterized by low self-esteem, depression, anxiety, and generally negative affect. Again, the overlap with Blane, with Cloninger, and with Knight is fairly clear.

Zuckerman (1979) described four types of alcoholism: *antisocial*, *developmental* (by which he meant a kind of transient problem with alcohol and/or drugs in adolescence that was outgrown, or matured out of, by most of those who manifested it), *addictive*, and *reactive*. This is a useful nosology. It is extremely helpful to distinguish among antisocial drug users; those who are going through a stage (as with Zuckerman's developmentals); those who are addictive (who look like Jellinek's gammas); and those who are self-medicating some sort of life crisis or neurotic conflict. Reactives can easily progress to the addictive if they do not get help or back off from their substance use (or preferably do both).

Could you comment on nonchemical addictions?

Some compulsive behaviors, such as compulsive gambling and compulsive sexuality, are strikingly similar to the chemical addictions. They are sometimes referred to as *process addictions* and sometimes as *behavioral addictions*. All of the psychodynamic theories cited in this primer and their clinical applications apply to these addictions as well as to chemical addictions. Nevertheless, they differ in that the pharmacology of the drug is not one of the etiological and consequential factors, although the compulsion itself plays somewhat the same role as a drug would.

What is codependency?

These days, codependency is saying good morning to your spouse.

Does codependency have any other meaning?

Codependency was once a very useful term, denoting a continuing relationship with an active alcoholic or drug addict for unconscious psychodynamic reasons, to the detriment of the codependent. It has become so generalized as to be meaningless, and I tell my patients that they cannot use that word because it has become too much of a wastebasket term. Its meaning is no longer clear and codependency no longer usually has much emotional reality for the person using the word.

The condition originally denoted by the word *codependency* is, however, a very real condition. This condition can usefully be seen as a form of addiction that needs to be addressed and treated.

The treatment process for codependency is very similar to that used in working with any other addiction; that is, the therapist must first form a therapeutic alliance; build enough rapport to have some salience; and only then begin to do some educational work, eventually confronting the co-dependent's denial, and then moving into an action phase in which the patient changes her (codependents are usually female) relationship to the addict, and finally a working-through phase.

Codependents are often more available for therapy than are substance abusers and make up a large percentage of outpatient psychotherapy patients. The therapist needs to be on the alert with codependents for addictions of their own, which not uncommonly surface in the therapy. Typically, the addiction of the codependent is sufficiently less severe than that of the identified substance abuser so that it hasn't come to anyone's attention; yet it may be an important part of the problem. It pays for the therapist to be alert to this possibility.

The codependency movement is riding high. There is a long list of best-selling books purporting to address it "scientifically." At its best, this movement has raised the consciousness of people in destructive relationships. At its worst, it is phobic about relationships and confuses what Karen Horney (1942) long ago called "morbid dependency" and healthy interdependence. Being overwhelmingly a female movement it is, to my mind, guilty of much barely subsurface male bashing.

What is comorbidity?

Comorbidity, also known as *dual diagnosis* and *mentally ill–chemically addicted* (*MICA*), refers to the existence of major psychiatric disorder or personality disorder along with addiction, and is probably more the rule than the exception. The most common comorbidities are depression and antisocial personality disorder with anxiety disorders of various sorts not far behind. There are also patients with major psychiatric illnesses, such as schizophrenia and manic-depressive psychosis, who are also substance abusers, but they are a relatively small percentage of the substance abusing population. Therapists see many more addicts who suffer from depression, anxiety, and personality disorders.

As delineated in other parts of this primer, borderline personality disorder is common in substance abusers. Narcissistic personality disorder, as

I have defined it (see pages 104–116) in terms of regression-fixation to Kohut's stage of the archaic nuclear self, is the psychodynamic correlative—the inner world structure—of the newly sober, so that narcissistic issues are central in their treatment. Narcissistic issues include such affective-structural aspects of being as self-esteem, self-cohesion, sense of ongoingness, the acquisition of the ability to modulate anxiety, the capacity to be alone, and, in general, what the twelve-step programs call "tools for living." The psycho-dynamic tradition calls twelve-step tools for living "psychic structure."

Antisocial personality disorder is another common comorbidity. The therapist must distinguish antisocial behavior secondary to the addiction and maintenance of a source of supplies from primary sociopathic disorder. In doing so, the therapist should keep in mind what Leon Wurmser (1987) calls the "flight from conscience," a condition that presents as a pseudo-antisocial character, while the underlying problem is an all too savage superego.

The therapist should also keep in mind that much psychopathology is induced by substance abuse and remits with sobriety.

Attention deficit disorder (ADD) and posttraumatic stress disorder (PTSD) are also common comorbidities with substance abuse and substance dependence.

Generalized anxiety disorder, panic disorder, and dysthymia are so frequently seen in active and recently recovering abusers that their presence is more the rule than the exception.

In each case the therapist must attend to the primary/secondary distinction and treat the "co" as well as the primary morbidity. Sometimes this is simultaneously, sometimes sequentially, but in any case recovery from or arresting of the comorbidity is not possible if the substance abuse continues.

Do porcupines drink?

No, but elephants do, or they at least ingest fermented palms, and sometimes go on rampages when they are high. The research in this area is rather scanty since most of the researchers have not survived. Then what do porcupines have to do with substance abuse?

The philosopher Arthur Schopenhauer (1851) compared human beings to freezing porcupines who try to huddle together to provide each other
with warmth, but who prick each other with their quills, forcing them to
separate.

A company of porcupines crowded themselves very close together,
one cold winter's day, so as to profit from one another's warmth and so
save themselves from being frozen to death. But soon they felt one another's
quills, which induced them to separate again. Before long, when the need
for warmth brought them nearer together again, the second evil arose once
more. So that they were driven backward and forward from one trouble to
the other, until they had discovered a mean distance at which they could
most tolerably exist.

Human beings also attempt to get close, stab each other with their
quills, and flee. Freud (1921) cited Schopenhauer's rather dour take on the
human condition in a discussion of ambivalence.

Although Schopenhauer and Freud are saying something about the
human condition, not about substance abusers, it is nevertheless the case
that Schopenhauer's metaphor applies with particular force to substance
abusers and addicts. With few exceptions, they are people who have extraordinary difficulties in being alone, and extraordinary difficulty in being
with others. They are caught between isolation and engulfment, between
aloneness and hostile interaction. In trying to understand the troubled and
often seemingly irrational interpersonal relations of substance abusers and
their preference for substances over people, remembering the pessimistic
philosopher's take on ordinary human nature (let alone troubled human
nature) reduces the therapist's anxiety and provides a means of understanding what one's patients are going through.

What are twelve-step programs?

Twelve-step refers to the twelve steps of personal or spiritual growth,
which is the basic ideology of Alcoholics Anonymous. Only the first step,
"Admit to ourselves that we were powerless over alcohol and that our lives
had become unmanageable," mentions alcohol or alcoholism. The other

eleven steps have to do with relationships with one's self, with other people, and with what AA calls the "Higher Power." These steps are modifications of the ten steps of spiritual growth of the Oxford movement, an upper-class revival movement of the 1920s, which AA's founder Bill Wilson had been a member of (see p. 127). Twelve-step has come to refer to any program that uses, in more or less modified form, AA's twelve steps as the backbone of its activity, such as Narcotics Anonymous (NA), Cocaine Anonymous (CA), Pot Anonymous (PA), Debtors Anonymous (DA), Alanon, Overeaters Anonymous (OA), and even a program called Arts Anonymous.

All these are self-help programs that can be understood in many different ways: as support groups, as cognitive behavioral therapies, as a kind of Kleinian group therapy, and as a self-psychological treatment. Many substance abusers do extremely well in twelve-step programs; others do not do well at all. Therapists need to understand the program, read its literature, and be familiar with local meetings and their ambiance so that they can make appropriate referrals, just as they need to be familiar with other ancillary supportive treatments. Generally speaking, twelve-step programs work best for those with some degree of mental health and interpersonal skills. Borderline patients often do extremely poorly, being unable to relate and to participate. Schizoid patients also do not do well, and those with major mental illnesses are generally unable to get much out of twelve-step programs. The programs seem to work best for those addicts who might be described as the "psychologically normal" addicts in Carl Rogers' sense of being "normal neurotics," and for those addicts with narcissistic personality disorders, using that term more in the Kohutian than in the *DSM-IV* sense. The programs seem to be aimed very much at Kohutian narcissists, a concept developed elsewhere in this primer, and are extremely effective with that population. But all sorts of people have been helped by twelve-step programs, and a referral is always worthwhile. It is, however, a mistake to insist on twelve-step participation for those who are resistant. Some people find the twelve-step's spirituality, perhaps more honestly called religiosity, objectionable, and they are uncomfortable with it. The therapist can suggest that it is much like a smorgasbord, to be used as a support group where you take what you can use and leave the rest. But, nevertheless, the push to participate in the belief system of the group, although subtle, is persistent and powerful and drives some people away.

Patients' values should be respected. But the therapist should also be aware that the most common reason patients don't want to go to twelve-step programs is that the people there are sober. This resistance must be interpreted and explored even though the therapist is flexible about the patient's participation.

Twelve-step meetings are of two types: open meetings, which are open to everyone, and closed meetings, which are open only to those who are trying to recover. Therapists working with substance abusers who are involved in twelve-step programs should attend some open meetings to acquire first-hand knowledge of the program. They should also read its literature, particularly the so-called Big Book, also known as *Alcoholics Anonymous* (Alcoholics Anonymous World Services 1955), and *Twelve Steps and Twelve Traditions* (Alcoholics Anonymous World Services 1952). The latter is an exposition by Bill Wilson of the steps and their dynamics.

II

Somatic and Psychological Consequences of Substance Use and Abuse

In physics, Newton's third law of motion states that for every action there is a reaction, equal and opposite in direction. A similar law pertains on the effects of drugs on the nervous system. Instead of the third law of motion, we have the concept of *opponent process* (Solomon 1977). If you depress the nervous system with a drug like alcohol, when you stop using the alcohol, opponent process takes over and the pendulum swings so that the nervous system goes into the opposite state of hyperactivity. This state of hyperactivity may be subjectively unpleasant and objectively dangerous and readily lead to more ingestion of the drug, in this case alcohol. In the case of uppers, the opponent process is depression. Withdrawal from drugs presents several dangers. First, it may set up an addictive cycle, because the user uses more to stop the cycle of withdrawal. Or, there may be serious physiological complications that can even be life threatening. This is particularly true in the case of down drugs. Withdrawal from alcohol, Valium, Librium, Xanax, and the barbiturates can put the nervous system in such a state of hyperactivity that convulsions can occur. Although the medical details of withdrawal from nervous system depressants is beyond the scope of this primer, it is vital that the nonmedical therapist know that withdrawal from depressants can be fatal. *The decision as to how and where detoxification should take place should always be made by a physician knowledgeable in substance abuse.*

Withdrawal from cocaine and amphetamines, although not medically dangerous, can result in very deep depression, usually known as a crash, which may set up an addictive cycle and can also lead to suicide. Withdrawal from opiates feels like an extremely bad case of the flu and is not something someone wants to undergo twice, but it is not dangerous in the way that withdrawal from central nervous system depressants is. The other drugs of abuse present fewer problems of physiological withdrawal and the consequences of withdrawal are much more psychological.

What is detoxification?

Detoxification is a medical procedure to get patients safely off whatever it is they're using. Generally speaking, this involves the use of another drug in the same class; for example, giving Librium to detoxify from alcohol, starting at a relatively high dose that is then reduced to zero over three to ten days in order to minimize the medical complications of withdrawal. Detoxification is often done spontaneously by tapering off, a procedure that runs the risk of resuming use to end the discomfort of withdrawal. A wiser course is for the patient to seek medical advice and detox either as an outpatient under supervision, with or without the assistance of medication, or in the hospital. The decision as to what form of detoxification is indicated should always be made by a physician.

Substance abusers' ambivalence toward detoxification is reflected by Benjy, an AA member who repeatedly slipped and who was probably to some degree "wet brained," who expressed a desire "to go into retox [sic]."

> *Could you give examples of seemingly irrational behavior*
> *during withdrawal?*

In the following two cases, the patients didn't realize that their behavior was driven by withdrawal and panic over the symptoms of unrecognized withdrawal.

David described how at the end of his drinking career he was faced each morning with a profound existential decision. It was the most momentous quandary of his day:

> I would wake up feeling like death. I knew that I was going to puke, but I had the shakes and I knew that I had to have a drink. I never dared go to sleep without something left in the bottle, but there wouldn't be much so I couldn't afford to waste it. I never knew whether to slug down the booze and hope I wouldn't puke it up before it hit, or keep shaking while I puked. Then I would know I had something to drink that would stay down after the dry heaves ended, but I worried the shakes would be so bad I wouldn't be able to set the bottle to my lips. I used to make important business decisions; now my life had come to this. The only thing that mattered was to decide whether or not to puke before I drank.

Sandy came from a wealthy politically prominent family. She was alone except for her young children in her country house. She was too ashamed to have the maid see how heavily she was drinking so she had sent her back to town:

> I hadn't shopped for days. I couldn't. I was feeding my kids hot dogs and canned beans for the sixth day in a row. That was all I had in the house. I was in the kitchen while I drank my God-knows-what drink of the day. I was almost out of liquor. As I reached for the pot on the stove, which was starting to burn, I knocked my drink over. It spilled on the floor. Without realizing that I was doing it, I got down on my knees and starting licking it up from the floor. I was afraid to miss a drop. When I raised my head, my 4- and 5-year-olds were staring at

me. Harry said, "What are you doing, Mommy?" Joyce was crying. I went into detox that night and I haven't had a drink since.

David and Sandy acted as they did because they were avoiding life-threatening withdrawal reactions. Neither of them fully realized this; all they knew was that they had to have a drink.

What is tolerance?

Tolerance is a phenomenon in which the nervous system habituates and accommodates to the effects of the drug so that more of the drug becomes necessary to obtain the same effect. The development of tolerance, although not pathognomonic in itself, should certainly lead the clinician to be suspicious of abuse or addiction. Some drugs build more tolerance than others. The opiates and some central nervous system stimulants such as cocaine build very high levels of tolerance and may necessitate the taking of many multiples of the original dose to get the same effect.

Another mechanism involved in the development of tolerance is change in the chemistry of the liver, the *induction*, that is, the increase in quantity, of the enzymes that metabolize the ingested drug, which enables the liver to detoxify the chemical more quickly. Whether tolerance is built through adaptation of the nervous system or induction of enzymes in the liver, the user needs to take more of the drug to get the same effect.

Late in an addiction, there is often a precipitous loss of tolerance. This is particularly true for alcohol and other central nervous system (CNS) depressants. This loss of tolerance is indicative of advanced alcoholism or drug addiction and is a sign that the user is in serious trouble.

What is cross-tolerance?

Cross-tolerance is the development of tolerance to all drugs within the *same class*. For example, if the patient builds a high tolerance to alcohol, which is a CNS depressant, he will have high tolerance for all CNS depressants. This can be of some practical importance, as is the case when an alcoholic is involved in an accident and arrives in the hospital needing general anesthetic, which is not effective because of the cross-tolerance to another CNS depressant, ethyl alcohol.

Tolerance to a CNS depressant does not build tolerance to CNS stimulants, or to drugs in other categories; but tolerance to one CNS stimulant (e.g., cocaine) does build tolerance to the other CNS stimulants (e.g., methamphetamine).

What is cross-addiction?

Cross-addiction is addiction to more than one drug. This is sometimes confused with cross-tolerance. Cross-tolerance means increased tolerance to all drugs in the same class, CNS stimulants, for example, while cross-addiction means addiction to more than one drug, for example, alcohol and cocaine. Polysubstance addiction is increasingly common.

What are blackouts?

Blackouts, or alcoholic amnesias, are memory losses during drinking episodes. In effect, the drinker has a temporary loss of the capacity for recent memory. Such loss can be partial ("grayouts") or total. Blackouts are also called *alcoholic palimpsests*. Palimpsest means sand writing in Greek. In a blackout, whatever is written in short-term memory is wiped out, like writing in the sand, because it cannot be converted into a more permanent engram; that is, it cannot be transferred to long-term memory. Blackouts are a common symptom of problem drinking. They are often casually dismissed by the drinker, although they may be prodromal signs of alcoholism. This casual dismissal often conceals profound apprehension. Psychologically, blackouts can be interpreted as failures of the synthetic function of the ego; experientially, they are disruptions in the experience of the self. They are often a source of great anxiety and guilt for the drinker, who does not know what he or she may have done during the blank period. The blackout drinker may then drink some more to anesthetize that anxiety and guilt, which unfortunately may have a basis in reality, since auto accidents and serious crimes have been known to occur during blackouts.

Could you give examples of a blackout?

Harry was a well-known journalist who was a "periodic," that is, binge drinker. Between binges or when recovering from them, he would sometimes do what his friends called "lying in state," which referred to Harry's mute immobilization for extended periods on his couch. Harry told me this story:

> One day I was lying in state when I felt a surge of energy and decided to go out for a drink. I went to my favorite bar. The last memory I have of the place was starting on my fourth beer. Then I was in a strange city, surrounded by high mountains. I knew from the architecture that it wasn't New York. I didn't recognize the language and it took me a long time to find anyone who spoke English. When I did, I discovered that I was in Katmandu. By the time I got home, I had put $5,000 on my credit card. I'm still paying it off.

David told the following story:

> I was going to take a trip to the Catskills with my buddy Jonah. On the way to his house I stopped for a drink. You know how it is. I had trouble getting out of the bar so I was an hour late. Jonah was furious. He started screaming, "You're an asshole, David—a total asshole—you ruined our trip." I said, "Oh, get off it, Jonah. It's only one o'clock and I was supposed to be here at noon." Then he really exploded. "For Christ's sake, David, you were supposed to be here at noon two days ago!" Doctor, I have absolutely no memory of those two days.

I was able to use both of these blackouts to confront these patients' denial.

What damage can alcohol do?

Alcohol is best described as a wonderful drug with horrendous side effects. It would not be nearly as popular as it is if people didn't like what it did for them, as its depressant effects on the higher brain centers make for disinhibition, mild euphoria, and for some, cessation of pain. Unfortunately, alcohol is a small molecule that readily pervades all parts of the body; it lacks a specific receptor site to bind it in the body, allowing it to wreak havoc all over. Alcohol can damage the nervous system, the liver, the blood, and just about every other organ and system.

The neurological effects of the alcohol are extremely important in terms of treatment. Although most cerebral damage from alcohol is reversed by sobriety, and is functional rather than structural, it is unfortunately the case that serious drinkers are not playing with a full deck, and that they have significant cognitive impairment, which is, one hopes, transitory. This, of course, makes the therapeutic process much more difficult. We are working with people with poisoned brains.

The other common drugs of abuse can also cause a wide variety of physical problems, for example, cocaine-induced convulsions, and depressed levels of testosterone secondary to chronic, heavy marijuana smoking. These medical complications are described in detail in my *Introduction to Alcoholism Counseling: A Bio-Psycho-Social Approach* (1995). From the therapist's point of view, the most important thing about the somatic complications is that they really do affect thinking, judgment, affect, and behavior.

What is the clinical addictive personality?

The clinical addictive personality, also known as the postaddictive personality, is an empirically determined cluster of traits repeatedly found in populations under treatment for addiction. These findings are robust and consistent across populations. They are statistical averages, and do not necessarily describe any particular addict. Most of this research has been done on white males.

As in much of the psychological literature, personality is operationalized here as scores on objective psychological tests, although sometimes it is operationalized as quantifications of projective test findings, for example the form level on the Rorschach test, reported as % F+.

It is necessary to distinguish the clinical addictive personality from the preaddictive personality, if there be one. Researchers tend to agree that there is a large degree of commonality in people at the end of the addictive cycle. Various psychological measurements on people in detox, rehab, or early recovery show a great deal of commonality. This should not be surprising since addiction is a process of progressive impoverishment, at the end of which the addict is left with an empty self, an empty world, and an empty bottle. Recovery is the converse, a process of progressive enrichment. A concomitant of the impoverishment is *dedifferentiation*, a process in which the addict loses his or her uniqueness, and becomes similar to everyone else in detox. This is, of course, something of an exaggeration; nevertheless, there is a cluster of findings that is quite consistent across populations and situations, which suggests either that those who become addicted started out much alike or that addiction strips and homogenizes.

Clinically addicted populations manifest pathology on the Minnesota Multiphasic Personality Inventory (MMPI), in particular, elevation of what is called the Psychopathic deviant (Pd) scale. This is one of the most consistent and robust findings in addictive populations. Sometimes referred to as the angry scale, it should not be interpreted as evidence that clinical alcoholics and substance abusers are sociopathic, or suffer from overt antisocial personality disorder, but rather that they manifest many signs of externalizing defenses, angry acting out, and a devil-take-the-hindmost attitude toward conventions, regulations, and laws. There is some evidence (Loper et al. 1973) that an elevated Pd is antecedent to addiction for at least some addicts, and that it persists, although in an attenuated form, well into sobriety. Alcoholics and other substance abusers also score strikingly high on the Depression (D) scale of the MMPI. However, the depression tends to remit with sobriety. Depression can be primary or secondary, and may be antecedent to the addiction for which the substance use is often a self-medication. Or the depression may be secondary to the substance use on both a pharmacological and lifestyle basis. Awfully depressing things happen to addicts, so they have realistic reasons—connected to declining health, economic loss, and broken relationships—to be depressed. Additionally savage self-hatred that is manifested in the superego's relentless battering of the ego, an unconscious process often coped with by projection, significantly deepens the depression. To add insult to injury, the very substance used to alleviate the depression exacerbates it.

Since cessation of use removes the pharmacological, lifestyle, and one intrapsychic component (self-hatred for the use itself) of the depression, it is not surprising that depression often lifts in sobriety. At least that is what average scores on various measures of depression show.

There are, nevertheless, a percentage of addicts who are primary depressives whose depression does not remit, and this will almost certainly lead to relapse if it is not treated psychologically or psychopharmacologically. Combining psychotherapy and psychopharmacology gives the patient optimal odds of remission.

High scores on the neuroticism (Pt) scale of the MMPI characterize high levels of anxiety, low self-esteem, obsessive worry, tension, indecisiveness, and concentration difficulties. This, too, is elevated in clinical addictive populations and tends to improve with sobriety.

MacAndrew (1965) constructed a scale of forty-nine items from the MMPI that accurately identifies 85 percent of male alcoholics. This group is reward-seeking, bold, aggressive, impulsive, and hedonistic, and clearly demonstrates many of the characteristics of those with elevated Pd scale. The 15 percent not identified by those items are identified by other items on the MMPI that are characterized by tension, fear, depression, and fear of punishment. MacAndrew called the first group *primary alcoholics* and the second group *secondary alcoholics*—an unusual use of the primary-secondary terminology.

The second consistent finding in addictive populations is that they are *field dependent* (Witkin et al. 1959). Field dependence refers to a cognitive style in which one does not trust internal cues but rather looks to the environment for guidance in construing a world. It reflects a mistrust of one's own perceptions of the world, and a global, cognitive style lacking in differentiation. Field dependence implies some degree of pathological fusion of self and object representations. There is a controversy in the literature whether field dependence correlates with pathological interpersonal dependence, either in the direction of defensive isolation or in the direction of symbiosis and loss of identity. Some researchers believe that it does, and that the findings of field dependency in alcoholics and other addicts clearly point to interpersonal difficulties that are, without question, present; other researchers, while not doubting the existence of the interpersonal difficulties, believe that field dependence refers only to cognitive style (Witkin and Oltman 1967). Field dependence is measured in several ways, one of which is the embedded-figure test. Field-independent people readily separate figure from ground, while field-dependent people do not.

The third major trait of the clinical addictive personality is *impoverished self-concept*. This is true whether it is measured by adjective checklist ("Check each item that applies to you"), by projective tests, or by interview. Addicts demonstrate diffuse self-concepts, empty self-concepts, and low self-esteem.

Another trait of the addictive personality is *ego weakness*, manifested by impulsivity; the inability to delay gratification; low affect tolerance; a propensity toward panic level anxiety and prolonged depression; an unclear, confused sense of identity; and lack of clear boundaries. Reality testing, an important ego function, is impaired in ego weakness. Another aspect of ego weakness is an external locus of control. That is, clinical addicts, on the average, see themselves as controlled by forces outside of themselves, rather than being in control of their own destiny. Of course addicts are not in control of their destiny, their addiction being the tail that wags the dog. Yet another aspect of ego weakness is confused identity. There is much empirical evidence for this in the form of data gleaned from figure drawings, which demonstrate permeable boundaries and lack of differentiation. This may include confusion as to sexual identity manifest in subjects drawing opposite-gender figures on the Draw-a-Person test.

Yet another finding of the clinical addictive personality profile is *stimulus augmentation*, meaning that addicts feel the impact of environmental stimuli more strongly than others. This has nothing to do with malingering, but appears to be a largely neurological, though perhaps partly developmental and environmentally determined, personality trait that is quite persistent and enduring. In short, the world impacts addicts hard.

In summary, the clinical addictive personality is characterized by elevated Pd, D, and Pt scales on the MMPI; field dependency; impoverished self-concept; low self-esteem; external locus of central; ego weakness; and stimulus augmentation. Clearly the addiction therapist is treating more than hangnails.

What is the preaddictive personality?

The preaddictive personality, if there be one, consists of traits that are found antecedent to the addiction and that presumably predispose to addiction. The notion of a preaddictive personality is much more controversial than the existence of a clinical addictive personality. One robust and consistent finding (Tarter and Alterman 1989) is the high rate of hyperactivity and attention deficit disorder (ADD) found antecedent to the addiction by those researchers who have done retrospective studies of the lives of men who are now diagnosed as addicted. There is additional evidence of cognitive deficits in children of alcoholics, although that finding is equivocal and inconsistent. Conduct disorder in childhood predisposes to addiction. In general, nonconformity, impulsivity, and reward-seeking characteristics, along with mild or moderate antisocial behavior, are often found in retrospective studies of preaddictive populations, as well as in longitudinal studies in which children are followed from an early age to maturity. Psychometric measurements made while the children are young can be used to determine antecedent traits in those members of the cohort who develop addiction.

At least one prominent researcher, Cox (1987), believes that there is compelling evidence of a prealcoholic male personality, characterized by nonconformity, impulsivity, and reward seeking. There is even more compelling evidence that clinical alcoholics are characterized by negative affect, depression, anxiety, and low self-esteem, as well as by a cognitive perceptual style that includes field dependence, external locus of control, and stimulus augmentation. According to Cox, negative affect and low self-

esteem are antecedent for the majority of female addicts, but are consequent for the majority of male addicts. In short, an angry, rebellious, externalizing, acting out constellation of personality traits and behaviors
renders one highly vulnerable to substance abuse. But so does depression, anxiety, low self-esteem, and poor interpersonal skills. It seems that
the high-rolling, devil-may-care types and the withdrawn, isolated, emotionally tormented types are equally prone to substance abuse, but for
somewhat different reasons. The substance use fits well into an externalizing lifestyle, while those in emotional pain use substances as self-
medication.

What is the pink cloud?

The pink cloud is twelve-step slang for the euphoria that many recovering persons experience in early sobriety. The pink cloud is a common but not universal phenomenon, as some people are seriously, even
suicidally, depressed without their substance or compulsive behavior. The
pink cloud probably reflects the ego's euphoria at having survived a potentially fatal disease or condition. It tends to last for three months to a
year, except in those who are genuinely manic, and is corrected soon enough
by the impingements of reality.

What should the therapist do about the pink cloud?

Therapists need to do two things with the pink cloud. First, to enjoy
it with the patient—not criticize it or point out its discrepancy with the
patient's reality. There are exceptions to this, such as when the pink cloud
seems too manic, or the patient seems too out of contact with his or her
actual situation. But these are rare. Ideally, the therapist allows the patient to fully experience the joy of early recovery and participates in that
joy; however, that participation is not uncritical nor does the therapist

lose his boundaries or objectivity in a merger with the patient's affective state.

The second thing the therapist must do, paradoxically, is to tell, or interpret to, the patient that, "The pink cloud is great, something to be enjoyed while it lasts, but sooner or later you are going to come down, and that may be very threatening to your sobriety. So, it is extremely important that we talk about other feelings you have about recovery, and the kinds of struggles you're undergoing when you feel those things. Life being what it is, you will sooner or later have disappointments, come up against obstacles, and find that living your life is, indeed, tough sledding. At that point you may feel panicky and very tempted to pick up a drug, but instead of you picking up, we will talk about what it's like to come down from the pink cloud. But for now . . . enjoy."

What is meant by drugs being biphasic?

Strictly speaking it is not the drugs but their effects on their users that are biphasic. Nevertheless, what you read in the literature is that "drugs are biphasic." What does this mean?

The biphasic nature of drugs refers to their initial giving of pleasure and relief, which they do in varying proportions for different users seeking different things in their use, followed by the very same drug coming to cause quite the opposite effects—pain, depression, anxiety, and despair. So the user continues using, and the drug comes to function in the psychic economy of the user as a means to alleviate the pain being caused by the drug itself. For example, patients frequently report that they use because they are anxious or depressed, and yet the very anxiety or depression that they are seeking to self-medicate may very well be—in fact, frequently is— caused by previous substance use. In short, they drug because they drug. This is highly interpretable, although this interpretation needs much repetition to be effective since it is not initially believed. Yet it can be mutative, indeed highly mutative. This is one didactic interpretation that the therapist should emphasize.

What is state-dependent learning?

State-dependent learning is a phenomenon in which knowledge acquired in certain physiological states is only accessible in those physiological states. For example, rodents trained to run a maze while they are high on a drug will not run the maze when they have not received the drug. But if you give them a martini or a line of cocaine or whatever their drug was, lo and behold they run the maze just fine. It has been suggested that something similar happens in human substance abusers, and that one reason that early sobriety is so tough is that it entails a steep relearning curve in which various activities that had been learned while intoxicated have to be relearned sober. This may be true of social skills; it may be true of sexual confidence and competence; it may be true of being able to dance, or drive a car (if one is very anxious); or it may be true of ease in public speaking.

I discuss the concept of state-dependent learning with my patients. I tell them it may be difficult at first for them to do certain things in sobriety that they were able to do drunk or high, but that after a while, even a long while, they will learn to do them sober. My experience with this educational intervention is that it is very comforting and reassuring, and that it reduces anxiety in such a way as to reduce the odds of patients' slipping when they begin to encounter reality situations that they have difficulty handling.

Explaining stage-dependent learning is a way of giving patients realistic hope and the cognitive structure to understand what is happening to them. It explains why certain tasks and activities are so difficult in early sobriety. I also usually note that among the things patients may never have learned to handle "straight" are their feelings, which, I reflect, are also going to take some time to be manageable.

What is the relationship between substance use and sex?

Well, that depends on the drug and on the stage of the use of the drug. Shakespeare probably got it right about alcohol when he has the porter in

Macbeth (II, iii, 34) say: "It [drink] provokes the desire, but it takes away the performance." And, indeed, Masters and Johnson (1970) report that excessive drinking is the single most common cause of sexual dysfunction in America. Alcohol is, however, disinhibiting, as are other central nervous system depressants, and for some people who are very anxious and uptight low dosages of it may indeed enhance sexuality. Otto Fenichel (1945) tells us that the superego is that part of the mind that is soluble in alcohol. Ogden Nash tells us, "Candy is dandy, but liquor is quicker," as a means of seduction. As Fenichel and Nash suggest, many people drink in order to be comfortable in bed. There is clearly a problem here. People who are so unable to engage in this basic life function without having so much anxiety or guilt that they have to drink, clearly require some psychotherapeutic exploration of their feelings about sex, perhaps along with some Masters and Johnson behavioral-style sex therapy (if their sexual dysfunction is serious enough to need this kind of intervention).

Heavy drinking over a long period of time can damage the sexual organs and lead to a permanent decrease in libido and sexual performance. Fortunately, this is not the usual outcome and most recovering alcoholics report that their early anxiety and sexual problems fade fairly quickly as they, perhaps, go through a kind of stage-dependent relearning, as described above. Most recovering alcoholics report that sex is more enjoyable in sobriety and "I remember what happened last night."

However, anxiety about sexual performance, particularly, but not only, in men, is a frequent cause of slips, and this needs to be discussed by the therapist. If the patient doesn't bring it up, the therapist should: "Having sex sober is a whole new experience and you may be having difficulties with it and you may be scared, and we need to talk about that."

Marijuana has long been used as a sensory enhancer, and although heavy marijuana smoking decreases the level of testosterone, many users report enhanced sexuality while smoking a joint. An earlier generation of couples therapists in the '60s and '70s frequently made a recommendation to patients that they "smoke a joint" during sex play if they were uptight. This is rarely recommended now for a variety of reasons, including changed societal attitudes toward drugs, exemplified by the "war on drugs" and the antidrug rhetoric of politicians. Nevertheless, therapists treat many patients who enjoy sex enormously while smoking marijuana, but then have a difficult time sexually when they give up the pot. These ex-smokers are similar to the central nervous system depressant ex-users who need to go through a kind of relearning to be sexual. The therapist can tell the former marijuana users about state-dependent learning, explore the sources of their inhibition, and reassure them that they are going to enjoy sex very much sober, but maybe not right away.

Cocaine initially enhances sexual performance, as does amphetamine, crack, and other stimulant drugs. However, as time goes on, users lose interest in both in sex and in their partner, and become almost exclusively interested in the drug, which then becomes the coke addict's love object. The abuser's sex life simply goes down the tubes along with everything else. This is true for all drug use. Once the drug becomes the beloved, not much else matters. In recovery, addicts' interest in sex comes back, but recovering cocaine devotees may be looking for the kind of ecstatic sexual experience they had early in their cocaine use, a level of ecstasy probably not available in sobriety. There is always the danger of a slip in an attempt to recapture that experience of ecstasy and intensity. The therapist needs to be proactive in this situation and raise the issue of such a motivated slip as a possibility, even if the patient does not.

Opiates, at least up to a point, do not interfere with erection, but they inhibit ejaculation. This phenomenon, known as "dope dick," is common in male heroin addicts and makes them highly attractive sexual partners for those who are looking for a copulating machine—whatever the emotional and object relational state of that machine. Sobriety ends this kind of prolonged potency, and this may be a cause of, or at least a rationalization for, a slip. This is the case in spite of the fact that sex is rarely very important to people who are heavily addicted to heroin. In fact, the shooting up of both cocaine and opiates is described as an orgasmic experience that becomes a substitute for sexual orgasm.

Not surprisingly, since substance use leads to major dislocations in every important life area, it does in the sexual area as well. Periods of readjustment in sobriety are more the rule than the exception and, carrying the kind of emotional charge that sexuality does, are minefields of potential relapse that need to be circumvented through active work on the patient's feelings about his or her sexuality—high and straight.

The therapist may also usefully suggest that sexual activity is not necessarily the first thing the patient needs to engage in in recovery and that, being an activity associated with such high levels of anxiety, it is perhaps more wisely postponed until sobriety is stable and comfortable.

What is the relationship between drug use and aggression?

Central nervous system depressants such as alcohol are strongly associated with violence and aggression of all kinds, including child abuse and spousal abuse. We know, however, from the expectancy literature (Pittman and White 1991), which deals with cognitive expectancies, that there are cultures in which drunkenness is not associated with violence, and, indeed, in these cultures there is none. So cultural expectations play a role here as well as pharmacology. Nevertheless, in our society, violence and heavy drinking are highly correlated. All aggression is not violent, and perhaps one reason that violence is associated with heavy drinking is that those very same heavy drinkers often have great difficulty in using their aggression in adaptive and self-enhancing ways. Therefore, helping patients in early sobriety get in contact with, own, and appropriately utilize and express their aggression is of the essence of therapy. If I were to single out two things that happen in therapy that are most life-enhancing and lead to the most fundamental changes and increase in life satisfaction, they would be helping patients get their aggression out front, and helping them mourn.

Unlike alcohol, marijuana tends to soothe and put people in a kind of dreamy state and is rarely associated with crimes of violence. Cannabis use is not much connected with aggression in our society. And, yet, we know that warriors in Islamic countries have been fired up into states of frenzy, in order to be better warriors, through the smoking of hashish. So, again, expectancies as well as pharmacology appear to play a powerful role in determining the psychological effect of a drug.

There is also the well-known phenomenon of loss of goal-directed behavior, the so-called amotivational syndrome, which is common in heavy pot smokers. Therefore, questions of motivation and mobilizing aggression in service of the ego in an adaptive way are central to the psychotherapy of marijuana addiction and the recovery from it.

Opiate use that leads to nodding out is not associated to any great extent with aggression or with fighting. However, the opiate user who is in a state of withdrawal and needs money to get supplies may commit violent crimes. This is probably much less common than the media would have us believe, but it certainly occurs. However, the nodding heroin addict is a danger to no one but him- or herself. Once again, we find an inhibition of aggression in opiate addicts, and an important part of their psychotherapy is mobilizing aggression and discovering why such heavy wraps have been put on it that the only form of aggression readily available to the addict is aggression against the self in the form of shooting up.

Cocaine and other stimulants increase the availability of dopamine and can lead to paranoid psychosis in which all sorts of violence can occur, but in my experience this is rare. As with the other drugs of abuse, cocaine and other psychostimulants are used more by those who have problems surfacing their aggression than by those who have problems controlling it. Those patients who are averse to—or afraid of—surfacing their aggression are more attracted to sedatives-hypnotics, marijuana, and hashish. The central problem with aggression and addiction, no matter what the drug, is an inhibition in the healthy use of aggression and the substitution of bluster or verbal and sometimes physical violence for any kind of effective action on behalf of rational goal-seeking behavior.

This inhibition may result from many factors, from skill deficits to oedipal guilt, and needs very careful exploration once the patient is stabilized. The therapist's first task is to contain inappropriate acting out and maladaptive expressions of aggression; the second task is the exploration of why there is such inhibition and dysfunction in accessing aggression in rational service of the ego.

What is the effect of drugs on cognition?

In short, not good. Drugs do neurological damage, in most cases transient functional neurological damage, in some cases permanent structural neurological damage, and almost inevitably they lead to confusion, memory lapses, difficulties with learning, and loss of the ability to abstract. This has implications for therapeutic technique in terms of making interventions short, clear, simple, and redundant. There is much repetition (or at least, seeming repetition) in all psychotherapy. In treating substance abusers, both active and early recovering, the therapist must remember that they are not playing with a full deck, and that their psychodynamic denial has as a handmaiden their neurological deficits. Therapists need to be extremely cognizant of the difficulties that their patients are having hearing them, and they need to try to find ways in which they can be heard.

Stimulant drugs, at least in low dosage, improve cognition and intellectual performance. In fact, stimulant drugs such as Ritalin are used in the treatment of such conditions as attention deficit disorder (ADD). There is a subcategory of substance abusers who are self-medicating their ADD; after stable sobriety is achieved, they need stimulant drugs in order to function at their highest cognitive level. But this is tricky, because it entails giving stimulant drugs to patients who have been addicted to stimulant drugs. A patient living with some degree of inefficiency and wandering attention may be preferable to the increased risk of relapse on Ritalin. This needs to be evaluated very carefully by an expert in this area, and then only after stable sobriety is achieved. Therapists tend to be more cautious about giving recovering drug users stimulants than are psychopharmacologists. But this is hardly surprising. There is also a relapse risk in not medicating ADD; the discomfort of living with the ADD may lead to a slip. My own very limited experience is that recovering patients on stimulant therapy do not relapse.

The longer we study it, the longer it seems to take for recovery to occur. There is a twelve-step saying, "It takes five years to get your marbles back, and the rest of your life to learn how to use them," which is not far off. Cognitive recovery is indeed slow, particularly from severe substance abuse, and patients report their own subjective experience of this when they say, "I thought I was pretty clear-headed after a year, and now that I'm sober three years, I realize how far I had to go." The therapist needs to recognize this and to encourage the patient to be patient about his or her learning and memory deficits clearing up. In most instances this is the case, and these difficulties will, indeed, remit with time. Therapists also need to recognize those cases that are more severe and irreversible, and to help those patients get suitable rehabilitation and remediation to make the maximal possible use of their remaining capacity.

What does alexithymia have to do with substance abuse?

Alexithymia, which is the inability to recognize or put feelings into words, is a major difficulty in substance abusers who, as a consequence of either affect regression or fixation to early stages of affect development (see the discussion of Krystal and Raskin in Part III), are unable to verbalize their feelings. The direct pharmacological effect of the drug used on the nervous system may also contribute to the alexithymia. Alexithymia easily lends itself to somaticizing, sexualizing, and acting out of feelings. Feelings that cannot be verbalized are overwhelming, and one of the most common ways of dealing with the inability to withstand the tension of unverbalized affect is to drink or drug it away; hence the importance of affect labeling (that is, the therapist giving the patient words for feelings) in the therapy of substance abuse.

What is anosognosia?

Anosognosia comes from the Greek, meaning, "without knowledge of the disease." It is a neurological condition, occurring most usually following a stroke, in which those parts of the brain that provide feedback circuits to the patient about his or her condition have been damaged by the stroke or other injury. Therefore, even though the patient may, for example, be paralyzed on the left side, the patient has no knowledge of his or her disability. Such patients continue to act as if they had full function on the left side. This is not denial, although it may contribute to psychodynamic denial; rather, it is a deficiency in self-awareness caused by neurological impairment.

How does anosognosia relate to substance abuse?

Substance abusers are notorious for their denial. Although I have never seen it in the literature, it has occurred to me that part of that denial might have a neurological basis. That is, the very substances used may poison certain brain circuits leading to their weakening or total dysfunctioning, and these circuits may be the circuits that are necessary for the patient to have self-awareness of his or her substance abuse. If this is indeed the case, then one aspect of denial becomes a special case of the cognitive impairment we know that drugs often induce.

What this means for treatment is that if there is some interaction between the neurological and the psychodynamic in the etiology of the denial, the lack of realistic perception of self and world, and the impaired concentration and ability to abstract, which is a common syndrome in advanced substance abuse, particularly alcoholism, then the therapist must aim his or her interventions in such a way that they can penetrate both psychodynamic denial and neurological impairment, including, perhaps, some degree of anosognosia. Therefore, a technique that uses simple, direct speech—sticks to the concrete and gives as many illustrations of the point to be made as possible from the patient's life, drawn from the material of the therapy sessions—is indicated. A high degree of redundancy in the therapist's interventions with the patient, particularly about the import of the substance abuse, is necessary to circumvent the psychodynamic denial, perhaps complicated by organic factors.

What is the effect of drugs on affect?

The "down" drugs take their devotees down, and the "up" drugs take them up, and all drugs whirl their abusers around and confuse them affectively as well as cognitively. Most substance abusers these days are poly-substance abusers, and this poly-abuse eventuates in severe affective metastability. Thus, what therapists see, in late addiction and early in sobriety, is in effect an organic brain syndrome characterized by cognitive deficits in memory, in abstraction, and in the ability to make connections, along with affective lability. The patient is up, down, and sideways. This emotional lability is an important part of the recovery process; that is, it is partly a sign of healing.

Unfortunately, emotional lability can also end the recovery process if the discomfort of the mood swings becomes so great that the patient returns to drugs rather than enduring the pain of the lability. Therefore, it is very useful to tell patients, "You are going to go through a lot of changes in your recovery, and we are going to talk about them in as much detail as we possibly can. And, sometimes we are going to find the reason you are so upset, whether that reason is something happening in your life, or something you remembered from the past, or some difficulty you are having in a current relationship. But sometimes, as clever and persistent as we may be, we are not going to find any reason for your emotional upset. Now, that may be because we are not clever and persistent enough, but that may not be the case because some of the changes that you are going to go through will simply be the result of the chemical changes of your brain in recovery. They are manifestations of your brain recovering; indeed, of you recovering. If you simply don't act on your mood swings and painfully intense feelings, and do something self-destructive like picking up and getting high, your periods of discomfort will become less frequent and less intense and eventually disappear."

That is a long and complicated intervention delivered to a patient who is likely not to be playing with a full deck. Therefore, it may need to be said in simpler terms, and certainly will need to be said more than once. This is an extremely helpful intervention because it gives a cognitive structure to a chaotic and frightening experience and helps the patient hold on during the recovery period.

What is the post-use syndrome?

The post-use syndrome comprises the various psychiatric and emotional conditions that can result from the substance use itself. For example, there is a postcocaine anxiety syndrome, which reflects changes in neuro-chemistry consequent on long-term, heavy cocaine use. This is a condition that remits slowly, if at all, and may require pharmacological as well as social and psychological treatment. Unfortunately, none of those treatments are very effective and the patient may simply need to learn to live with chronic anxiety. It may be the case that the best that can be done is for the patient to learn coping skills to deal with this persistent anxiety. There are many other post-drug syndromes in which some form of emotional discomfort or psychiatric disability is consequent on the drug use, and these conditions tend to be very treatment resistant. The *DSM-IV* recognizes these post-use syndromes and has a whole section devoted to them. This is an innovation; it is the first official acknowledgment of the existence of post-use psychiatric illness.

What is the prolonged abstinence syndrome?

The prolonged abstinence syndrome is the continuation of dysphoria of various sorts well into sobriety. It differs from acute withdrawal in being less dramatic, less dangerous, and less painful. The main danger of the prolonged withdrawal syndrome is it readily leads to relapse.

Sleep disturbance is extremely common, as are cognitive disturbances and emotional lability. This syndrome is also characterized by irritability, poor affect tolerance, and little capacity to tolerate stress. All of these states can quickly lead to relapse unless they are dealt with in therapy. The best way to do this is for the therapist to discuss the prolonged abstinence syndrome (also known as the prolonged withdrawal syndrome) with the patient: "There will be a lot of ups and downs to go through, but they are a normal part of your recovery. If you just don't use, they will gradually get better. Come in and bitch about the changes you are going through—talk to me about them—but don't use."

What is the relationship between regression and substance abuse?

The vector goes both ways. Regression to Heinz Kohut's stage of the archaic nuclear self (see Part III), or regression to Melanie Klein's paranoid-schizoid position as the dominant mode of functioning and being (see Part III), or regression to Freud's oral stage all predispose to substance use. So does fixation at any or all of these development stages or positions.

On the other hand, substance use, as it proceeds into abuse, is a profoundly regressive process. Defenses become more primitive: adaptive behaviors are lost; functioning becomes more erratic; the object relational world (that is, the internal world of object representations) becomes less differentiated, simpler, more primitive, less adequate to deal with the complexities of reality; fusion and merger takes place between self and object representations; there is affective regression (as delineated by Krystal and Raskin [1970]) back to a state of primitive *Ur-affect* characterized by dedifferentiation, deverbalization, sexualization, and somatization (see p. 90). The depth of this regression must be taken extremely seriously. It is often missed by therapists, particularly when they are dealing with well-educated, well-dressed, middle-class patients who are glib talkers and want to impress with their educational and vocational attainments. Emotional regression is omnipresent in active and early recovery substance abusers along with neurological and cognitive regression. These patients experience fusion and confusion. If the therapist misses the depth of the regression/fixation in affect, cognition, self-representation, object relations, and psychosexual stage, the treatment will fail, because the therapist will be addressing someone who is not in the room. If the therapist keeps in mind the enormous disorganizing effect of prolonged substance abuse and addresses patients at their developmental stage, patients will feel understood and begin to redifferentiate and reintegrate as they come back up the developmental ladder.

Many substance abusers are cases of fixation rather than regression. These are the patients who have been described by Robert Knight (1937, 1938) in his delineation of "essential alcoholism" (see Part III). In terms of Otto Kernberg's (1975) typology of character types, they are at the lower range of the borderline spectrum. These patients are difficult to treat, often needing some form of institutional treatment as well as individual psychotherapy. They are the patients who are said to need habilitation rather than rehabilitation.

What is the relationship between substance abuse and self-esteem?

There are very few statements that I would make categorically about substance abuse. There is, however, one that I am comfortable in asserting: there are no serious substance abusers who do not have abysmally low self-esteem. As is so often the case in substance abuse, this is both cause and effect. As Rado (1933) pointed out, substance use is driven perhaps more by the need to raise self-esteem than by any other dynamic. Tragically, the cure exacerbates the disease, and the addictive career is one long assault on self-esteem as the abuser suffers loss and wounds and contempt and rejection piled upon loss and wounds and contempt and rejection. By the time the patient begins therapy, there is barely enough self-esteem to sustain life, and sometimes not even that.

What can the therapist do to increase the patient's self-esteem?

The recovery process itself increases the patient's self-esteem. Each day patients stay away from drugs, they will feel a little better about themselves—less out of control, and more in command of self. Group therapy can be very helpful in raising self-esteem, giving patients an opportunity to share guilt and shame and to get positive feedback from peers, an experience that is different from, and sometimes more effective and believable than, feedback coming from the therapist, who is not a peer and who does not share (at least qua therapist) the cycle of despair and redemption that patients traverse.

But at best, the acquisition or reacquisition of self-esteem is a long and uneven process. The acquiring of a reasonably constant and reason-

ably high level of self-esteem is one of the results of transmuting internalization of healthy self-selfobject relationships in early life according to
Kohut (see Part III). Lacking such relationships, transmuting internalization of selfobject functions including modulation of satisfactory levels of
self-esteem has often not taken place in the lives of substance abusing
patients. Amelioration of these deficits takes place by indirection throughout the long process of transmuting internalization (i.e., taking in good stuff
a little bit at a time) during the therapy. Somehow, the therapist's regard
for the patient has to get inside the patient.

The aspect of low self-esteem consequent upon the abuse itself disappears naturally with the cessation of use and is slowly replaced with good
feelings about the self. The acquisition of an identity as a recovering person and as a healer of other people, as happens to those who are in a twelve-
step program, does wonderful things for self-esteem, but that's not the only
route. Self-esteem is raised by analysis of the genetic (historical) roots of
self-hatred, accomplishment (especially in the area of emotional growth),
and self-forgiveness (sometimes entailing reparation), and by more consistently facing reality.

What is the relationship of narcissism to substance abuse?

This is a topic discussed at a number of points in this primer. It is my
belief that narcissistic problems, particularly those around self-esteem and
self-cohesion, are absolutely central to the psychodynamics of substance
abuse and must be addressed in the therapy. Here, I am talking about the
internal world and the way it manifests itself in subjective states and in
behavior. But usually when mental health professionals talk about narcissistic personality disorders they are talking about feelings of entitlement,
the need for omnipotent control, the devaluation of other people, shallow-
ness in emotional relations, exploitiveness in emotional relations, and the
rest of the *DSM-IV* description of narcissistic personality disorder. Narcissists in the *DSM-IV* sense are not very likable characters. Substance
abusers have received bad-enough press without my adding to it, and they
themselves believe that bad press, so I do not wish to say that all substance

abusers are narcissistic personality disorders in the *DSM-IV* sense. That is contrary to fact, and it is very damaging. There are a significant minority of substance abusers who are narcissistic personality disorders in the *DSM-IV* sense. However, there are far more substance abusers who suffer from pathological narcissism in Kohut's sense, as elaborated in my discussion of Kohut (see Part III). Further, the addictive process itself exacerbates pathological narcissism, as the addict becomes self-involved of necessity. There is nothing else the addict can do or be except be absorbed with him- or herself and the acquisition of the drug, which is identified with the self in advanced stages of addiction. This is necessary to survive psychically, even physically, in the later stages of drug addiction.

Treatment focuses on reducing narcissistic vulnerability through the ego-building effect of psychodynamic psychotherapy. This ego (self) strengthening is a by-product of the entire therapeutic process. It is surprising how much narcissistic pathology including the *DSM-IV* description is secondary to and a defense against narcissistic vulnerability.

What is the relationship of antisocial personality disorder to substance abuse?

Antisocial personality disorder (ASP), also called sociopathy, is frequently comorbid with substance abuse and dependence; however, the meaning of this is complex and less than certain. ASPs commonly drink and drug to excess and in socially irresponsible ways as a manifestation of their sociopathy. It is merely another antisocial behavior, although biologically oriented researchers have suggested that both antisocial behavior and the substance abuse are consequent on a common neurochemical abnormality probably involving low levels of serotonin. Here, the substance abuse is driven by the antisocial personality disorder.

On the other hand, in their desperation to get supplies, substance abusers frequently commit antisocial or even criminal acts they would never otherwise engage in. Here, the antisocial behavior is secondary to the addiction. This primary-secondary distinction is of great importance clinically; the substance abuser who engages in antisocial behavior in defense and support of (usually) his addiction, is a very different patient than the ASP patient who drinks and drugs. For further discussion of this matter, see the sections on the preaddictive personality (p. 47); on the postaddictive personality (p. 43); on classifications of drug use, particularly by Winokur and Cloninger (pp. 26, 27); and Leon Wurmser's notion of dynamic of flight from conscience in substance abuse (p. 94).

Therapists must be cautious in working with substance abusers who display strong antisocial tendencies.

Ted had come to me with a drinking problem and apparent guilt (which in retrospect may have been pseudo-guilt), about his anti-social behavior, particularly in money matters. Foolishly, I let him run up a modest but meaningful bill, in spite of having been forewarned, a mistake I have not repeated. He always had an excuse. When I finally confronted him, saying that he must make a substantial payment or the treatment would have to be suspended, Ted became indignant, replying, "You have some nerve! I told you I was antisocial when I came here and I wanted you to treat me for it. The fact that I'm stiffing you proves you haven't helped me, so why should I pay you? Since you didn't cure me, there is no reason I should give you a cent!" I didn't get paid.

Ted notwithstanding, therapists should remember that the majority of substance abusers suffer from overly punitive super-egos rather than the opposite.

What is the relationship among depression, manic-depression, and substance abuse?

As noted elsewhere in this primer, depression may be secondary to substance abuse, or substance abuse secondary to depression, and they both need to be treated if recovery is to occur. The same is not quite true about manic-depression.

Manic-depression closely follows the addictive cycle: manic high on the drug, succeeded by depressive crash or hangover characterized by remorse, guilt, and self-hatred. Both the manic-depressive and the addictive cycle consist of intense euphoria and a sharp rise in self-esteem followed by a precipitous decline in self-esteem with concomitant self-hatred. Many authors, starting with Rado (1933), have noted the isomorphism between manic depression and addiction.

It is known that many manic-depressives become alcoholic or become addicted to other drugs, and it is known that drug use, particularly of central nervous system stimulants, can set off manic episodes. In the case of manic depressives who are addicted—usually, but not always, to alcohol— there is little hope of recovery unless the addiction can be treated. The converse is also true; manic-depressive substance abusers cannot stay clean unless their mood disorder is treated. The usual treatment is psychopharmacological. For most manic-depressives, lithium carbonate (Li_2CO_3) is the drug of choice. For those manic-depressive addicted patients who are in twelve-step programs, that can be a problem. I have known patients who were told by their AA or Narcotics Anonymous (NA) sponsors to discontinue taking lithium because they were supposed to be living a drug-free lifestyle. Those who did so went into manic episodes. So when the dual diagnosis is manic-depression, the therapist must be very alert to the attitudes of the patient's twelve-step group toward the use of psychotropic medication. The same would be true of a dual-diagnosis patient who had schizophrenia.

Having said that, and certainly believing that treatment with lithium is a rational therapy for manic-depression, I think it is also the case that the psychodynamic side of manic-depression tends to be ignored these days and should not be. A great deal can be accomplished psychotherapeutically, uncovering the repressed affective and object relational determinants of the cyclothymia. Cyclothymia is the neurotic equivalent of full-blown manic-depressive psychosis. The central issues in the psychotherapy of cyclothymia are stabilizing self-esteem and building defenses against narcissistic injury. These patients are excessively vulnerable to narcissistic injury. The essence of the treatment is the gain in ego strength and self-cohesion that allows the patient to weather various sorts of narcissistic injuries without going into a manic defense against the underlying fall in self-esteem.

Henry J. Richards (1993) has written that addiction parallels the three major mental illnesses: the manic phase in which the patient becomes high, the depressive stage in which the patient is coming down from the drug (and which may also have preceded the drug use), and the schizoid isolation into which substance abusers sooner or later enter. (The schizoid isolation is parallel to the schizoid personality disorder concomitant with schizophrenia.) Richards is quite right on that point, and in substance abuse therapy the therapist needs to talk about the mania, the depression, and the schizoid isolation.

> *What is the relationship between suicide and substance abuse?*

Suicide and substance abuse, particularly alcoholism, are strongly correlated; that is, a substantial proportion of suicides are alcoholic or other substance dependent. This is over and above what Karl Menninger called the "chronic suicide" of alcoholics (see Part III). Of course, the majority of alcoholics do not suicide. Similar correlations and relationships pertain between child abuse (physical and sexual), and spousal abuse and alcoholism.

Suicide is also a danger in early recovery when the addict, now stripped of defense and coping mechanism, is overwhelmed.

Jack was speaking of his early days of recovery:

> Doctor, I went into detox after my therapist said, "You think you drink because you're crazy. Did it ever occur to you that you're crazy because you drink?" When I came out of detox, I was really shaky. I returned to Bierer House, a sort of oddball halfway house named for the psychiatrist who, with Maxwell Jones, pioneered social rehabilitation of mental patients in England. It was a wild, wonderful, but totally unstructured brownstone in the West 20s. Marion Tanner, who was the model for Auntie Mame, was the "housemother." She was then in her late eighties and her free-flowing white hair fell to her buttocks. She ran the place, sort of, with Libby Lyon, a far-out

social worker who combined social radicalism with real-estate shrewd-ness. Marion played Don Quixote to Libby's Sancho Panza. Marion had a real gift for soothing distraught people, but I didn't think of availing myself of her services.

The house always had a fascinating mix of recently discharged mental patients, the recently separated and divorced, students, bohe-mians, and sundry drifters—mostly alcoholic. You could get a chess or bridge game or a philosophical debate at three in the morning.

I had responded to an ad in the *Village Voice*, "Betwixt or be-tween? Try Bierer House." I had arrived drunk and woke up in a semi-blackout, not quite sure where I was or how I got there. Several months later I went into detox. The day I got out was okay. I pretty much spent it in my room on the fourth floor staring out the window at the Gen-eral Theological Seminary across the street. But I was increasingly aware of the concrete sidewalk below. When I awoke the window was talking to me, "Jack, come and jump out." I tried to sleep despite the voice, but to little avail. I don't think I was really crazy because I knew it was a projection, but I couldn't turn it off. Then I felt sucked to-ward the window as by a giant vacuum cleaner. I tried to fight the suction, but I kept getting closer to the window. I knew others had jumped from Bierer House windows and I thought, "I'm going to have to jump, I have no choice. I have to kill myself!" Some vestige of sanity must have saved me. I braced my legs, resisted the pull toward the window and fled. When I got out on the street—nobody was around—I started running and I didn't stop until I got to the Mustard Seed, an AA "clubhouse" in midtown, which was miles away. I walked into a lunchtime meeting populated with prosperous-looking business types. I was unemployed, my career in ashes, and looking at the people fill-ing the meeting made me feel even worse. I was still sure that I would have to kill myself. My attention kept going back to that window, and the "speaker's" words hardly registered. Then I started getting the drift of what he was saying—he was talking about his own suicidal thoughts. My attention became riveted on his story:

When I first got sober, I just couldn't hack it. My life was a shambles, but the worst thing was my feelings, I just couldn't stand them and I didn't know what to do with them. I couldn't even name them, all I knew was that they were awful—not to be borne. So I decided to kill myself. I had always drunk when I felt shitty, but now I couldn't do that. Drink had always been my escape hatch and now it was closed. I knew I couldn't drink; I don't know why, but I had shut that door forever and I knew it. I guess I knew that a return to alcohol meant an even worse death—the damn stuff just didn't work any more. So I had nowhere to run until I thought of killing myself. Death was a place to run. The old door was closed and sealed, so I opened a new one. I was really going to do it until I realized that what I really wanted was to drink. Then I remembered that I knew what to do about that so I started going to more meetings and talking to my sponsor. He told me that I wanted to kill myself because I didn't know how to cope sober and I wasn't used to staying with pain. He said he could help me to cope and stay with my feelings. My suicidal obsession lifted. It took me a long time and a lot of meetings until I felt halfway decent; but— a day at a time—it happened, and today I'm doing pretty well.

I sucked in the speaker's every word. I felt enormous relief. By the end of that meeting I knew that I didn't have to and wouldn't kill myself. In AA they say that there are no coincidences. I don't believe in that mystical crap—what did Jung call it . . . synchronicity?—but who knows? I sure got to the right meeting, and however it happened, I was able to identify.

Therapists would do well to reflect on Jack's story. Patients in early recovery who are really concerned that they cannot go back to alcohol or drugs and who are overwhelmed by long-anesthetized feelings are suicidal risks. They feel that they cannot live with drugs and they can't live without them. It is sometimes helpful for the therapist to articulate this for the patient and warn that suicide may seem like the only way out— but it is not.

Jack's therapist's line (oversimplification that it is), that brought him to detox also has its uses in substance abuse treatment.

Jason had stuck a quarter of a million dollars up his nose in the form of cocaine. He suffered postcocaine anxiety syndrome and extensive psychopathology. I was an expert witness at his divorce hearing. He was asking for alimony from his wife on the basis of his disability and half of the value of their expensive condo. She was on the stand, testifying that Jason had trashed the condo during his cocaine sprees, greatly reducing its resale value. In the most innocent of little-boy voices, Jason interrupted the proceedings to say, "Your honor, the only damage I ever did to the apartment was when the hook pulled out of the ceiling when I tried to hang myself."

Jason got a decent settlement.

Could you comment on addiction and interpersonal problems?

As in so much about substance abuse, the vector goes both ways. Difficulties in interpersonal relations lead to substance use, which in turn becomes abuse; and the abuse leads to difficulty in interpersonal relations, leading to yet more substance use. A vicious cycle has been set up. Substance abuse patients often spend most of their time complaining about their mate or significant other. It is useful to interpret: "Mr. Smith, you have two problems; one is your marriage and the other is your substance abuse, but I should really put that in the opposite order. Even though your wife says all the problems in your marriage are caused by your cocaine abuse, it is quite possible that that is not the case and that there are problems in your marriage that would be there whether you were using or not. But you can't do anything about that situation one way or another unless you deal with your cocaine use. Only after you stop getting high can you sort out what is going on at home, and see whether your wife is right, or you are right, or as is most likely, you are both right." What the therapist is doing is not falling into the trap of blaming everything on the substance use, which the patient has been hearing from everyone for years, yet while acknowledging the fact that there may be (and probably are) other things going on, not for one minute letting go of the notion that the substance abuse is a major problem that must be dealt with. Therapists err in two directions here. The more naive therapist will sometimes buy the patient's rationalization for the substance use, while the therapist who is more committed to the disease model may put everything on the substance abuse, which denies the patient's subjective experience and, indeed, often the objective reality.

What is the relationship between impulsivity and compulsivity in substance abuse?

Substance abusers are impulsive. They have difficulty staying with their feelings and have little tolerance of delayed gratification. As has been frequently noted, mature adults postpone gratification and are miserable. Yet, those who do not delay gratification tend to be even more miserable; to wit: substance abusers. Yet substance abuse is clearly often compulsive. It involves repetition over and over again of the same activity. The Kohut–Levin (Levin 1987; also see p. 110) model of the psychodynamic correlative of addiction being regression-fixation to Kohut's stage of the archaic self makes sense of this phenomenon of simultaneous impulsivity and compulsivity. According to the model, failures of internalization lead to self-deficits that make the control of impulse extremely difficult and tenuous at best, while the compulsivity is driven by a desperate attempt to fill in the gaps in psychic structure—an attempt doomed to failure. In recovery, patients frequently become even more compulsive. The ritual of the twelve-step programs is about as compulsive as you can get. I have had patients who have heard the same preamble read literally thousand of times and yet go back to hear it at more and more meetings. Ritual is soothing and satisfying, at least for some people.

Therapists treating substance abusers need to support compulsive defenses for a long time because the alternative is a return to impulsivity, which means a return to active substance use. The patient's compulsive defenses are there for a reason, to keep his or her impulsivity under wraps. It is only much later in the treatment that the maladaptive nature of the compulsive defenses is appropriately interpreted. Such interpretation is only timely after stable and secure sobriety has been achieved (it is much better to have 10,000 rituals than to start shooting up again after a year of sobriety). Then and only then should the therapist help the recovering addict look at his or her maladaptive compulsivity.

> *What is apraxia and how does it relate to substance abuse?*

Apraxia, which is Greek for "not acting," is a technical term in neurology that denotes an inability to carry out purposeful movements in the absence of paralysis. It is particularly applied to a situation in which the patient is unable to use an object, such as a fork. It is a cognitive deficit secondary to organic impairment. The psychoanalyst John Gedo (1997, Gedo and Goldberg 1973), has borrowed the term to denote psychological and emotional inabilities to act rationally. He believes that these psychological apraxias are also cognitive deficits. To act sanely one must know *how* to act sanely. Gedo understands emotional apraxias as partly neurological, perhaps congenitally so, and partly experiential, the result of faulty learning and disturbed early relationships. Substance abusers demonstrate many apraxias.

Gedo sees apraxias—the inabilities to self-soothe, modulate anxiety, regulate affect, and anticipate consequences—as essentially learning deficiencies complicated and exacerbated by constitutional weaknesses. He sees apraxias as the root pathology in severe neurosis and in addiction. The core apraxia, the one with the most saliency, is a deficit in the ability to regulate affect. This is a devastating deficit, rendering its sufferers vulnerable to chronic and acute depression, mania, anxiety disorders, and personality disorders understood as failed attempts at adaptation to deficit.

Gedo originally specified only three apraxias: problems in tension regulation, difficulties in organizing a coherent program of action, and the inability to renounce illusions. Substance abusers commonly demonstrate all three of these apraxias. Later, Gedo added disorders of thought, communication, learning, planning, affectivity, and encoding of bodily signals to what was now an open list of apraxias.

Apraxias are close relatives of—or alternate ways of conceptualizing—alexithymia (Krystal and Raskin), ego and self deficits (Khantzian), failures of internalization of psychic structure (Kohut), and failure to acquire "tools for living" (twelve-step programs). (See sections in this primer on these authors and concepts.) So there is widespread agreement that substance abuse on its psychodynamic side can be best understood as a misdirected attempt at compensation and adaptation. Gedo's unique contribution is his emphasis on the biological basis of at least the vulnerability to apraxias evidenced by his borrowing of the term from neurology, and understood as difficulties in subcortical functioning. Attention deficit disorder and posttraumatic stress disorder, which are highly comorbid with substance abuse, can also usefully be conceptualized as apraxias.

Working as a five session per week analyst, Gedo's treatment recommendation is essentially an increase in insight brought about by making the patient aware of his or her apraxias and how they impede the patient's quest for smooth functioning and a sense of well-being. Symptoms ranging from phobias to substance abuse are interpreted as either avoidances of apraxic weaknesses or compensations for them. The patient who previously had no understanding of what was wrong or of the need for remediation experiences relief—understanding soothes—or as the great slogan of Austrian liberalism put it, "*Weissen macht frei*," knowledge liberates. The patient can now institute appropriate remedial actions and learnings with the analyst's support and guidance. To modify the most famous of twelve-step "slogans"—the Serenity Prayer—the patient accepts the things he cannot change, and changes the things he can. With some modifications this is a treatment model, a therapeutic strategy, of great utility in working with substance abusers.

Gedo's "models of the mind" and the treatment recommendations flowing from them also have applications to substance abuse treatment. Gedo, looking at the internecine theoretical battles within psychoanalysis, concluded that the competing models were accurate ways of understanding *differing* developmental stages—their mutual contradictions being only apparent. In his hierarchical epigenic (meaning that each developmentally later stage incorporates all earlier stages) model, Gedo envisions human functioning as best conceptualized as a succession of stages that find representation in the following schemata: (1) the reflex arc (for preverbal, presymbolic functioning as well as nonverbal, nonsymbolic functioning in later life) suggested both by Freud's (1900) *Interpretation of Dreams*, and Jean Piaget's sensorimotor stage of cognitive development; (2) the object relations model of internal representations of self and object as developing from fused and split precursors (see sections on Klein and Kernberg in Part III); (3) Freud's structural model of id, ego, and superego, which best accounts for the emotional conflicts of the oedipal stage and of later life; and finally (4) Freud's topographical model of dynamic unconscious, preconscious, and conscious realms of the mind, which best represents the postoedipal mind and nonpathological, albeit inherently limited, maturity. The patient needs to be understood as functioning at all of these levels.

Gedo derives important treatment recommendations from his hierarchical model. He is thinking of the techniques of analysis, but his suggestions apply quite well to substance abuse therapy.

He recommends that the therapist use:

1. *Pacification* to quell the turmoil and acting out that is concomitant with the inability to regulate affect characteristic of the preverbal, presymbolic reflex arc stage and its survivals into later life;
2. *Unification* to facilitate the patient's integration of split self and object representations;
3. *Disillusionment* of the primitive idealization characteristic of early object relations;
4. *Interpretation* to make conscious the intrapyschic conflicts characteristic of the oedipal and later stages as explicated in the structural model; and
5. *Introspection* by the reasonable, healthy adult to continue to make conscious the unconscious as depicted in the topographic model.

This sequence of interventions, sequential conceptually although not temporally, that is, the therapist mixes as needed pacification (cf., Winnicott's holding environment and Scharff's [1992] contextual transference), unification, disillusionment, and interpretation, is an excellent guide to technique in substance abuse therapy. Substance abuse patients are desperately in need of pacification. They are chaotic, unstable, and racked by affect storms. The therapist provides pacification through the holding of the therapeutic relationship; facilitating additional support as needed through referral to AA, NA, detox, group, or inpatient rehabilitation; making sense out of chaos through didactic interventions, especially those explaining the disease model of addiction; and calling attention to apraxias and demonstrating their effects on the substance abuser's life and use.

People, and substance abusers more than most, need mother's milk and corrective feedback all their lives, preferably from the same person. Therapy provides this, which pacifies, too.

The therapist facilitates unification by connecting the splits manifest in the substance abusing patient's relationship to self, therapist, drug of choice, and other people. The therapist enables the patient's disillusionment with his or her idealized substances and compulsive activities by pointing out the unrealistic nature of the user's "belief" in the magical qualities of the substance and by providing the security necessary for such disillusionment to take place. Interpretation of conflict, the last of Gedo's therapeutic techniques not only provides insight, it pacifies and facilitates unification, as does sobriety itself.

Introspection in such guises as self-analysis and "working" AA's tenth step ("continue to take personal inventory . . ."), is part of every spiritual and psychodynamic tradition and a necessary condition of mental health.

III

Psychodynamic
Theories of Addiction

There are many dynamic theories of addiction, some of which derive from drive theory, some from ego psychology, some from object relations theory, and some from self psychology. One of the earliest formulators of a dynamic theory of addiction is Thomas Trotter, already referred to (see p. 10) in the context of his being one of the ancestors of the disease concept of addiction. In his work, Trotter (Jellinek 1943) stated that addiction, in this case to alcohol, was the result of premature weaning and heredity. It was not a bad guess he made, that the causes of addiction lie in early trauma and in constitutional predisposition. Other theorists who have written importantly about the dynamics of addiction include Freud, Karl Abraham, Edward Glover, Karl Menninger, Thomas Szasz, Sandor Rado, Henry Tiebout, Henry Krystal and Herbert Raskin, Leon Wurmser, Peter Hartocollis, Edward Khantzian, Robert Knight, Ernst Simmel, Otto Fenichel, and Heinz Kohut.

What does Sigmund Freud say about addiction?

In *Civilization and its Discontents*, Freud (1930) stated:

> The service rendered by intoxicating media in the struggle for happiness and in keeping misery at a distance is so highly prized as a benefit that individuals and peoples alike have given it an established place in the economics of their libido. We owe to such media not merely the immediate yield to pleasure, but also a greatly desired degree of independence from the external world. For one knows that, with the help of this "drowner of cares" one can at any time withdraw from the pressure of reality and find refuge in a world of one's own with better conditions of sensibility. [p. 78]

Freud, the cocaine devotee and nicotine addict, was most certainly not oblivious to the pleasures of substance use.

What else does Freud tell us about addiction besides the fact that it allows us to escape external reality and to retreat to an inner world of narcissistic fantasy?

In a letter to Wilhelm Fliess, Freud (1897) states that all later addictions are displacements of and reenactments of the original addiction to masturbation. This may seem far afield from our everyday work with substance abusers; however, it is a dynamic that highlights the dead-end nature of addiction, its compulsive repetition, the guilt and shame that accompanies the failure to follow through on the resolve, originally not to masturbate, later not to use, a failure that is driven by withdrawal into a world of fantasy and narcissistic pleasure. Just as one's love object in masturbation is one's self, or one's fantasy of another, but not an actual other, one's love object in addiction is that substance experienced as an extension of self. In his essay on the great Russian writer, *Dostoyevsky and Parricide*, Freud (1928) analyzes Dostoyevsky's compulsive gambling and plays upon the word *play*, saying Dostoyevsky's gambling addiction is a displacement and reenactment of his addiction to and inward conflict about masturbation. But Freud complicates the picture by condensing masturbatory guilt with oedipal guilt and with guilt for the addictive activity itself. He points out that Dostoyevsky's violent alcoholic father was murdered by his peasants, enacting Dostoyevsky's unconscious wish to kill that father, and that the enactment in reality of the fantasy, inculcated guilt—overwhelming guilt—in Dostoyevsky. This analysis allows Freud to focus on the payoff in Dostoyevsky's compulsive gambling, namely losing. The pleasure is in the pain. Addictions offer one a rare opportunity to express aggression and be punished for it simultaneously. This is an extraordinarily powerful hook.

In *Beyond the Pleasure Principle*, Freud (1920) speaks of the repetition compulsion as a manifestation of the death instinct. He uses addiction as one of his examples of the repetition compulsion. The centrality of guilt and the use of substance abuse for self-punishment is highly salient, and its interpretation is often mutative in treating substance abusers. Additionally, many addicts describe themselves as "doing nothing but jerking off." The masturbatory nature of addiction is often recognized by patients and can sometimes be usefully interpreted. Of course, if one were dealing with a 250-lb. truck driver who is an angry man, it is probably unwise to interpret, "When you drank, all you did was whack off," even though it may be dynamically true.

Whenever I ponder whether or not to interpret an addiction to a substance as a displacement of an addiction to masturbation, I think of the probably apocryphal story of Ms. Henderson who sat in the front row of Bruno Bettelheim's lecture hall at the University of Chicago, ostentatiously knitting as the august professor held the rest of the auditorium spellbound. Week after week the universally feared Dr. Bettelheim would glower at Ms. Henderson, but to no avail. Finally, he could take it no more and halted his presentation to address the offender. Speaking in his coldest and most contemptuous manner, the professor said, "Ms. Henderson, do you know that knitting is symbolic masturbation?" The hall was enveloped in a silence you could cut with a knife until Ms. Henderson, totally unruffled, replied, "Professor Bettelheim, when I knit, I knit; and when I masturbate, I masturbate." Some addicts use when they use and masturbate when they masturbate, but then some don't.

What has Edward Glover contributed to our understanding
of addiction?

Glover, an English analyst chiefly known for his notion of ego nuclei, self precursors that coalesce into an ego, also highlighted a central dynamic in substance abuse, namely, drinking or drugging in order to express rage at someone. Glover (1928) speaks of oral and anal sadism as the central dynamic in addiction. I prefer to talk of the "Fuck you martini." Most slips, that is, relapses, are driven by unconscious and sometimes conscious rage. They are angry acts, eating or drinking or smoking or drugging or sexing against somebody. That somebody may be an external object or an internal object and the therapist needs to be alert for the possibility that the rage directed at the external object is transferential and really belongs to one or more internal objects. The patient's rage, usually over some narcissistic injury, must be interpreted. That rage often comes from narcissistic vulnerability, from feelings of worthlessness, from low self-esteem, or from an inability to deal with the slings and arrows of outrageous fortune. In that state of narcissistic vulnerability, the injury, real or imagined, is often, by any reasonable objective standard, slight indeed. But in the addict's mind, it is an overwhelming offense to "His or Her Majesty, the Baby" (Freud 1914), and elicits narcissistic rage. "Off with their heads" is the sentiment behind the "Fuck you martini."

What does Karl Abraham have to say about the
dynamics of addiction?

Abraham (1908) wrote one of his first psychoanalytic papers on addiction, his topic being the relationship between sexuality and alcoholism. Abraham teaches us two very useful things. First, he amalgamated and bridged the sociological and the psychological. His analysis of alcoholism is in terms of male drinking in the beer *stubba*, the taverns of Berlin, around the beginning of the twentieth century. His awareness of the social dimen-

sions of that behavior very much informs his paper, just as we need to in-
form our understanding of our addictive and substance abusing patients
by understanding their cultural setting. Second, Abraham emphasized the
use of alcohol, and by extension, any drug, to express forbidden wishes—
explicitly, forbidden homosexual wishes. He pointed to a more or less open
expression of homoeroticism in the bleary-eyed camaraderie of the beer
stubba, and this in a highly homophobic society. Only with the consumption of alcohol were these men capable of putting their arms around each
other, sometimes kissing each other, and of expressing love toward each
other. Abraham points out the psychosexual regression that accompanies
drunkenness, as the component instincts (see Freud 1905) come to be expressed directly. Abraham here is thinking primarily of sadistic enactments,
but also of masochistic ones, as well as of the expression of ego-dystonic
homosexuality. He also highlights delusions of jealousy in the alcoholic.
As the alcoholic's potency diminishes as a consequence of his drinking,
he now accuses his wife of being with other men. This too is a defense
against homosexual wishes—"It is she, a woman, and not I, a man, who
desires another man."

The 1990s, of course, are another time and place. Nevertheless, we
encounter many patients who drink in order to express forbidden sexual
desires—sadistic, masochistic, homosexual, what have you. They then
discount them. I have treated many men who have had homosexual experiences while drunk who disclaim that experience totally, it had nothing to
do with them, it was just the booze. The same is true for other drugs. The
therapist needs to interpret the unconscious wish that finds expression in
the state of being high and help the patient own the wish, or fantasy, or
drive.

What does Karl Menninger teach us about the
dynamics of addiction?

Menninger (1938), one of the few American analysts to subscribe to
Freud's (1920) notion of the death instinct, wrote a book, *Man Against
Himself*, depicting many forms of self-destruction. Both alcoholism and

drug addiction receive prominent treatment in that text. Menninger more than almost any other dynamic thinker emphasizes the self-punitive and self-destructive dynamic of addictive behavior. He calls addiction "chronic suicide." This is also known as suicide on the installment plan. Drug addiction is highly correlated with suicide, as is alcoholism, and such suicide may indeed be acute rather than chronic. There is a debate in the literature about the meaning of addictive self-destructive behavior. Some thinkers, such as Edward Khantzian (1981), believe that the self-destructive behavior is a by-product of the addict's use of the substance for adaptive purposes. The behaviorally oriented researchers believe that addiction is biphasic in the sense that it initially provides pleasure, and only much later in the addictive process does it have serious negative consequences. Therefore, it is perfectly rational for users to continue doing something (drugging or drinking) that provides them with positive reinforcement. If users are addictively inclined, they continue to seek that positive reinforcement (euphoria and/or anxiety reduction) until they are hooked, that is, addicted. Only later do the negative consequences come, and by then they cannot escape them because they are now addicted. So, from both an ego psychological and a behavioral point of view, the self-destruction, which is certainly real enough, of the addict is not dynamically motivated.

Menninger believes the opposite. I believe the two positions are not incompatible. As we know, contrarieties do not trouble primary process thinking. Thus, one may be using a drug in an adaptive fashion to meet some ego need one cannot meet on one's own, and one may be destroying one's self, in terms of health, financial well-being, relationships, and relationship with self simply because one is hooked and doesn't know how to escape, *and* one may be motivated by the dynamic unconscious to destroy one's self—all at the same time. It is vital that the therapist be alert to each of these possibilities and to discuss and interpret them all.

Randy "slipped" repeatedly, and I suggested that her slips were motivated, or at least rationalized, by claims to special privilege— "A princess has the right to go on a bender"—a hypothesis for which there was much evidence, although she denied it. When I went on to suggest that her slips were acts of aggression ("Fuck you martinis") against me and sundry others, she also denied it, offering the counter-suggestion that she drank when she simply couldn't find another way to cope (drinking to remediate or self-medicate self and ego deficits). I agreed with her and told her so (although I continued to believe that her slips were "overdetermined" and that the dynamics I had suggested were also operative). After acknowledging the adaptive function of the slips, I suggested that they had yet another purpose— self-punishment and self-destruction. She ran with that ball as my interpretation resonated. Our mutually constructed understanding of the complex dynamics of Randy's slips proved highly mutative and those slips became progressively less frequent.

What does Sandor Rado teach us about the dynamics of addiction?

In a prescient paper of 1933, Rado captured in a highly poetic way the tragic trap of addiction—the viciousness of the addictive cycle. He spoke of a state of tense depression, a sort of agitated depression that is felt to be intolerable, and its concomitant feelings of worthlessness or, at best, of very low self-esteem. The drug is then taken for its euphoric properties. It is an elatant. The user rises from tense depression to manic joy. In that manic joy, the constraints of reality are obliterated. So far, so good. Who would not want to be in such a state of elation? Unfortunately, it cannot be sustained and there is the crash, returning the developing addict to an even tenser and deeper depression. The claims of reality come back in spades, necessitating another round of drug use. But it is less effective this time, and the manic or euphoric state is more tenuous, briefer, and less effective, necessitating yet more use of the drug, ad infinitum, until there is almost no euphoria and almost continuous bleak and black depression. In his elucidation of this cycle, Rado noted the close similarity between drug addiction and manic-depression. And, indeed, there is a far greater than random correlation between manic-depression and addiction, particularly alcoholism. But even if the patient is not technically manic-depressive, his addiction is a manic-depressive process.

Further, Rado underlines the centrality of self-esteem in the entire process. What the drug does is to raise self-esteem. That is the single most salient quality it has, and is the primary reason the user uses. The therapist will never go wrong in centering on self-esteem; there is almost nothing I would say without qualification about drug addiction with this exception. There are no addicts who do not have absolutely abysmal self-esteem, however defended against by bluster and bravado. It is vital that the therapist interpret this: "You think so little of yourself that you have to have, or at least believe you have to have, cocaine in order to feel better about yourself." "When you drink you feel you are on top of the world." "The only time you really like yourself is when you're smoking pot." Correlative to pointing out or interpreting the function of the drug in raising self-esteem, the therapist also needs to help the patient experience his or her abysmally low self-esteem, indeed, self-loathing. Karl Menninger, concentrating more on aggression, particularly aggression against the father and self-punishment for it, stated that the first step in recovery was for the alcoholic to realize he was "a real bastard." Interesting choice of words by Menninger, but that's not very relevant here. Somewhat similarly, focusing now not on the angry acted out aggression but on the self-loathing, patients need to be able to feel how really bad they feel about themselves in order to begin to move toward a more realistically based self-esteem. Therefore, the therapist needs to say things like, "You really feel like shit, and therefore you have to make all sorts of claims of greatness so you won't know that you are shit."

> *What has Robert Knight contributed to our understanding of addiction?*

Knight was one of the first analytically trained psychiatrists to work with alcoholics. He was also one of the first to describe the borderline syndrome. There is no accident that Knight's interests were in both borderline and addictive problems. There is, indeed, a substantial overlap between borderline and addictive populations. As stated elsewhere, it is not the case that all substance abusers are borderlines, but it is the case that the vast majority of borderlines develop substance abuse, if not dependence. Working in a closed setting of the Menninger clinic in the 1930s, Knight treated many male alcoholics. Knight (1937, 1938) commented on their dynamics, and realized that they were roughly distinguishable into two different types. The dynamic that Knight saw was self-punishment for forbidden aggression against the father. That aggression took place on both the level of fantasy and the level of reality. In the latter it was acted out in terms of living a lifestyle that embarrassed the father, necessitated rescue, and generally made the father's life miserable. This aggression against the father added a layer of guilt to the son's already guilt-ridden psyche, although there was also satisfaction in that aggressivity. This new level of guilt echoed earlier oedipal guilt, building layer upon layer of guilt until the burden was intolerable. The answer, of course, was to continue to drink. Guilt can be anesthetized with alcohol. And this drinking to deaden the guilt of previous aggression is only yet another aggression, but it is not only that—it also leads to failure, humiliation, shame, and often poverty. The male drinker hurts not only the father but himself. Knight is not too far from his boss Karl Menninger's notion that alcoholism and other addictions are forms of chronic suicide as punishment for forbidden death wishes toward the father.

Life doesn't offer many deals this good. Where else but in addiction can you express your forbidden murderous wishes and be simultaneously punished for that expression? This dynamic is an extraordinarily powerful hook that keeps some people drinking/drugging to death. This dynamic is interpretable and that interpretation is often heard and acted on, that action being movement toward sobriety.

In his study of his patients' families, Knight noticed that the fathers were very erratic, as well as erratically punitive, and that the mothers tended to be passive, subordinate, and ineffectual. Although we work in a different time and place, this is a family constellation we still very commonly see in the families of male addicts.

Knight also noticed that in spite of the fact that all of his patients had very serious alcohol problems necessitating hospitalization, they were not the same. In fact, his population seemed to be bimodal. Elucidating this bimodality, Knight distinguished between what he called *essential alcoholics* and *reactive alcoholics*. Essential alcoholics were those alcoholics who had been in trouble with booze from their first drink, who had very spotty educational and vocational histories, and whose interpersonal relationships were stormy, distant, symbiotic, or otherwise highly disturbed.

In short, they never really matured into anything approximating healthy adulthood. The reactives, on the other hand, often had substantial, even spectacular, academic and career success. They had, for the most part, succeeded in marrying and establishing families, and, at least until their addictions had progressed, had behaved in more or less caring and responsible ways; that is, they appeared to be capable of love, even if they were no longer so. They were simply a different population than the essentials. Knight called this syndrome reactive because he believed that this type of alcoholism was a reaction to some major narcissistic wound. Although this was probably true in some cases, it is more likely that Knight was describing patients who had been functional alcoholics until their disease progressed and they had deteriorated to the point where admission to the Menninger Clinic was necessary.

Almost all workers in the field have made similar distinctions, both for alcoholics and for other substance abusers. The way this is sometimes put is that some patients require habilitation and others rehabilitation. Clinically, the two groups feel very different. The essentials require a very long period of time to make even minimal gains, while the reactives, if they stop drinking, often turn their lives around rather spectacularly and rapidly, which is not to say that many emotional and psychological problems do not remain.

Another way of looking at Knight's differential is that the essential alcoholics are probably borderline, while the reactive alcoholics are probably narcissistic. Borderlines and narcissists do indeed make up much of the addicted population. In general, borderlines have a terrible problem functioning in any area of life, while narcissists often do quite well in school and work, but run into trouble in their interpersonal lives. Knight really doesn't present us with much data about the marital and parental relationships of his reactive alcoholics, but one suspects that even though when compared to the essentials they seem like upright, responsible citizens, they probably had highly troubled relationships with both their families of origin and families of procreation.

Knight's treatment recommendations are also of interest. For the essentials, he believed that abstinence was the only possible cure, and that the best psychological treatment was an expressive, supportive therapy with many didactic and educational components, more or less what a modern substance abuse counselor does.

Knight's essentials may have been people who had a constitutional predisposition to alcoholism, and it may be the case that part of their difficulties around drinking resulted from biological vulnerability. This would support Knight's intuitive feeling that abstinence was their only hope.

The reactives, according to Knight, had once drank normally, and he thought that if it was important to them perhaps they could drink normally again. His treatment for reactives was psychoanalysis. Believing that their core problem was intrapsychic conflict between id and superego, analysis made perfect sense as a treatment modality. But Knight was hardly a fool, and he had these patients under lock and key for a long period of time, often up to, or in excess of, a year, during which the analysis was going on. They did not have an opportunity to drink during that time. From our perspective, the practicality of a return to controlled drinking by this population is questionable. There are, of course, some reactives who, with insight, can drink without getting in difficulties, but the therapist must be cautious in negotiating treatment goals to not give the patient unrealistic hope that he or she can become a social drinker with impunity. For most, this is not possible, although for a few it is.

> *What does Otto Fenichel teach us about the*
> *dynamics of addiction?*

Fenichel (1945) is credited with the observation, "The superego is that part of the mind which is soluble in alcohol" (p. 379). In the sections on alcoholism and drug addiction in his classic text, *The Psychoanalytic Theory of Neurosis*, Fenichel points to the use of drugs to resolve irreconcilable id-ego conflicts. He also discusses at length and was the first to highlight the narcissistic regression in alcoholism and drug addiction. By narcissistic regression, Fenichel means the relinquishing of the object world (reality) for an inner world of fantasy. Drugs enable this living in fantasy. Typically these fantasies are about omnipotence and grandiosity. In exchange for the world, the addict becomes the ruler—*His or Her Majesty*—of an empty world, empty self, and empty bottle.

What does Thomas Szasz teach us about the dynamics
of addiction?

Szasz (1958) wrote a fascinating paper on the counterphobic mechanism in addiction in which he postulates that a great deal of addiction is
driven by a desire to master overwhelming fears. The addict is essentially
making the statement, "I am indestructible. I can engage in the most dangerous self-destructive acts and emerge unscathed." This feeds into and
strengthens denial. There is a kind of grandiosity in that position that can
be very resistant to therapeutic intervention. It is perhaps heroic to defy
the gods once, but to do it on a daily basis is madness, and that is exactly
what the addict does. I would elaborate on Szasz's notion of a counterphobic
mechanism and postulate that many addictions are enactments of a drama
of death and resurrection. The substance abuser, at least in his more advanced state, ingests the drug until he or she collapses and goes into a state
of oblivion. This is certainly an enactment of death, a kind of little suicide.
In a way, the addict's little suicide is similar to Dostoyevsky's epileptic
fits, which were also a little death, as interpreted by Freud (1928), as a
punishment for his murderous wishes toward his father.

The most powerful part of this drama lies in the fact that the addict,
at least most of the time, comes out of the stupor and is resurrected, prov-
ing that he or she is immortal. It is an extremely powerful dynamic. The
addict who is tormented by fear of death enacts death counterphobically,
and miraculously is resurrected from the underworld. This drama not only
reinforces the addiction but affirms the addict's grandiosity. After all, one
who can die and be reborn is indeed a powerful and wonderful being. The
therapist can interpret this drama and say to the addict, "Like all of us, but
perhaps more so, you are absolutely terrified of death. Yet, when you drink
yourself into unconsciousness, you in effect kill yourself, choose death,
enact death, render yourself unconscious and insensate. So, in drinking,
you go into the very fear that is most powerfully in you. Yet, you wake up
in the morning, however hung over, and you've survived, and that's enormously reassuring to you. It also affirms how powerful you are. But you
don't really feel powerful; on the contrary, you feel profoundly powerless

and need this reassurance. Ironically, your very attempt to master your fear of death is killing you. Given your cirrhotic liver, you know and I know that you can't live much longer if you continue to drink the way you do."

> *What does Harry Tiebout teach us about the dynamics of addiction?*

Tiebout was the psychiatrist of the founder of AA, Bill Wilson. Wilson was a lifelong depressive, perhaps what we would now call a dual-diagnosis patient who went to Tiebout for treatment of his depression long after he was a world-famous figure. The two men taught each other a great deal. From Tiebout, Wilson heard the phrase, "His or Her Majesty, the Baby," from Freud's 1914 essay, "On Narcissism." He incorporated it into the AA literature, which sees pathological narcissism as the central dynamic of addiction. Tiebout, in turn, learned a great deal from Bill Wilson about the "surrender" experience, the experience in which the addict throws in the towel and admits he or she is powerless to control that addiction and reaches out for help. This is also known as hitting bottom.

Tiebout (1949, 1957), in his papers on surrender, emphasized the grandiosity in addiction, the saliency of "His or Her Majesty, the Baby." Tiebout called for "ego deflation in depth." He was using ego not in the sense of the executive part of the mind, as it is used in Freud's structural model, but in the everyday sense in which one says, "He has a big ego." Tiebout's emphasis on ego deflation has an unpleasant, moralistic, even sadistic, tone to it, a kind of crush-'em-and-rub-their-noses-in-it flavor, which I find offensive; nevertheless, he has something important to say. Reactive grandiosity, as a defense against underlying feelings of worthlessness, is an extremely potent dynamic in addiction, and must be dealt with in one way or another. In deflating this grandiose ego, one can simply inflict more narcissistic wounds and do more harm than good. Yet, the therapist must confront that grandiosity, at least during the phase of active addiction, because that grandiosity will keep the substance use going forever, making it impossible to work through the grandiosity in a more accepting and neutral way. So, something like Tiebout's ego deflation is often a vital part of substance abuse treatment. Fortunately, that deflation often comes about spontaneously and is a by-product of both treatment and the addictive process, rather than through the therapist self-consciously pin-pricking the balloon of ego inflation.

What do Henry Krystal and Herbert Raskin teach us about the dynamics of addiction?

Krystal and Raskin (1970) made one of the most clinically useful contributions to the literature on the dynamics of addiction when they spoke of affect regression as a central dynamic. What they were alluding to cannot be understood unless we look at their developmental theory. It is the theory about the development of affect in which it is postulated that affect is originally a massive, undifferentiated, vague, and overwhelming experience that they call an *Ur*-affect, a primitive precursor of more finely discriminated feelings and emotions. This *Ur*-affect is preverbal, experienced as somatic, and undifferentiated. In the normal course of development, affect is differentiated so that, for example, Rado's tense depression becomes anxiety and depression, now experienced as qualitatively different. Further, the differentiated affects can be verbalized. By giving feelings labels, they can be spoken of, instead of being experienced as bodily states, and they become available for psychic elaboration and working through, obviating the need for somatization and/or acting out.

The process of affect development not only involves the unfolding of an innate biological potential, but, importantly, is an interpersonal or object relational process. We learn what we are feeling by being given labels for our feelings, words for them, by empathic caregivers. When a mother says, "You're crying because you're feeling blue, and you're feeling blue because your doll broke," or "You're crying because you're angry," she is giving her child the means by which to verbalize feelings.

For many substance abusers, this process went poorly. The loving caregivers were not there to help them sort out and verbalize their feelings, so the feelings remained massive and undifferentiated, somaticized and unverbalized, or they became differentiated and verbalized, but weakly and insecurely so. In other words, substance abusers commonly suffer either fixation at a stage of primitive affect, or have a vulnerability to affect regression consequent upon early trauma and deprivation. In traumatization of all sorts, there is affect regression. Addiction is a form of chronic traumatization. This is true even though it may not seem so, and it may appear that the trauma is mostly inflicted on others; nevertheless, it is traumatic to the self, which experiences one narcissistic wound after another as the addiction progresses. This in addition to historical trauma—either acute or chronic, or both.

Thus, there are many reasons for substance abusers to be vulnerable to affect regression, including the addiction itself and its pharmacological effects. By the time they seek treatment, we find that they have alexithymia, that is, they cannot put their feelings into words or can do so only in a confused and imprecise way. Further, resomatization is the rule, rather than the exception, and anxiety, in particular, is experienced not as a signal but as overwhelming. Such anxiety is commonly experienced as a bodily catastrophe such as imminent heart attack or stroke. Leon Wurmser believes that sexualization is also an aspect of affect regression. It is necessarily the case that the addict coming for treatment at the end of the addictive process, or deep into it, is suffering from affect regression characterized by dedifferentiation, resomatization, deverbalization, and sexualization. The therapist's job is to help the patient reverse this process and move up the scale of affect development into differentiation, verbalization, desomatization, and desexualization. That sounds complicated but in practice is fairly simple. One simply helps the recovering substance abuser find labels for feelings. One interprets the patient's affects: "You're sad," or "You're angry," or "You're confused." These are interpretations and the therapist may misperceive the active or recovering addict's emotional state, but with experience this happens infrequently. Generally speaking, the therapist is on target and has a better sense of what the patient is feeling than the patient does. Even more importantly the therapist has words for those feelings. In the reverbalization, discriminations are made and differentiation takes place. Also in the verbalization, a means of symbolization and working through comes into being, and somatization is no longer necessary. Similarly, the sexualization of affect diminishes with its differentiation and verbalization.

There is a famous experiment by the social psychologist Stanley Schachter (Schachter and Singer 1962), in which he assigned research subjects to one of four conditions. Two groups received adrenaline, two groups received sterile water, and every group had a confederate who was placed among them as they were told they were waiting for the experiment to take place. One confederate was happy and jolly, and when those that received the adrenaline were asked what they were feeling, they said they were happily excited. The other confederate was angry and complaining and cursing out the stupid scientists, and when those who received adrenaline were asked what they were feeling, they said they were feeling angry and unhappy. Those that received sterile water were not very influenced by either confederate. This would seem to argue that affect is a result of an interaction between physiological arousal and cognitive labeling, and very much supports the theory of Krystal and Raskin.

What is Leon Wurmser's contribution to our understanding of the dynamics of addiction?

Wurmser (1978) addresses the degree to which the addict externalizes internal conflict and looks for external solutions, and how our society so often reinforces such an externalizing defense in its denial of the saliency of the inner world, particularly of the unconscious inner world. Further, Wurmser describes a complex process depicting and elaborating the addictive cycle, a cycle that begins with a narcissistic crisis (stage one), a state in which self-esteem plummets and the integrity of the self is threatened. This is intolerable, and leads to instant defense. This narcissistic crisis leads to a breakdown of affect defense (stage two), so that affects become overwhelming and the addict undergoes affect regression. Then affect is experienced as massive, archaic, somatic, sexualized, deverbalized, and dedifferentiated. At that point, the patient feels uncontrollable intense rage, or shame, or despair, but cannot put those feelings into words. In the third stage, the affect disappears and is replaced by a vague, unbearable tension, as the addict begins a frantic search for excitement and relief and experiences craving. At this point, there is massive denial of inner reality and a frantic search for an external solution. This leads into the fourth stage, the wild drivenness for action, for an external concrete solution to the internal conflict.

There is a great deal of magical thinking in the fourth stage. The addict swings into action, which is characterized by both self-destructiveness and by aggression. It is a breaking out, in which boundaries are transgressed, social limits are violated, others are attacked, the self is destroyed, and the addict is consumed with hurting and being hurt, humiliating others and being shamed. Then despair takes over, and there is a splitting of the superego to allow for whatever action must be taken to end this intolerable state of affairs. This eventuates in feelings of entitlement. Finally, the drug is found, consumed, and the narcissistic crisis is ended, self-esteem is restored, and manic-euphoria results in pleasure. In summary, the cycle consists of acute narcissistic crisis, affect regression, search for affect defense and the use of denial and splitting, the use of externalization as a defense in a search for magic power, the mobilization of aggression, the split of the superego, and finally the pleasure of being high. At that point, the substance abuser is in the state of even greater narcissistic vulnerability, consumed with shame and guilt, albeit unconsciously. The pleasure soon ends, and the next acute narcissistic crisis occurs, likely because of the greater narcissistic vulnerability. It is truly a horrible situation in which to be trapped.

Wurmser is reminiscent of Rado in his sensitive and, underneath the technical language, moving depiction of the addictive cycle and the entrapment in which addicts find themselves. His recommendations are twofold: multimodal treatment (because addiction is a very hard condition to combat and requires heavy artillery for its successful resolution) which might include self-help, group therapy, family therapy, psychopharmacology, or analytic, or modified analytic, therapy, and psychodynamic treatment. Wurmser feels that analysis, or at least psychodynamic treatment, is essential in order to help the addict move from externalization to contact with the inner world of affect, cognition, aspiration, and fantasy.

Wurmser makes other points, which are highly salient in the treatment of substance abuse. He believes that much contemporary analytic and psychodynamic theory focuses too much on deficit and not enough on conflict. His belief is that much that appears to be deficit, that is, to be holes and gaps within the patient, often turns out to be defenses against conflicts, or to be unconscious potentials that need to be realized. Wurmser is not unaware of deficit, as in his citation of affect regression based on vulnerability derived from early trauma, which he borrows from Krystal and Raskin; nevertheless, his emphasis is on the uncovering of unconscious conflict. He takes this position partly because he views it as more hopeful. Conflict can be surfaced and worked with, while deficit is much harder to ameliorate.

Wurmser also emphasizes a dynamic he calls "flight from conscience" as driving not only substance abuse, but severe neurosis in general. The problem is not that patients lack a superego, but that the superego is so harsh, primitive, and unforgiving that there is a flight from that superego into sometimes gross and outrageous antisocial behavior. Patients act out to escape their conscience. Wurmser's notion of flight from conscience is perfectly consistent with his emphasis on working with conflict and with his view that many contemporary analysts and psychodynamic therapists miss conflict in their all-too-ready acquiescence in the patient's self-estimation. To focus on deficit can be a way of devaluing the patient— "He can't do this, that, and the other thing; he's missing parts; he's a mess."

Wurmser also coined a term, *psychophobia*, which refers to our culture's repudiation of the inner world of fantasy, of drive, of unconscious conflict, and of unconscious aspiration. Substance abusers are highly psychophobic. They externalize and act out in every possible way to avoid contact with their inner worlds, particularly with the stringencies of the superego. The psychophobia of a culture that emphasizes manipulation through technique and behavioral change (as desirable as that may sometimes be) reinforces the patient's unwillingness to look inside and experience the inner world.

What is the contribution of Peter Hartocollis to our understanding of the dynamics of addiction?

Hartocollis (1968) was one of the first to point out the high prevalence of borderline and narcissistic personality disorders in addiction. It is counterfactual to say that all addicts are borderline. It simply is not true, but the contrary tends to be true. Most borderlines become substance abusers, usually polysubstance abusers. It is also contrary to fact to say that all substance abusers are narcissistic personality disorders in *DSM-IV* terms. Nevertheless, narcissistic difficulties seem to be at the core of addiction, and there is a reactive narcissism that goes with the addiction that may or may not be ameliorated by recovery in and of itself. Elsewhere in this primer I argue that regression/fixation to pathological narcissism, in Kohut's sense, is the psychodynamic correlative of addiction. Hartocollis emphasizes that the borderline and narcissistic character elements of the addict must be dealt with psychodynamically if any sort of satisfactory stable sobriety is to become possible. Hartocollis also noted that alcoholic denial is a denial not only of the drinker's alcoholism but of the drinker's need for help; that is, it is a form of counterdependence and pseudo–self-sufficiency, both of these states being characteristic of borderline and even more of narcissistic pathology.

What has Edward Khantzian contributed to our understanding of the dynamics of addiction?

Khantzian (1981, 1999) is the author of the *self-medication hypothesis*, the notion that people use drugs to remediate ego deficits and developmental arrest. In his view, the taking of the substance is an initially adaptive attempt to cope with a deficit state. He sees these deficits as involving both ego and self. Although these deficits encompass many areas of functioning and of self-regulation, they are primarily deficits in the areas of self-care, affect regulation, self-esteem, and a subjective sense of well-being. The self-medication hypothesis has also been called the prosthetic theory of drug use and abuse. In this formulation, the drug is seen as a prosthesis that supplies the missing part or the missing function. Khantzian is very clear that the motivation, conscious or unconscious, driving substance abuse is the attempt to relieve suffering.

Khantzian's view is of the utmost clinical saliency. If the therapist does not recognize, as one of the most central dynamics of addiction, the adaptive nature of drug use and the attempt at self-cure through that use, there is no way in which the alcoholic or drug addict will feel understood.

However mistaken the belief, however many years have passed since the drug ameliorated, rather than exacerbated, deficit and conflict, the taking of the drug was at one point a rational attempt to cope despite developmental disability. The therapist must acknowledge this and, indeed, reflect it back to, or even interpret it to, the patient, who may have no conscious awareness that that was what he or she was trying to do. This in no way negates the importance of confrontation of denial, or of the need to repeatedly point to all of the negative consequences of the addiction. Nor is it incompatible, though Khantzian would probably think that it was, with interpretations around self-hatred and psychodynamically motivated self-destruction. One may indeed have begun using drugs in an attempt to cope, and either simultaneously or sequentially have come to use the drug as a self-punisher.

Khantzian's emphasis on the suffering driving substance abuse, on addicts trying, however futilely, to alleviate their pain, powerfully alters the therapist's countertransference. Frustration and rage at the seemingly irrational behavior of the substance abusing patient evanesce, and the therapist's ensuing calm and acceptance is communicated to the patient.

Khantzian highlights the specificity of the attempt at self-medication; for example, the use of amphetamine, crack, or cocaine is an unconscious attempt to treat attention deficit disorder (ADD) and hyperactivity. For Khantzian, the drug of choice says a lot about the substance abusing patient that the therapist needs to attend to, both to understand and to treat the ADD or depression or anxiety psychopharmacologically and/or psychotherapeutically. Khantzian makes an interesting and clinically useful distinction in the use of cocaine as self-medication. One group of users is self-medicating depression, while another group is sensation-seeking and on the manic side. They are looking to get even higher. The therapist needs to be alert to which of these dynamics pertains as well as to be on the lookout for self-medication of ADD.

Khantzian's colleague John Mack (1981, Khantzian and Mack 1989) has developed with him an elaboration of the notion of deficits in the areas of the capacity of self-care and self-governance driving addiction. Part of being sane is knowing how to be sane, and the basic idea here is that the alcoholic or drug addict simply does not know how to be sane. There is, in behavioral language, an enormous learning deficit, or, speaking more psychodynamically, there are massive failures of internalization of parental functions, so that self-care and self-governance have never been internalized. It is not possible to internalize that which never existed externally, and in the case of many substance abusers who grew up in chaotic, even violent, homes in which there was little consistent care, there was little opportunity to internalize the ability to care for oneself. The parallel between Mack and Khantzian's deficits and Gedo's apraxias (see p. 71) is evident.

In Kohut's terms, there has been a failure to transmutably internalize the functions of the selfobject (see the sections on Kohut, below). Mack and Khantzian elaborate the notion of self-care, and amalgamate it, to some degree, with other ego and superego functions to arrive at the notion of self-regulation as an ego function, with perhaps some superego aspects to it. In their view, self-regulation, which includes limits on behavior, is, even in the best of circumstances, not completely internalized and always depends on external reinforcement. That is to say that some ego functions and some superego functions constantly require reinforcement from the environment. To take a trivial example, few of us are so self-regulated or superego restrained as to always observe the speed limit; only the possibility of getting a ticket slows us down. Khantzian and Mack are saying that something like this pertains to many areas of life. If we are not part of a social system that gives you feedback, we are not going to be able to regulate ourselves effectively. And that will be the case no matter how fortunate our early circumstances, or how well we have internalized regulatory ego and superego functions. Human beings always need a social context and corrective feedback from that context.

In Khantzian and Mack's view, it is precisely the people who have the weakest internal structures that are most likely to be alienated and in a state of anomic isolation. Those who need it most lack social support for their precariously internalized ego and superego functions, rendering them highly vulnerable to turning to substances to make up for both internal deficit and current environmental deficit.

In Khantzian and Mack's analysis, it is precisely the power of the twelve-step programs to provide an auxiliary ego and, to some degree, auxiliary superego that makes them so highly effective for recovering persons. Khantzian and Mack's term for this amalgamation of ego and superego functions seen to be both internal and external is *self-governance*. Addicts are radically disabled by their deficits in their ability to self-govern, and it is precisely the genius of the twelve-step programs to provide the external component of that self-governance, which in the course of time becomes internalized, but never completely. As is the case for all of us, the recovering addict continues to need the external support, feedback, and constraint that the program provides. This seems to me to be very realistic. Whatever other ways there may be in which we are necessarily interdependent, it is most certainly the case that ego and superego functions are not completely internalized, as a classic psychoanalytic model would maintain, and indeed they require continuous environmental reinforcement. This reinforcement permits them not only to maintain their existence, but to evolve into more mature forms.

What is Stephanie Brown's contribution to our understanding of the dynamics of addiction?

Brown (1985) emphasizes the developmental arrest in addiction both of the addict and of the children raised by the addict. She considers it absolutely vital that the therapist figure out when growth stopped and the arrest began. Only then can the therapy successfully put the addict back on the pathway to emotional maturity. She understands the Twelve Steps as facilitating ego growth in a way parallel to that of a psychodynamic therapy informed by psychoanalytic developmental theory. In the case of patients raised in alcoholic or addicted homes, the therapist should determine what age the patient was when the family became overtly dysfunctional. The arrest occurs at that point.

Brown also emphasizes the traumatization ineluctably consequent on being out of control—and every addict is out of control. The therapist should make the patient aware of this. Brown regards every case of addiction as a case of post traumatic stress disorder—the trauma being the experience of being out of control—and treats the addicted patient accordingly.

> *What is Ernst Simmel's understanding of the*
> *dynamics of addiction?*

Simmel created the first inpatient drug rehabilitation center, Schloss Tegel, outside Berlin in the 1920s. He didn't think of Schloss Tegel as a rehab. Rather, he considered it a psychoanalytic sanatorium. In both his understanding of the dynamics of drug addiction and in his treatment, he emphasized the symbolic meaning of the drug. Simmel noted that many of his patients could taper down to such a low dosage of their drug, usually alcohol, that its pharmacological effect was minimal, yet they clung to it and refused to give up the "last drop." This suggested that the drug served a psychodynamic function quite apart from its pharmacological action. It had some symbolic meaning—mother, magic potency, elixir of life, elixir of love, selfobject, semen, blood, milk, magic, or preserver of the integrity of the self. Central to Simmel's treatment was interpretation of the symbolic meaning of the drug. This is no less useful now than it was 70 years ago. Interpretations around the symbolic function of the drug are often mutative. It takes a good deal of listening before the clinician has the knowledge necessary to make an accurate interpretation. Simmel, treating people in the sanatorium, was in perfect position to wait them out as he worked with them analytically. This is much less feasible in an outpatient setting where the patient's ongoing use may make such interpretation irrelevant.

It is of some interest to note that Freud, coming to Berlin for an adjustment of his prosthesis for his ablated jaw, which had been removed to treat a carcinoma secondary to his addictive smoking, stayed in Simmel's sanatorium, Schloss Tegel, while he was having his mouth worked on. Ironically, Freud had no insight that he too, was an addict and his resting in his friend's sanatorium for addiction was entirely appropriate. Then again, perhaps Freud did know at some level.

Simmel created a milieu therapy in which every member of the staff was part of the treatment team, from the cook to the gardener. He built in feedback loops so that his patients learned about themselves in all of their activities. Similarly, in modern recreational therapy or occupational therapy, how patients play the game or make the vase reveals an enormous amount about them, and this is very usefully commented on or interpreted by recreational and occupational therapists.

In creating his milieu, Simmel did something unique. He split his staff into a highly supportive nursing team that indulged the patients, self-consciously infantilized them, and tried to meet all their needs, in an attempt to belatedly remediate early environmental deficit and trauma, and a medical team. The first component of the staff provided a corrective emotional experience. It was, indeed, a *nursing* staff. The second component, the physician (in that time and place almost certainly a male), was, on the other hand, the representative of reality, the setter of limits. So, part of the staff represented the pleasure principle and part the reality principle. Simmel's notion was that addictive patients, at least the ones in his sanatorium, were too regressed to deal with reality, including the reality of their own addiction, unless they were embedded in a highly supportive environment. That notion still has utility, perhaps not in such a direct form as Simmel prescribed it at Schloss Tegel. But most certainly something like this happens in most inpatient rehabilitation units, and the twelve-step programs very much provide support and reality checks simultaneously. As Claude Miller, a wise analyst, was fond of remarking in his seminars at the American Institute for Psychotherapy and Psychoanalysis, "All of our lives, we need mother's milk and corrective feedback, preferably from the same person." Simmel intentionally did not provide it from the same person, yet all of his staff were part of the same institution, and in the patient's transferential fantasies were surely amalgamated in some way.

Simmel came to the United States when the Nazis came to power in Germany, and continued his interest in the treatment of alcoholism in New York City. Here, too, he anticipated and, indeed, made possible some of our current understanding of addiction. Shortly after World War II, he wrote a paper, part sociology, part psychology, continuing in the analytic tradition of bridging these realms of discourse, a tradition going back to Karl Abraham (1908), in which he forecasted a huge increase in addiction and severe psychopathology following the end of the war. He hypothesized that the kind of dislocation the war had brought, and the unleashing of primitive aggression concomitant with it, combined with the difficulties that the veterans would have reintegrating into civilian society, would lead to an increase in all kinds of acting out behaviors, including addiction. He proved to be entirely right. Something similar to that happened after the Vietnam War, when the veterans who used pot and heroin in Vietnam returned to the United States and, for the most part, put aside the narcotics, but showed up in Veterans Administration hospitals a few years later as alcoholics. These veterans, like Simmel's World War II veterans, often suffered undiagnosed posttraumatic stress disorder, which they sought to self-medicate with alcohol and other drugs.

Simmel did not live to finish his 1948 paper, but in it he reached out to the self-help community, then barely known, and attempted to interpret the twelve steps of Alcoholics Anonymous in terms of ego development. In our own time, Stephanie Brown (1985) has continued this work and has elaborated such a developmental hypothesis (see above). Simmel, in his advocacy of collaboration between mental health professionals and self-helpers, has much to teach us about how to deal with our countertransference to the twelve-step programs. If we are to successfully work with addicts, it is necessary that we come to terms with that countertransference. Simmel's attitude toward the twelve-step programs is one worth identifying with. He neither abdicates his professional stance nor condescends to the self-help movement; on the contrary, he is entirely open to learning from it, while feeling that he, as a professional and analyst, has much to teach self-help movement members.

What does Erich Fromm teach us about the dynamics of addiction?

Fromm's (1941) best-known book is entitled *Escape from Freedom*. There are few more total escapes from freedom than addiction. Fromm's central notion, written in the shadow of the totalitarian movements of the mid–twentieth century, elaborates a social-political dynamic in which the anxiety of being free, having to make choices, and being responsible is more than people are sometimes able to bear. In that state, they all too readily abdicate freedom, and enter into an orgy of submission to authoritarian figures or movements. This is a pattern that we have seen over and over again in the twentieth century with enthrallment to figures as diverse as Hitler and David Koresh, who led his followers to mass suicide. Fromm was right. Human beings do have a difficult time bearing the responsibility of being free. Whatever the ultimate truth of the free-will determinism debate, experientially we have feelings of agency, and those feelings often frighten us. Addiction is very usefully understood and interpreted as a flight from freedom. Fromm was elaborating not only a social dynamic, but a psychological one.

Dostoyevsky had a similar insight into the dread of freedom. In the Myth of the Grand Inquisitor in his novel *The Brothers Karamazov* (1881), Christ returns to Earth in the midst of the Spanish Inquisition and offers men freedom and responsibility in exchange for relinquishing mythological hope. Christ is sent away. Dostoyevsky's Grand Inquisitor tells him that what he offers human beings is too difficult, they cannot manage it; only the elite, the Inquisitor and his peers, can know the truth of the human condition. The rest of us must be protected, infantilized, and reassured. Something similar goes on in the 1990s in the United States, just as surely as it did in Dostoyevsky's vision of fifteenth-century Seville. People find all sorts of ways to relinquish their freedom—addiction preeminent among them. What the Danish philosopher Søren Kierkegaard (1849) called the "dizziness of freedom" has led to many a slip. Addiction is total enslavement. All of the addict's actions are predetermined by his or her need to obtain the drug, to use the drug, to recover from using the drug. The same is true of the "process addictions" such as compulsive gambling. Choices there are not. The addict's world becomes progressively narrower and more constricted. In recovery the process is reversed and the recovering person becomes more and more aware that a range of choices is open in every area of life. This can, and frequently does, cause enormous anxiety. The drive to escape from this anxiety commonly leads to a return to drug use. The twelve-step programs tell people not to make major decisions in the first year of sobriety. The manifest reason for this is that people change a lot during the first year of sobriety and it is therefore unwise to make avoidable major decisions during this state of transition. But the latent reason is even more powerful: the anxiety of making choices is so overwhelming for people in early recovery whose egos are still too weak to withstand it, that choosing makes them vulnerable to relapse. Therapists should interpret the danger of the dizziness of freedom in early sobriety and support delaying making major decisions until the recovering addict has his feet on the ground.

> *What is the dependency conflict theory of the etiology of addiction?*

The dependency conflict theory states that people who cannot find healthy interdependent interpersonal ways of meeting their dependency needs are prone to turn to substances. Rather than turning to people, they turn to drugs, doing so from a stance of pseudo–self-sufficiency. Denying their need for human support, they consider themselves self-sufficient, meeting all their needs for support and security through the use of substances or by engaging in compulsive activities. Such counterdependents are blind to their dependency on chemicals.

As the addiction plays itself out, the counterdependent user slowly, or sometimes rapidly, collapses, and winds up overtly dependent on other people for care. At the end of a spree, the user often has to be nursed. The whole cycle is played out right back to the infant nursing at the breast.

Howard Blane, in a classic book, *The Personality of the Alcoholic: Guises of Dependency* (1968), describes three types of dependency in alcoholics: (1) *Open dependents* are characterized by an attitude of "take care of me." "Here I am at my therapy session so I can collect my welfare check." Blane's open dependents are much like Robert Knight's essential alcoholics. He considered their prognosis poor. (2) *Counterdependents*, whom therapists frequently encounter in their clinical practices, are characterized by an attitude of "Fuck you, I don't need anyone." However pathetically and transparently untrue, it is a powerful defense that is extremely difficult to penetrate. The best the therapist can do is to try and address the fear behind the counterdependency, interpreting how deeply afraid the addict is of any form of closeness, intimacy, or indeed of any relationship. The reasons for that fear need to be uncovered and explored. The twelve-step programs are extremely good at addressing counterdependency with such slogans as "We need each other," "Keep coming back," and "Nobody graduates." The twelve-step programs continually try to make interpersonal dependency acceptable to a counterdependent population and to undercut the pseudo self-sufficiency. Therapists need to work with patients on this issue also. Blane considers counterdependents to have a poor prognosis. Although the more extreme of counterdependents are fairly antisocial, and more or less unworkable in most therapy, not all counterdependents are unreachable. Addressing the underlying fear is the key. (3) *Dependent/ counterdependents* are those addicts who are in great conflict about how to meet their dependency needs. Blane considers them by far the most treatable because their conflict is the most active and unresolved, and they can be engaged in psychotherapy because they are in pain.

The cowboy with his horse and bottle who rides off into the sunset needing nobody is the classic counterdependent. But the same scenario gets played out in New York City in the 1990s just as it once got played out in Silver City in the 1880s. Those cowboys who look back, however furtively, to town, are the ones that are most likely to succeed in treatment.

What does Heinz Kohut teach us about the dynamics of addiction?

Kohut was a classical analyst who came to see that classical theory could not account for what went on his analyses. He realized that certain patients, whom he later identified as having narcissistic personality disorders, did not relate to him as a separate person, but rather as if he were an extension of themselves. Kohut (1971, 1977) called these ways of relating *narcissistic transferences*. (He later called them *selfobject transferences*.) He built a whole developmental theory from this analysis of the transference. He distinguished between two kinds of such transferences: *mirror transferences* and *idealizing transferences*. In the mirror transference, the therapist's only function is to reflect back (mirror) the patient's wonderfulness. What the patient seeks is affirmation of archaic, infantile grandiosity. In the idealizing transference, the patient puts all of the wonderfulness—omnipotence and omniscience— in the therapist, and then fuses with him or her. I would suggest that the addict's relationship to the substance can usefully be understood as a combined mirror and idealizing transference.

Kohut spoke of the *transmuting internalization* of psychic structure. By transmuting internalization he meant a gradual taking into the self, so to speak a grain at a time, of the functions once performed by selfobjects, by which Kohut meant not internal representations but people to whom one relates in a special, undifferentiated way. Each nontraumatic failure of the selfobject to meet a psychological need results in the acquisition of some capacity to meet the need oneself, for example, tension regulation once the function of the loving caregiver (selfobject) of the infant becomes an internalized ability to achieve such tension reduction. Kohut's notion was one of optimal frustration: no frustration, no internalization—there is no need for it; too much frustration, no internalization—what is absent can't be taken in. As Winnicott suggests, parents and therapists both succeed by failing.

Kohut would have been more accurate had he referred to psychic structure as psychic *capacity*, for that is what he meant. He conceptualized most psychopathology, and certainly narcissistic pathology, as a deficit state—something is missing inside. It is missing inside because something went wrong developmentally. Some phase of early object relations went awry. Of course, it makes perfect sense to take something in—alcohol, for instance—to remedy an internal lack. The only trouble is that what is missing can only come from people, from a certain kind of relationship, not from a chemical. So the treatment of addiction must be, in some sense, a replacement of rum with relationship. Kohut compared an addiction to a futile attempt to cure a gastric fistula by eating. The food might taste good, but it falls right out the hole without either nourishing or repairing the hole. As Kohut put it, "No psychic structure is built" (1977b, p. viii).

What is narcissistic rage?

The Kohution notion of narcissistic rage illuminates much addictive behavior. Narcissistic rage, unlike mature aggression, is not instrumental in the service of reality-based goals; rather, it is the response of the unmirrored, unnurtured self to narcissistic injury (see Levin 1993). Narcissistic injury is injury to the core self, which is characterized by deep pain, intense feelings of shame, a precipitous fall in self-esteem, and an unquenchable desire for revenge. It is the response of the offended monarch, "Off with their heads." Kohut (1972) uses as an example Captain Ahab in *Moby Dick*. Ahab's insane desire for revenge on a "dumb brute," the white whale, destroys him and all but one of his crew.

Narcissistic rage turned against the self can result in suicide. Addictive rage is multidetermined; part of it is pharmacological, the result of the drug's effect on the central nervous system; part of it in defense of the addiction; part of it from the accumulation of unexpressed anger (addicts have a lot of bluster, but rarely are effectively communicative or assertive); part of it is self-hatred projected outward; part of it is historical (that is, unconscious rage over childhood injury); and part of it is narcissistic rage as a consequence of narcissistic vulnerability. Since most slips are rage responses, helping the patient recognize, contain, and appropriately express, rather than act out, narcissistic rage is of the essence of addiction therapy. I have built upon Kohut's metapsychology to construct a theory of the dynamics of addiction. Kohut inferred a developmental sequence based on his experience of the transference of adult patients. One of the stages in that development is the stage of the archaic, nuclear, bipolar self. I believe that this is the psychodynamic correlative of addiction. This psychodynamic correlative may or may not be etiological. That is, it may be caused by the addiction, rather than be the cause of it. However, in many cases, pathological narcissism as here defined, meaning regression fixation to the stage of the archaic, nuclear bipolar self, plays a powerful role in the etiology of many addictions.

Can you elucidate Kohut's developmental scheme?

Kohut defines the self as a unit cohesive in space and enduring in time, the center of initiative and the recipient of impressions. It can be regarded either as a mental structure superordinate to the agencies of the mind—the id, ego, and superego—or as a content of those agencies. Kohut believed that these two conceptualizations were complementary. However, in his later work, he emphasized the self as the central or superordinate principle. It is, so to speak, the organized and organizing center of human experience and is, itself, experienced as cohesive and enduring. According to

Kohut, the infant develops a primitive, fragmented sense of self very early. Each body part, each sensation, each mental content is experienced as belonging to a self, to a "me," as mine; however, there is no synthesis of these experiences yet. They are selves, but no unitary self. Nor are there clear boundaries between self and world. Kohut designates this stage the *fragmented self*; this is the developmental stage at which psychotic persons are fixated, or to which they regress.

The next stage of development, an *archaic nuclear bipolar self*, arises from the infant's experience of being related to as a self, rather than as a collection of parts and sensations, by empathic caregivers. This self is cohesive and enduring, but is not securely established. Therefore, it is prone to regressive fragmentation. It is nuclear in the sense of having a center, or nucleus, and it is archaic in the sense of being primitive, that is, a grandiose and undifferentiated precursor of the mature self. The archaic nuclear self is bipolar in that it comprises two structures: the *grandiose self* and the *idealized parental imago*. The grandiose self is a differentiated self that is experienced as omnipotent, but there are no truly differentiated objects. Objects are experienced as extensions of the self, as selfobjects. The child's grandiose self attempts to exercise omnipotent control of his selfobjects, including the people who care for him. In healthy maturity, all love objects have a selfobject aspect. However, in maturity, the experience of the object as selfobject is a reversible regression in the service of the ego that lacks the rigidity that characterizes experience of objects as selfobjects in pathological narcissism. Pathological narcissism is regression/fixation to this stage of the archaic bipolar nuclear self.

The internalization of psychic structure, that is of the capacity to perform the functions performed by selfobjects, is codeterminous with the formation of the nuclear self. As Kohut (1977a) puts it, "The rudiments of the nuclear self are laid down by simultaneously or consecutively occurring processes of selective inclusion and exclusion of psychological structure" (p. 183). Failure to adequately internalize functions originally performed for the child by selfobjects results in deficits of the self. Addiction is a futile attempt to compensate for this failure in internalization.

It is the inner emptiness, the missing parts of the self experienced as a void, that addicts try to fill with food, with alcohol, with drugs, or with compulsive sexuality. It cannot be done. Whatever is compulsively taken in goes right through, and no psychic structure is built; that can only be done by internalization of relationships. It is their abysmally low self-esteem, their doubts about being real or existing at all, and their terror of regressive fragmentation that addicts try to remediate by their addictions. They always fail.

What is it that addicts have failed to internalize?

What the addict suffering from pathological narcissism in the Kohutian sense is lacking is the ability to self-soothe, the ability to modulate anxiety, the ability to maintain a reasonably stable, satisfactory level of self-esteem, a consistent feeling of cohesion and ongoingness, a sense of agency, and the capacity to be alone. It is these self functions that are deficient in the addict that the addict attempts to remediate by substance use.

What does Kohut's notion of the mature self
tell us about addiction?

According to Kohut, the two poles of the archaic nuclear self develop in healthy maturity into realistic ambition derived from the archaic grandiosity, and into values and ideals derived through depersonalization from the idealized parental imago (representation). It is striking, in working with substance abusers, how deficient their ability to be realistically ambitious is. We frequently find one of two extremes. Substance abusers are either grandiose, overreaching, unrealistic, and live in fantasy, indicative of fixation at the level of the grandiose self, or they are at the opposite pole, exhibiting an equally unrealistic underestimation of their capacities, resulting in little attempt at appropriate achievement, indicative of failure to integrate archaic grandiosity into the mature self. Similarly, the pole of idealization in the addictive self has not reached maturity, and substance abusers concomitantly frequently experience radical difficulties in the area of values and ideals. Here, too, we find the two extremes of unrealistic grandiosity and its opposite, the lack of any sort of livable ego ideal. According to Kohut, the experience of idealizing parents is a necessary developmental stage, necessary to the achievement of mature ideals. Children need to be able to look up to their parents and to only gradually become nontraumatically disillusioned with them as they go from being ideal to being real objects. In the stormy childhoods of many substance abusers, often in homes rendered chaotic by parental substance abuse, there is little opportunity for idealization, just as there is little phase-appropriate mirroring of the child; the result is massive deficits in the self. The child growing into adolescence then discovers substances that are readily idealized, and just as readily provide mirroring in the form of reassurance and the raising of self-esteem.

> *What do you and Kohut mean by fragmentation?*

Fragmentation is a notion of Kohut's (1971, 1977). It refers to the fragmentation of the self, that is, the regressive falling apart of the archaic, bipolar, nuclear self into an earlier stage of self experiences without cohesion. This is an important notion in substance abuse, both because substances can lead to such fragmentation, and because they are commonly used for self-medication in an attempt to abort the panic terror induced by threat of fragmentation. Fragmentation is experienced as psychic death in the sense that it means the loss of the self. So the dynamic import of drugs on fragmentation goes both ways: it causes it, and is often used as an attempt to cure it, an attempt that inevitably fails.

Fragmentation can be understood in many ways, and is clearly a metaphor; therapists do not literally see the fragments (although they sometimes feel that they do), but therapists can see evidence of the process of fragmentation. One example Kohut gave was hypochondriasis, in which the patient becomes the various aching body parts and has difficulty experiencing him- or herself as in any way integral or whole.

This brings to mind the story of the man who goes to the doctor and says, "Doctor, I have these terrible headaches, and my bowels bother me, and my legs ache all the time, and to tell you the truth, I myself don't feel so well either." In the state of fragmentation there is no "I myself," there is only the headache and the explosive bowels and the aching feet. Ordinary language also alludes to fragmentation in such phrases as "I'm falling apart" and "I'm going to pieces."

> *How does your model of regression/fixation to the stage of the archaic nuclear self account for the empirical findings on the addictive personality?*

The clinical addictive personality is delineated on pp. 43–47. Its empirically supported traits include elevation on the Psychopathic Deviant (Pd) and Depression (D) scales on the Minnesota Multiphasic Personality Inventory (MMPI), field dependence, confused gender identity, ego weakness, and stimulus augmentation.

Elevation in the Psychopathic Deviate (Pd) scale of the MMPI, in both active and recovering addicts, can be understood as a manifestation of the overtly grandiose self with its arrogance, isolation, and lack of realistic goals. The elevation on the MMPI Depression (D) scale reflects both the psychopharmacological consequences of active addiction and the impoverishment of the self, riddled with structural deficits and impaired in its capacity for self-esteem regulation, found in pathological narcissism.

Developmentally, the depression reflects the disappointment that results from inadequate phase-appropriate mirroring (approving confirmation) of the child's grandiose self by selfobjects. Additionally, addiction gives one much to be realistically depressed about. Empirical findings, using adjective checklists and self-reports, of impoverishment of the self are to be understood in the same way. The structurally deficient self of pathological narcissism is experienced as an empty depression and is reported as lack of interest, activities, and goals. Even the self is uninteresting to the self. The regression to pathological narcissism concomitant with addiction progressively strips the already enfeebled ego of its investment in objects and activities.

Another consistent finding in substance abusers is field dependency. Field dependence involves a relative inability to utilize internal resources, as well as impairments in the differentiations of body image, of figure and ground, and of self and world. By definition, the field-dependent person experiences the environment as a selfobject, which is precisely the way in which the person who is fixated or regressed to pathological narcissism experiences the world.

Confused gender identity is another frequent finding in addictive populations. This confusion also can be understood in terms of pathological narcissism. Developmentally, the archaic self arises before the establishment of firm gender identity. Hence, regression or fixation at the stage of the archaic self entails a blurring of gender identity. Failure to adequately internalize the ideal selfobject of the same sex, which is postulated as etiological in the person's vulnerability to pathological narcissism, renders difficult the establishment of firm gender identity.

Ego weakness is a construct that integrates several empirically confirmed characteristics of the active and early sobriety addict: impulsivity, lack of frustration tolerance, lack of affect tolerance, and lack of differentiation of the self representation. In terms of pathological narcissism, ego weakness in the addict is understood as encompassing the structural deficits in the self. In other words, the failure to internalize by a process of selective and depersonified identification, which Kohut calls transmuting internalization, the functions of affect regulation, self-soothing, boundary maintenance, and maintenance of satisfactory levels of self-esteem, once performed from the outside by the mother and other caregivers, results in ego weakness. In the case of weak or incomplete internalization of the functions of the selfobject, the self is subject to regression to pathological narcissism.

Stimulus augmentation, another characteristic of substance abusers, can also be understood in terms of pathological narcissism as a failure to internalize the mother's function as an auxiliary to the innate stimulus barrier. Although constitutional factors play a role in stimulus augmentation, failures in internalization and structuralization just as certainly play their role.

> *What are the practical applications of the notion that pathological narcissism is a psychodynamic correlative to addiction?*

There are a number of interventions that are extremely effective when working with addicts and that logically follow from this theoretical understanding. In their respective ways, these interventions address what theory understands as narcissistic deficit and narcissistic injury and the attempt at their self-cure through drug use; the attempt to fill the inner emptiness consequent upon failures of internalization and transmuting internalization; the acting out and turning against the self of narcissistic rage; idealizing and mirror transferences to the drug; attempts at omnipotent control through substance use and abuse; attempts to boost abysmally low self-esteem through the use of drugs; and the centrality of shame experiences, both antecedents to and consequences upon, the drug abuse. The following generic ways of translating theory into concrete interventions need to be modified so that each patient can hear them; nevertheless, they are models of great utility when working with addicts.

Most of these interventions are addressed to "actives," those still using, yet their maximum effectiveness is with the "recovering," particularly those in early sobriety. By varying the tense from "you were" to "you are," they can be used with both groups.

1. This intervention addresses the narcissistic wound inflicted by not being able to drink "like other people." In many subcultures, the inability to drug like other people is just as deep a narcissistic wound. The admission that one is powerless over alcohol or drugs, as twelve-step programs put it, or that one cannot use without the possibility of losing control, as I would put it, is extremely painful. It is experienced as a defect in the self, which is intolerable to those who are as perfectionistic as addicts usually are. The self must not be so damaged and deficient. Additionally, to be able to "drink like a man" or "drink like a lady" may be a central component of the alcoholic's self-concept—his or her identity. This is particularly so for macho men, but is no means

restricted to them. The therapist must recognize and articulate the conflict between the patient's wish to stop using and the patient's feeling that to do so entails admitting that he or she is flawed in a fundamental way. The therapist does this by saying, "You don't so much want to use, as not want not to be able to use." This intervention makes the patient conscious of the conflict in an empathic way and allows him or her to struggle with this issue, and often opens the way for the patient to achieve a more comfortable, stable recovery.

2. All addictions are one long experience in narcissistic injury. Failure stalks the addict like a shadow. As one of my patients put it, "When I drink, everything turns to shit." It sure does: career setbacks, job losses, rejection by loved ones, humiliations of various sorts, ill health, economic decline, accidental injury, and enduring bad luck are all-too-frequent concomitants of addiction. Each negative experience is a narcissistic wound. Cumulatively, they constitute one massive narcissistic wound. Even if the outward blows have not yet come, the inner blows—self-hatred and low self-regard—are always there. The addict has all too frequently heard, "It's all your fault." The therapist must empathize with the addict's suffering. "Your disease has cost you so much," "You've lost so much," and "Your self-respect is gone" are some ways the therapist can make contact with the substance abuser's pain and facilitate his experiencing this pain instead of denying, acting out, or anesthetizing it.

3. Addicts feel empty. Either they never had much good stuff inside, or they have long ago flushed out the good stuff with alcohol or drugs. "You drink so much because you feel empty" makes the connection, as well as brings into awareness the horrible feelings of an inner void. After sobriety has been achieved, the historical (that is, childhood) determinants of the paucity of psychic structure that is experienced as emptiness can also be interpreted.

4. Addicts lack a firm sense of identity. How can you know who you are if your experience of self is tenuous and its partly unconscious inner representation lacks consistent cohesion? The therapist can comment on this and point out that being an addict

or substance abuser is at least something definite—having an identity of sorts. When AA members say, "My name is———, and I am an alcoholic," they are affirming that they exist and have at least that one attribute. The manifest purpose of twelve-step members so identifying themselves is, of course, to deal with denial. But, the latent meaning is existential. Not being sure of their very existence, addicts need to assert it. With sobriety, many more attributes of the self will accrue—the self will enrich and cohere. One way of conveying this to the patient is to say, "You're confused, and not quite sure who you are. That is partly because of your drug use. Acknowledging your addiction will lessen your confusion as to who you are, and give you a base on which to build a firm and positive identity."

5. Many people use substances because they cannot stand to be alone. They drink to enjoy someone's companionship (see discussion of Winnicott on pp. 116–117). This should be interpreted. "You use so much because you can't bear to be alone, and getting high gives you the illusion of having company, of being with a friend." "After you stop using, it will be important for us to discover why it is so painful for you to be alone."

6. Addicts form selfobject (narcissistic) transferences to drugs and compulsive activities. Relating to drugs as a friend can be regarded as a form of what Kohut called the twinship transference, one form of the mirror transference. Addicts also form idealizing and mirror transferences to their drugs of choice. The image of the archaic, idealized parent is projected onto the drug and it is regarded as an all-powerful, all-good object with which the user merges in order to participate in this omnipotence. "Heroin will deliver the goods and give me love, power, and whatever else I desire" is the user's unconscious fantasy. The therapist should interpret this thus: "Heroin feels like a good, wise, and powerful parent who protects you and makes you feel wonderful, and that is why you love it so much. In reality, it is a depressant drug; not all the things you thought it was." The therapist can go on to say, "Now that getting high isn't working for you anymore, you are disillusioned, furious, and afraid. Let's talk about those feelings."

7. One of the reasons that addicts are so devoted to the consumption of their drug is that it confirms their grandiosity—in other words, they form a mirror transference to the substance. One alcoholic patient told me that he was thrilled that a sixth Nobel Prize was to be added to the original five. He read this while drinking in a bar at 8 A.M. His not so unconscious fantasy was to win all six. The therapist should make the mirror transference conscious by interpreting it. "When you drink, you feel you can do anything, be anything, achieve anything, and that feels wonderful. No wonder you don't want to give it up."

8. Addicts, without exception, have abysmally low self-esteem no matter how well covered over by bluster and bravado it may be. Self psychology understands this as an impoverishment of the reality ego that is a consequence of failure to integrate archaic grandiosity, which is instead split off by what Kohut calls the "vertical split" and which manifests itself as unrealistic reactive grandiosity. This low self-esteem persists well into recovery. At some point the therapist needs to say, "You feel like shit, and think that you are shit, and all your claims to greatness are ways to avoid knowing that you feel that way. You don't know it, but way down somewhere inside you feel genuinely special. We need to put you in contact with the real stuff, so you don't need drugs or illusions to help you believe that the phony stuff is real." The particular reasons, which are both antecedents to and consequences of the addiction, that the patient values him- or herself so little need to be elucidated and worked through.

9. Sometimes the patient's crazy grandiosity is simultaneously a defense against and an acting out of the narcissistic cathexis of the patient by a parent. In other words, the patient is attempting to fulfill the parent's dreams in fantasy, while making sure not to fulfill them in reality. This is especially likely to be the case if the patient is the adult child of an alcoholic. Heavy drinking or drugging makes such a defense or acting out easy. If the recovering person's grandiosity does seem to be a response to being treated by either parent as an extension of themselves, the therapist can say, "One reason you feel so rotten about yourself is that you're always doing it

for Mom or Dad, not for yourself. You resent this, and spite them by undermining yourself by getting high."

10. Many addicts have a pathological need for *omnipotent control*. The drug is simultaneously experienced as an object they believe they can totally control and coerce into doing their will, and an object they believe gives them total control of their subjective states and of the environment. This can be seen as a manifestation of their mirror and idealizing transferences to substances. Addicts frequently treat people, including the therapist, as extensions of themselves. The twelve-step slogans, "Get out of the driver seat" and "Let go and let God," are cognitive-behavioral ways of loosening the need to control. Therapists should interpret this need to control in the patient's relationship to the drug, in the patient's relationship with other people, and in the patient's relationship with the therapist. For example, "You think that when you drink you can feel anyway you wish." "You go into a rage and get high whenever your wife doesn't do as you wish." "You thought of mainlining because you were upset with me when I didn't respond as you thought I would."

11. Substance abusers and their children suffer greatly from shame experience. Addictive patients are shamed of having been shamed, and often use drugs to obliviate feelings of shame. Therapists need to help substance abusing patients experience, rather than repress, their feelings of shame now that they no longer anesthetize them. One way to do this is to identify feelings of shame that are not recognized as such. For example, "You felt so much shame when you realized you were alcoholic that you kept on drinking so you wouldn't feel the shame."

> *What does Donald Winnicott contribute to our understanding of addiction?*

Although there are many aspects of Winnicott's theoretical and clinical writings that have application to the understanding of treatment of substance abusers, by far the most salient is his short essay, "The Capacity to Be Alone" (1958). In it, Winnicott postulates that the capacity to be alone is a paradox. It comes from the experience of being alone in the presence of another person. If we are fortunate enough to have been with a loving, non-impinging parent who allowed us to be alone as we explored the world, even as they were there with us, we slowly internalize that parent so that we can now be alone without really being alone, because mother or father is inside of us. This process can go awry in either of two ways. The parent may be, to use Winnicott's term, too impinging, too controlling, too unable to let the child be, or the parent may not have been available. In either case, there will be pathological deficit in the capacity to be alone. Counterintuitive as it may be, the capacity to be alone is not a given, is not innate, but is a human achievement. It is important to note that Winnicott's capacity to be alone is not defensive isolation; it is quite the opposite. It is the kind of being alone that is necessary for creativity, for inner peacefulness, for serenity, for contemplation. Defensive isolation occurs out of fear and is what the twelve-step programs call isolating, which they quite rightfully see as a danger to sustaining sobriety.

> *What does failure to internalize the capacity to be alone have to do with substance abuse?*

One of the most frequent reasons that people use drugs is to be companioned. One of the capacities that must be internalized during development, namely, the capacity to be companioned by the self and its internal objects, never occurs, so that aloneness becomes terrifying abandonment. It cannot be tolerated and must be immediately alleviated by providing one's self with the companionship of reefer, line, or a sexual partner. The therapist should interpret this.

> *What does Erik Erikson teach us about the treatment of substance abuse?*

There are many aspects of Erikson's developmental scheme that are highly relevant to substance abuse treatment, but I will highlight only two. The first is the development of basic trust at the very beginning of life, or the failure to do so. As Erikson tells us, his is an epigenetic scheme in which each succeeding stage enfolds even as it builds on earlier stages. It follows that if we miss out on, or fail to successfully master, an earlier developmental task, it will make mastery of all the later ones more difficult. Many substance abusers have severe problems with trust. That is one reason they use substances instead of relationships to meet their needs, an insight that gives us another perspective from which to view the counterdependency so often concomitant with substance abuse. The substance abuse therapist needs to be aware that many, if not most, of these patients have never developed basic trust, and that makes for extraordinarily fragile therapeutic relationships (which are fragile enough on many other counts, including defense of the addiction). And that failure to successfully master this first developmental task means that all of the subsequent developmental tasks will be fraught with difficulty and achieved tenuously if at all.

The other Eriksonian developmental task particularly relevant to work with substance abusers is the achievement of identity, or the failure to do so, which Erikson variously calls *identity defusion* and *identity confusion*. Whether as fixation or regression, identity disturbances are ubiquitous among substance abusers. When an AA member says, "My name is John, and I am an alcoholic," he is performing what the ordinary language philosopher John Austin (1961) called a "performative utterance." A performative utterance is a use of language that actually does something, and does not merely denote something. When the judge says, "Ten years," he's not merely pointing to something in the statute book; he is speaking a performative utterance. When John says, "I am," he is not only denoting his existence, he is creating, or at the very least, affirming it. Further, he is specifying his existential assertion by naming one characteristic of that existence—being alcoholic. This is the beginning of having an identity.

Substance abusers are very confused about their identity, partly because of the confused state that the substance induces by its cognitive damage and partly because of developmental deficit. To be something—an alcoholic or an addict—is better than to be nothing, and this affirmation of existence as an addict is the beginning of accruing a more complex identity. We have empirical evidence (Conners 1962) for this. If patients in a drug rehabilitation unit are asked to fill out an adjective checklist of self-descriptive terms, they check very few items on the list, indicating a vacuity in their self-concepts. If the same people are tested five years later (if they remain sober), they now have a very rich self-concept, and check many adjectives.

Problems around identity, even existence, are absolutely crucial in the treatment of patients early in recovery from substance abuse. Over and over again, the therapist needs to return to issues of identity, changing identity, and the confusion of having been one person drunk and one person straight, and to emphasize to patients that once they have a core identity as an alcoholic or an addict, then they can, and will, add all sorts of attributes to their identity as they slowly accrete and accrue an enriched self-concept.

Erikson's epigenetic developmental scheme has more implications for substance abuse treatment than those derived from difficulties around the establishment of basic trust and identity, transcendentally vital as they may be. Failure to successfully negotiate any of Erikson's psychosocial stages, which is more the rule than the exception for substance abusers, renders the work of negotiating each of the succeeding stages all the more difficult. This is especially apparent in working with adolescent substance abusers struggling with the vicissitudes of the identity crisis without having mastered the previous stage of industry vs. inferiority, the stage in which Erikson tells us that the "tools" necessary to function in a given culture are acquired. The failure manifests as massive educational deficits that must be remediated if the youngster is to have any shot at a stable and satisfying sobriety. This task seems so daunting that many youngsters give up and relapse. The therapist needs to be empathic to the seeming impossibility of playing catch-up, as well as to be able to offer the teenager a realistic plan of remediation that kindles hope.

At the other end of life, imagine the virtual impossibility of arriving at final integrity, which Erikson counterposed to senile despair or disgust and which he tells us entails "the acceptance of one's one and only life cycle and of the people who have become significant to it as something that had to be and that, by necessity, permitted no substitutions" (1968, p. 138), without having reasonably satisfactorily mastered the stages of intimacy and generativity because of substance abuse. For the older patient in early recovery, the sense of its being too late can be crushing. The best the therapist can do is to engage the patient in major mourning for lost opportunity, while paradoxically focusing on the now, and perhaps suggest that the patient read *King Lear.*

What does James Masterson contribute to our understanding of substance abuse and its treatment?

Masterson's (1976) theory of the dynamics of borderline personality syndrome is highly relevant to work with many substance abusers. Masterson postulates that the borderline has been raised in a situation in which separateness and autonomy are punished and symbiosis is rewarded, and that the borderline patient has internal representations reflecting these experiences that are activated in current interpersonal relations. The internal representations are both enacted and projected in these relationships, including the relationship with the therapist in which they can be usefully interpreted. People with such internal worlds have great difficulty with their interpersonal relations and are quite prone to turn to substances. Substance use gratifies and rewards the drive toward symbiosis, yet simultaneously gives the illusion of autonomy and separateness. Drug use thus provides (at least in the beginning) a way out of the dilemma of the Masterson borderline who is trapped between fear of abandonment and fear of engulfment. If the therapist detects such a pattern in the patient, interpretation of the drug as yet another rewarder of fusion and being a substitute for and reincarnation of the parent who would not let go will be mutative. For borderlines with the kind of internal world Masterson describes, drug use is perfectly ego-syntonic behavior. The fact that the substance use provides a pseudo–self-sufficiency, a kind of artificial and illusionary sense of separation without the accompanying punishment by abandonment by the love object—now the drug—is an extraordinarily powerful hook that makes it extremely difficult for the user to relinquish the use. Naturally, not all substance abusers fit this rubric, but surprisingly many do, and the addictions therapist needs to be alert for this pattern of internal object relations that Masterson characterized as a split between a maternal part-object that is attacking in the face of efforts at separation-individuation and a maternal part-object that offers approval and supplies for regressive and clinging behavior. The borderline's part-self representations are also split between the bad, helpless, guilty, and empty, and the good, passive, compliant child. We see this all the time in work with substance abusers.

> *What does Otto Kernberg teach us about the dynamics*
> *and treatment of substance abuse?*

Kernberg (1975) sees substance abuse as a correlative of borderline personality disorder, although he realizes that this correlation is imperfect. A great deal of Kernberg's work has been on the treatment of borderlines. And as we have seen, most borderlines are substance abusers, although the converse is not the case—most substance abusers are not borderline—so that it is natural for Kernberg to concentrate on the internal world and dynamics of the borderline in his discussions of substance abuse. He has definite treatment recommendations, the most important of which is that the patient may not use while he or she is in treatment. He greatly encourages his patients to take part in twelve-step programs and does strict limit setting. His way of handling substance abuse is strikingly like his way of handling attempted suicide. He tells his patients that if they attempt suicide, he will do everything possible to save their lives, but the treatment will be at an end. He is not quite so strict on terminating if the patient breaks the contract by drinking or drugging, but he holds a fairly tight line, and being a therapist with a great deal of charisma and one who projects a great deal of power he may be able to get away with things that other therapists cannot. Nevertheless, the recommendation that the patient must be abstinent in order to participate in the treatment is quite prevalent in the substance abuse treatment field, and often makes sense. But I do not believe it always makes sense. There are times when one must work with the user while he or she continues to use, even if the ultimate goal is abstinence. This is a controversial treatment recommendation with which Kernberg would not agree.

In looking at the borderline personality aspect of substance abuse, it is useful to look through the lens of Kernberg's theory of the dynamics and development of the borderline personality structure. According to Kernberg, an object relations theorist who speaks of internal object representations, we start out with an undifferentiated, amalgamated selfobject representation, which essentially is without boundaries and without demarcations. Those fixated or regressed to this developmental stage are, by definition, psychotic, since reality testing is not possible without separation of self and object representations. Kernberg calls this stage one of object relations development.

In Kernberg's second stage of development, there is division of the undifferentiated stage one representation along affective lines, resulting in a separation into a good selfobject and a bad selfobject representation. That is to say that differentiation has not yet occurred in terms of separation of self and object, but that affective differentiation has taken place in a kind of global way. The infant experiences a good mother who feeds and soothes, and a bad mother who frustrates. These experiences are internalized as selfobject representations in which both the good and bad mother become part of me and of my internal representation of myself. Fixation/regression to this stage of object relations development also results in psychosis, because there is still no separation of self and object.

In Kernberg's third stage, there are four internal representations, namely of the good object, the bad object, the good self, and the bad self. Now there is separation, but not yet integration of the positive and negative aspects of our experience of the world and ourselves. Kernberg, being a drive theorist in spite of his object relations orientation, depicts the goodness or badness of these representations as resulting from the cathexis by libido or by aggression of self and object representations. This is the internal world of the borderline patient, and, in Kernberg's view, it is responsible for the chaotic interpersonal experience and the wild fluctuations in self-evaluation borderlines experience. There is no integration of good and bad self representations, nor of good and bad object representations. The patient is not psychotic, reality testing being possible, but his or her affective life is chaos. When the twelve-step slogan speaks of there being only two people who can get a person in trouble, the great "I am" and "poor me," it is speaking of Kernberg's good self representation (here grandiose), and bad self representation.

Kernberg's treatment is aimed at the integration of these representations so the patient can move into a mature internal world. This stage four internal world consists of complex self representations in which the positive predominates over the negative, but that are, nevertheless, amalgamations of the good and the bad. People who reach stage four of object relations development are capable of ambivalence. Similarly, the representations of others become complex as good and bad object representations are integrated.

Melanie Klein, whose work has been one of the major influences on Kernberg, would conceive of the developmental move from stage three to stage four as a move from the schizoid position to the depressive position. In Klein's depressive position, ambivalence and mourning become possible.

Kernberg's way of working and facilitating motivation is to interpret the transference in here-and-now terms. He makes few genetic interpretations; that is, he rarely comments on the historical source of what is happening now in the treatment. Rather, he interprets extensively, and often at length, what is going on between the patient and the analyst or therapist. These interpretations serve to make maladaptive defenses conscious. Manifestations of splitting into all good and all bad, the most characteristic borderline defense, are confronted. Kernberg talks about the borderline defenses of devaluation, primitive idealization, and denial, as well as of splitting, considering these pathognomonic of borderline personality disorders when they are the predominant defensive mechanisms.

These are precisely the defenses we see in substance abusers: the primitive idealization of the substance; the primitive idealization of the grandiose self; devaluation of others (including the therapist) as a defense (a manifestation of negative transference, which Kernberg is particularly prompt and vigorous in interpreting); and denial. All are highly characteristic of substance abusers, as is projection. Denial is the defense most characteristic of substance abusers.

Kernberg also addressed narcissistic personality disorder. In his view, the narcissist's internal world is dominated by a pathological representation that is an amalgamation of ideal self, real self, and ideal object. The real and ideal are confused, boundaries are blurred, and the grandiosity characteristic of the great "I am" is a natural consequence of having such a selfobject representation.

Kernberg sees substance abuse as common among and very characteristic of many narcissistic personality disorders, as he defines them.

Peter Hartocollis (1968), whose work I have already cited, sees the internal world of substance abusers similarly to Kernberg. However, his presentation is more ego psychological than object relational. He sees the characteristic difficulty of the borderline as historical, as rising from disturbances in parent–child relations. The borderline adult interpersonal difficulties are derivatives of difficulties in the rapprochement subphase of separation-individuation. Hartocollis is here drawing on Margaret Mahler's well-known developmental schema, of the autistic stage, the symbiotic stage, and the stage of separation-individuation with its four substages—differentiation, practicing, approchement, and separation-individuation proper. In Hartocollis's view, the borderline has suffered either traumatic rejection and abandonment or a refusal to let go in the rapprochement subphase, and this makes for the very stormy interpersonal relations driven by fears of abandonment and engulfment. The borderline turns to substances because he finds his relationship to them more manageable. This is strikingly similar to Masterson's presentation of what he calls the "partial object relations unit" in which separation is punished and symbiosis rewarded (see above).

So these four thinkers—Kernberg, Masterson, Hartocollis, and Mahler (by implication, as I don't know anywhere she writes explicitly about substance abuse)—all see the difficulties of the borderline substance abuser as arising quite early in development, and being more determined by developmental arrest and deficit in object or ego development than by intrapsychic conflict. That is not to say that borderlines do not experience intrapsychic conflict. Like all human beings they do, but these conflicts are not central to their dilemma.

The treatment implications of all of this is to be aware of these various ways of thinking about what happens, internally and interpersonally, to people with borderline and narcissistic characteristics. That is where substance abusers tend to be, and even if their level of object relations and ego development is a regression consequent upon the drug use, it is what therapists have to deal with. This knowledge lessens the therapist's anxiety in face of the patient's irrationality. The therapist looks for the unfolding of the patient's internal world in terms of relationships to self, to others, to therapist, and to the substance. All of these relationships and their interconnections can be usefully commented on. My own model (see above), based on the developmental theory of Kohut, which understands all of this as regression/fixation to the stage of the archaic grandiose self, is not in conflict with the position of these ego and object relations theorists. It is another way of organizing the data, and, I think, a more useful one, but there really is not that much conflict between the models. There is more difference in the treatment approaches, with Kernberg and his followers being more confrontive than Kohut and the self psychologists.

What does Carl Jung teach us about the psychodynamics of addiction?

Jung played an interesting and important role in the creation of Alcoholics Anonymous. In the 1930s, an American businessman, known in the AA literature as Roland H., developed a serious drinking problem in middle life. Roland was a highly successful, seemingly not deeply disturbed man, who simply could not stop drinking. He went to Zurich to enter analysis with Jung. After a period of intensive analytic work, Roland terminated, to the satisfaction of both his analyst and himself. He was "cured." Within a very short time he returned to Zurich, hopelessly drunk, begging Jung for further help. Jung refused, saying to him, "I have done everything medicine can do for you by the way of psychological help, and I have nothing further to offer. Either you will drink yourself to death, or you will end your life in a sanatorium." Roland became desperate and begged Jung for a ray of hope. The wizard of the Alps declined to give Roland that hope. After a further period of Roland's tears and begging and pleading, Jung finally said, "Well, there is one possibility. If you were to undergo a profound transvaluation of values as Nietzsche put it, or a psychological reorganization at a deep level, as I would put it, then you could recover." In essence, Jung was telling Roland H. that he had to undergo some sort of "peak" or conversion experience resulting in a profound alteration in his inner world. One could describe such a change as a change in existential stance.

Roland H. left Zurich in despair. He continued to drink, wandered from place to place, and finally visited Oxford University. At that time, the Oxford movement, a sort of upper-class revival movement that held that if you convert the "leading people" in a community and move them to live a more spiritual life, then you could raise the spiritual tone of the entire community, was flourishing. Also known as the moral rearmament movement, the Oxford movement, after having started at the university, spread worldwide and became a fairly potent social force in the 1920s and 1930s. It had ten steps of spiritual growth that later became, in modified form, the twelve steps of AA and its various spinoffs. Roland did, indeed, join the Oxford group, and had his transvaluation of values, his psychological reorganization, and his change in existential stance, and he became sober, remaining sober for the rest of his life. He returned to the United States and encountered Ebby Thacker, a wealthy drunk. He related his story and Ebby, too, joined the Oxford movement and stopped drinking.

Thacker then went to visit his old friend Bill Wilson, then living in his father-in-law's house in Brooklyn Heights, drinking around the clock. Wilson was no longer able to function. His wife Lois meagerly supported them with a sales job at Macy's. When Thacker arrived, Wilson, a former stockbroker—now impoverished, ill, and close to death—was delighted. His drinking buddy had arrived. But, lo and behold, his drinking buddy did not want to drink. It was a scene reminiscent of Eugene O'Neill's (1946), *The Iceman Cometh*. In O'Neill's play, Hickey, a traveling salesman, visits Harry Hope's End of the Road Bar once a year. His annual visit is eagerly anticipated by the residents of Harry's whose perspective is epitomized by Jimmy Tomorrow. Hickey, like Ebby Thacker, arrives one year without liquor and unwilling to buy drinks, having found salvation and no longer needing alcohol. He persuades each of the rummies in Harry Hope's bar that they don't need their illusions, or as O'Neill calls them, their "pipe dreams," and that they can go out tomorrow and realize them in action. Needless to say, it doesn't work, and Hickey himself turns out to be fleeing from the murder of his wife; he too, is living a pipe dream. O'Neill's point seems to be that human beings cannot live without illusions or delusions or modifications of consciousness induced by substances because reality is simply too painful. There is a reiterated cry throughout *The Iceman Cometh*: "Hickey, what have you done to the booze?" It doesn't work anymore. *The Iceman Cometh* presents us with human life as inextricably tragic. O'Neill, who was an alcoholic himself, is perhaps here reflecting a personal vision, rather than a metaphysical one, but he believed that he was describing reality, not his own take on it.

Bill Wilson, like the dying rummies in Harry Hope's bar, was delighted to see his drinking buddy and then equally crushed and disillusioned as Ebby began to tell him the story of his having joined the Oxford movement. Somewhere along the way, Bill started listening to Ebby, and decided he had little to lose by being open to experiencing an inner change. He returned to Knickerbocker Hospital to be dried out for the umpteenth time, and on this occasion had a peak or mystical experience in which he felt a sense of overwhelming value in the universe, which was somehow within him as well as without. He thought perhaps he had gone insane, and spoke of the experience to Dr. Silkworth, the director of the hospital. Silkworth told him he didn't understand what had happened to Bill, but he seemed to be in better shape now than before his conversion experience, peak experience, what-have-you, so it must be a good thing. Wilson left the hospital and joined the Oxford movement, never to drink again.

Being a leader, rather than a follower, it was inevitable that he would break with the Oxford movement and found his own institution, which he did. The reasons he gave had to do with what he saw as a talking down to alcoholics, and by extension, to substance abusers in general, by the "saved" of the Oxford movement, and he pioneered the idea of sharing one's own experience, rather than preaching, which is certainly more effective communication.

Wilson went on to found AA when on a business trip to Akron, Ohio, he had an intense yearning to drink and feared succumbing to this ultimate thirst. He sought out another drunk to help as a kind of diversion. The way he did it was very characteristic of Bill Wilson. He called the Firestones, the leading family of Akron, with whom he had had some contact, and asked if they knew someone who needed help. Bill was forever the poor boy aspiring to be part of the gentry. They referred him to a physician, Bob Smith, who was on one of his periodic benders. Bill went to see Dr. Bob, shared his experience, and Dr. Bob, too, got sober. The two of them rode to the hospital the next day where Smith, who was scheduled to operate, was fighting the shakes, so Wilson fed him a few bottles of beer en route to the operating room, and as far as we know the patient survived. Smith, too, became sober, and the experience of sharing a common problem became the basis of the twelve-step movement, which grew very rapidly once Wilson institutionalized it by writing the twelve steps and the other early AA literature. Smith, incidentally, was a proctologist, though he did other kinds of surgery, so if you had hemorrhoids in Akron in the 1930s, you were in trouble.

Many years later when AA was a potent social force with meetings on every continent, Wilson wrote to Jung telling him of his indirect influence on the founding of Alcoholics Anonymous through Roland H. having spoken to Ebby Thacker, who in turn told his story to Bill Wilson. Jung wrote back thanking Wilson for his letter and the news of what had happened to Roland H. and said, "Craving for alcohol is the equivalent on a low level of the spiritual thirst of our being for wholeness, expressed in medieval language: The Union with God. . . . You see, 'alcohol' in Latin is 'spiritus' and you use the same word for the highest religious experience as well as for the most depraving poison. The hopeful formula therefore is: *Spiritus contra spiritum*" (Jung 1961, p. 623). The spiritual against the spirits.

Jung's essential theory of the dynamics of addiction is that it is a result of repressed or pathological spirituality. It is a search in the wrong place for a legitimate human need. To grossly oversimplify, psychopathology for Freud is the outcome of repressed sexuality, and for Jung, repressed spirituality. Thus the "cure" has to be some kind of refurbishing of the user's spiritual life. How much one cares for this approach is a matter of taste; I am ambivalent about it. I think Jung is a verbose, obscure, often hypocritical and dishonest writer whom I simply do not care for, yet he may be on to something here.

The twelve-step program emphasizes cure through spiritual growth. One does not have to be otherworldly to agree that some sort of emotional growth and maturation is a necessary, if not sufficient, condition for recovery from substance abuse. There are, of course, many people who want no part of that approach; they are not looking for salvation or spiritual growth and just want help with their substance abuse, and they certainly should not be pushed into this kind of religiosity if it is antithetical to their values. Other people find the Jungian approach, as institutionalized in the twelve-step programs, extraordinarily helpful and do very well with it. Clearly, it is not for us as therapists to impose value systems on our patients and both groups do well coming from very different standpoints and going toward very different goals, although control or abstinence from the substance is the goal with all patients.

What does Melanie Klein teach us about addiction?

Klein's (1975a,b) developmental theory is a useful adjunct to the developmental theories of Mahler, Kernberg, Masterson, and Kohut. Klein believes that that death instinct must be projected out onto the environment, lest it destroy the neonate. The projected death instinct then becomes the persecutory object (otherwise known as the bad breast), and the persecutory object is hated, feared, and envied.

The death instinct is also projected in order to protect the good within from destruction. But the good aspects of the self can also be projected outward, creating ideal objects and the good breast. So the child is now living in a world of split part-objects (all good and all bad). According to Klein this is a biologically programmed developmental sequence that is reinforced by the inevitable frustration of the world, in this case the frustration of mother not always being there. The good and bad breast are now identified with and introjected by the infant so that they now become internal objects. Kleinian developmental theory starts out as an instinct theory, but it does not remain one. It becomes an object relations theory. Instinct essentially drops out, leaving internal objects and external objects.

The abused substance is experienced as the good breast until it turns on and fails the user. It then becomes the bad breast.

Once the inner badness is projected, the infant lives in a split (or schizoid) and persecutory (or paranoid) world. This state of being is called by Klein the *paranoid-schizoid position*. It is both a developmental stage and a state of being that stays with us throughout life.

Klein originally called this development stage and existential stance the paranoid position until Ronald Fairbairn (1940) suggested that the aloneness of the infant greatly added to anxieties of psychotic proportion, and that schizoid defenses were instituted to protect the infant from persecution by the bad breast. Accordingly, he suggested that Klein change the name of the position to paranoid-schizoid, which she did.

In Klein's developmental scheme the next stage involves a recognition that the good breast is the bad breast and that there is only one breast, which entails an integration of self and object representations. The characteristic defenses of the paranoid-schizoid position are splitting, denial, and devaluation, and the affective states accompanying it are terror, hatred, and envy. In the depressive position, which Winnicott (1963) called the acquisition of the capacity for concern, not only are good and bad integrated and splitting healed, but there is a realization that I have created the bad breast by spoiling the good breast through my hatred and envy. This results in primitive guilt, which leads to savagery against the self by the primitive superego.

According to Klein, who based her theory on clinical evidence from her analysis of children, in my realization that I have transgressed against and spoiled the good breast—feelings derived from my desire to bite, piss on, and shit on the good breast—I develop a wish to make reparation for that spoiling. Thus an important part of arriving at and living in the depressive position is the making of reparation for my aggression.

But my envy of the good breast prevents me from making that reparation. Melanie Klein is to the breast what Freud was to the penis—both theorists putting great emphasis on envy of those body parts by those who do not have them, either by reason of their gender or their infantile state. (The Spanish existential philosopher Unamuno wrote of male womb envy.) But Klein goes a step further and says that that reparation becomes possible because I am able to overcome my envy and hatred through feeling gratitude for the goodness of the good breast—and later, gratitude for whole objects.

This sounds like it has an awful lot to do with the dynamics of substance abusers. Substance abusers are often filled with primitive rage, hatred, and envy, and they aggress in all kinds of ways against the good things of their lives and this world. They also live in a split world of part-objects—

split not only into good and bad, but into less than whole units, this being seen particularly clearly in sexual addictions in which the person is irrelevant and the genitals are the only area of interest. But substances, too, are part-objects in the minds of those who abuse them, most often good breasts or good penises, but not infrequently bad breasts and bad penises. Perhaps even more to the point is the degree to which substance abusers live in the Kleinian paranoid-schizoid position, that is, in a state of terror in a persecutory world.

In the Kleinian vision, that persecution is entirely the product of the projection of the death instinct and of aggressive and murderous wishes, and certainly substance abusers struggle with murderous wishes. As their addiction progresses, they regress to living almost exclusively in the paranoid-schizoid position. Users often become overtly paranoid, refusing to answer the door, being afraid to open their mail, and hiding from the world and from themselves.

All of us live throughout our lives, except for the very earliest months, in dynamic equilibrium between the depressive and the paranoid-schizoid positions. Creativity and spontaneity, discontinuity and novelty, are more a product of paranoid-schizoid functioning, something we would not wish to live without, while steadiness, reliability, responsibility, and rationality are all concomitant with existence in the depressive position. There is, so to speak, more sanity in the depressive position, and substance abusers are not any too sane, so they are definitely not spending most of their time in the depressive position. The difficulty in substance abuse in terms of the Kleinian developmental scheme is the predominance of paranoid-schizoid functioning rather than its presence, which is universal. Some substance abusers never reach the depressive position, or do so only insecurely. They are the patients described as essential alcoholics, as primary addicts, as habilitation cases. But most substance abusers have regressed to predominantly paranoid-schizoid functioning.

Thomas Ogden (1986) has added a position even more primitive than the paranoid-schizoid to the Kleinian developmental scheme, which he calls the *autistic-contiguous position*, a coming-into-being phenomenon. But this is not terribly relevant to the treatment of substance abuse except to explain the utter lostness of those substance abusers who have regressed all the way. They have literally lost themselves and must come back into being.

Klein also discussed a phenomenon she called *projective identification*, in which an unacceptable part of the self is projected onto another and then is actually evoked in that person by some sort of behavioral maneuver on part of the projector, so that the object of the projection actually feels the hatred, anger, or envy that is being projected onto him or her. The part of self or affective state thus projected can now be identified with and reintrojected. Such a process of projective identification (which also goes on with the therapist in a kind of counterprojective identification) plays an extremely important role in therapy, and we need to explore our countertransferences to see what is being induced in us by the patient—to see how much of it is our stuff and how much of it is theirs—and perhaps through our containment of that projection and pacification of it enable the patient to own this unacceptable part of self.

Substances are ideal targets for both projection and projective identification. In that case, the projective identification is more of a fantasy business, and obviously the substance does not change its emotional state in response to the user's thoughts and feelings and actions toward it, but it does in the user's fantasy and the scenario is acted out in the addict's mind. All of this is very useful in treating substance abusers, in understanding their experiential world, and in formulating interpretations of the addict's relationship with self, therapist, other people, and substance.

In what way is AA a Kleinian therapy?

Alcoholics Anonymous can be usefully understood as a therapy that helps people move from the paranoid-schizoid to the depressive position. The twelve steps serve to attenuate primitive guilt, to soften the superego, to help members forgive themselves for the aggressions they have committed (real and imagined), and to reach a state of self-acceptance. They do that through the sharing of guilt and through the "making of amends." AA's making of amends is Melanie Klein's reparation for aggression against the good breast motivated by hatred and envy. AA puts great emphasis on gratitude. Klein tells us that it is gratitude that allows us to overcome envy, and to mourn our damage—our spoiling—of the good breast, and that it is gratitude that enables us to recognize that good and bad are aspects of others and of ourselves experienced as integral, and to reach an acceptance of that complexity and ambiguity.

Twelve-step programs, just like Kleinian therapy, seek to integrate splits and to move their members from predominantly paranoid-schizoid to predominantly depressive functioning. They do this by surfacing positive affect (primarily gratitude) in order to contain and overcome hatred and envy. Envy of the good breast—and by extension envy of the power and potential of others—can be extraordinarily disabling if that envy prevents identification with the achievements of others. Identification enables realistic emulation of those achievements. Thus, envy gets in the way of educational and vocational accomplishment. Therapists frequently see this in substance abusers working far below their potential who are so filled with hatred and envy that they cannot allow themselves to learn. The pain of this dilemma is then self-medicated with one drug or another, and away we go in the addictive cycle.

Alcoholics Anonymous and other twelve-step programs put great emphasis on gratitude, carrying it to what often seems to the therapist an extreme when its members express gratitude that they are alcoholics or addicts. This must seem very strange to most therapists who (partially correctly) see a manifestation of denial when a patient says, "Doctor, I'm really grateful that I'm an alcoholic." What patients mean by this is that their addiction eventuated in hitting bottom, forcing them to take a look at themselves and to undergo a psychological and emotional reorganization, a kind of transvaluation of values. Their gratitude flows from the fact that the life they are now leading has a kind of integrity and worth that they were probably incapable of attaining without having gone through the addictive process. One can say that this is nonsense, and that the damage to self and others that that addictive process entails is hardly something to be grateful for, and that one can grow in other ways than by shooting up for ten years. That is certainly true, but the therapist would be making a great error to dispute the patient on this, although there are tactful and empathic ways of pointing out the denial side of that expression of gratitude.

The flip side of the coin is the genuineness of at least some recovering persons' feelings that they have, indeed, reached a developmental state that they probably would not have reached without having been ill. They know that their addiction has forced them to make changes they never would have made without it and they are grateful that this has occurred.

One could argue that all effective therapies are regressive in one way or another. This is most certainly true of electroconvulsive therapy. Many psychopharmacological treatments (particularly of the psychosis) are probably reductive in the sense of simplifying the patient's world even if they are also corrections of neurochemical aberrations, and most certainly psychoanalysis is, whatever else it may be, a regressive treatment. To a lesser extent, other psychodynamic treatments use regression to allow patients to let go of their present gestalt (their present take on self and world), which is by definition limiting and incomplete. Promoting and facilitating the pieces, so to speak, falling apart, provides an opportunity to do some reorganization and reintegration at a higher level. A reintegration that encompasses more truth, in the sense of being more congruent with the infinite complexity of internal and external reality, is, indeed, a curative process, but this is not possible without prior disintegration of a lower level of organization—in the sense of encompassing a less reality-existential stance, that is, a way of being in the world and relating to self. Addiction may be an unconscious search for health through regression and reorganization. If one survives, one may be better than one otherwise would have been. On the other hand, it is all too easy to romanticize a potentially fatal illness.

The twelve-step emphasis on gratitude is highly congruent with Klein's view of the emotional concomitant of moving into the depressive position, and twelve step can be usefully seen as a social therapy that enables people to move from predominantly paranoid-schizoid to predominantly depressive position functioning.

> *What does Wilfred Bion contribute to the understanding and treatment of substance abuse?*

Bion was a psychiatrist and psychoanalyst who pioneered group therapy during World War II, when he was treating soldiers suffering from combat neurosis. He published a book, *Experience in Groups* (1959), in which he described group dynamics in a way that helps therapists understand and work with the addicted family. Bion's approach is also useful in leading therapy groups for substance abusers. Bion says that every group—from the family to General Motors—works at two levels, corresponding to the conscious and unconscious levels of individual existence: the task group level and the basic assumption level. The task group (or work group) is the rational organization pursuing rational goals, for example, the family with an addicted member trying to help that member get clean. However, the task group simultaneously is a basic assumption group and at an unconscious level is engaged in fight or flight, dependency, and pairing. That is, the group is always concerned with issues of safety, which it meets either through fleeing or through aggression, or both, with being taken care of, and often with denying the need to be taken care of, and with separating from the group to form pairs, in short, sexuality, which the group tolerates because its own unconscious fantasy is that the pair will conceive the Messiah. David Scharff (Scharff and Scharff 1991) has added fusion/fission as a fourth basic assumption in every group.

The therapist can also look at the inner world of the drug addict and the addict's relationship to the drug as a combination of task orientation and a series of basic assumptions. At the task—or rational—level, the patient is trying to be less anxious, less depressed, to have more self-esteem, to be more social, or to fulfill some other seemingly and, perhaps in reality, reasonable agenda by using the drug. At the same time, there is a whole host of basic assumptions going on in this two-person group. The drug—being presumably inanimate—does not participate in the fantasy, but the patient does, and the patient uses his or her relationship with the drug to meet needs for fight and flight, for being dependent, for bonding sexually, and for fusion or fission, that is to achieve symbiosis or to disintegrate into what Bion called "bizarre bits" and Kohut called "fragments."

Bion also speaks of the container and the contained. By this, he means that human beings from infancy on need to project parts of themselves and states of their being they cannot cope with into a safe container. At the beginning of life, the container is usually the mother. Bion points out that throughout all of our lives we oscillate between being the container and contained. This gets played out between the user and the drug with the drug often being a container for a multitude of unmanageable aspects of self.

Could you comment on addiction and psychosexual regression?

The psychodynamic theorists, who subscribe to drive theory, characterize substance abusers as having arrived very insecurely, if at all, at the genital stage of psychosexual development. The ease at which substance abusers leave heterosexual relationships and marriages to return to their family of origin or their favorite substance is cited as evidence for the weakness of their genitality.

The regression substance abuse therapists see most often is to adolescence, and then to latency, in which sexuality is often more or less relinquished and the patient proceeds to play with his (to borrow a word from Harry Stack Sullivan) "chums," and the "bottle gang" replaces the heterosexual coupling. Sometimes the regression goes further, perhaps to the phallic stage (now characterized by narcissistic exhibitionism), feelings of phallic prowess manifested in various forms of antisocial aggression. Regression may then continue back into anality, a level of psychosexual development unconsciously recognized in the twelve-step slogan characterizing the goals of the treatment as becoming "clean and dry." The regression or fixation to anality may be quite apparent and this is often exemplified in the general messiness of the patient and the patient's lifestyle. Sometimes the patient is, quite literally, covered with shit; sometimes, the patient is more metaphorically covered with shit and patients often tell their therapists that this is so. Regression can go back even further to orality in which the drug becomes a breast substitute. In fact, the regression concomitant with addiction may recede to yet earlier developmental stages, right back into a psychic state congruent with intrauterine existence.

As the user regresses from orality to primary narcissism, there is a manifestation of a different kind of narcissism, not now phallic aggressiveness, but a primitive kind of self-absorption in which the object world is pretty much lost. All that is left is fusion with the substance, which is the only object left to the addict at that point in the regression. Finally, there can be a regression to autoeroticism, where even the primitive structure of the narcissistic self is lost, and there is what Kohut (1971, 1977) called

fragmentation and Freud (1905) called autoeroticism, and yet further regression into a kind of ultimate passivity of intrauterine existence, which
is seen in drug stupor.

Often forgotten these days, is Freud's observation that regression is
one of the ego defenses, and that regression can be a defense against oedipal conflict. This is a subject not usefully spoken of with active substance
abusers, but can be highly salient in working with recovering people in
which the context allows for an interpretation: "Your drug use allowed you
to relinquish the relationship you had with your wife [or husband] or girlfriend [or boyfriend], because that aroused too much anxiety in you; and
may very well be connected with your feelings about your parents (oedipal strivings) and guilt about those feelings." Such an interpretation is an
invitation that, if the patient allows it, will open up a whole new area for
psychotherapeutic exploration. The therapist can also suggest that the
patient's guilt over sexual and aggressive feelings toward the parents necessitated failure and regression. Here, the regression is both a punishment
and a defense, and that can be interpreted.

---

*What does Daniel Stern's theory of self contribute to our
understanding of addiction?*

For Stern, the self is experiential. He defines it as the sense of agency,
the sense of physical cohesion, the sense of continuity, the sense of affectivity, the sense of a subjective self that can achieve intersubjectivity with
another, the sense of creating organization, and the sense of transmitting
meaning. Definitions are prescriptive as well as descriptive, and Stern opts
for a self or series of selves that are sensate, vaguely inchoate, or sharply
experienced sensations and organizations of sensations. These selves are
essentially preconscious most of the time, although for the most part they
can emerge into consciousness without difficulty. It is not clear how or how
much the Sternian selves are dynamically unconscious. Perhaps figure and
ground is a better metaphor than conscious and unconscious; Stern's selves
most commonly serve as ground, albeit an active and organizing ground,
but they become figure in some situations.

Stern's selves correspond to discontinuities—quantum leaps in development. The sense of the emergent self comes into being during the first two months of life. It is a "sense of organization in the process of formation" (Stern 1985, p. 38). Stern emphasizes the experience of the process more than he does the product. This process is an ongoing organization of bodily concerns resulting in experiential cohesion of the body, its actions, and inner feeling states. These will form the core self that is now emerging. The emergent self is both the process and the product of forming relations between isolated events. It is the giving of cohesion. In adult life, the emergent self is the basis of creativity and potential for ongoing development.

In the next stage, that of the core self, there is a consolidation of that which has emerged from the emerging self. The core self is characterized by experiences of self-agency ("I can do things"), self-cohesion ("I have boundaries; I am a physical whole"), self-affectivity ("I have patterned inner qualities of feeling that are the same across experiences"), and self-history ("I endure, go-on-being, because there are regularities in the flow of my experience, in the stream of my consciousness"). These four self-experiences of the core self are preconceptual. They are "senses of," not concepts, not cognitive knowledge or self-awareness. They are not reflexive or reflective. The core self is a self without self-consciousness. In normal development, it is consolidated at about 8 months.

Stern's inclusion of affectivity as one of the most salient aspects of self-experience has important implications for the experience of the continuity of the self. Stern maintains that affect is the most constant experience we have, in the sense that affects remain more the same across time than any other experience. That is, our experiences of anger, sadness, joy, and pain are essentially the same in infancy, in childhood, in adolescence, in young adulthood, in maturity, and in old age. Therefore, our experience of affect very importantly determines and is constitutive of our experience of going-on-being. There is clinical implication in this as well, in that putting patients in contact with their feelings, their affects, in addition to whatever else it may do, should increase their sense of self-cohesion and self-continuity.

The subjective self develops from 8 to 15 months. Essentially, infants discover that there are inner subjective experiences—thoughts and feelings—that are theirs alone. Simultaneously, or slightly later, infants "discover" that others also have minds (i.e., inward, private thoughts and feelings that are potentially the same as theirs). This opens up the possibility of intersubjectivity. They can share (or not share) or connect (or not connect) with other creatures who are subjects like them, who have an inner world of sensations, feelings, and thoughts. For Stern, self and objects are co-emergent, not from a symbiosis, but from genetically and temporally prior, less organized, inward experiences of self and others. There is a prior primitiveness of self and others (primitive in the sense of less organized and less self-aware), but no prior confusion or merger. In the state of the subjective self, the subjectivity of the other is also established, and multitudinous possibilities for relatedness come into being. It is only now that merger or symbiosis becomes possible, but only as a union of that which was initially experienced as distinct.

During the second year of life, the verbal self comes into being. Now the self can be represented as a narrative: the story one tells to oneself about who and what one is. The narrative self is reminiscent of Freud's notion of the secondary revision of dreams, the process by which the dreamer gives the dream more cohesion and a better narrative line than it actually has. In a sense, the verbal self is a secondary revision of the dream that is one's life. The verbal self cannot adequately represent the other selves. It creates a world of concepts and abstractions that carry with them the danger of alienation from the vividness, uniqueness, and vitality of the preverbal experience characteristic of the emergent, core, and subjective selves. Thus, the four selves are equally necessary. The temporally later does not supplant the temporally earlier; rather, they provide different self-experiences. The four selves endure and mutually enrich each other across the life span. In the full flower of the Sternian self, it is simultaneously the experience of coming into being, the experience of being, the experience of interiority of self and others, and the experience of having or creating a history verbally, a narrative.

Stern's theory of the four selves helps the therapist make sense of some aspects of the addictive experience and the addict's behavior. Most substance abusers seem to have mastered the stage of the emergent self. It has been noted by many authors that creativity and substance abuse have not infrequently been linked. And the reason for this may be that substance abusers live a great deal in the world of the emergent self. And, indeed, the very experience of getting high—changing one's state of consciousness and then returning to the sober state—is a whole process of emergence and reemergence. Therefore, it is possible that the dynamic behind some substance abuse is the drive for mastery of Stern's very first developmental stage—the coming into being—by its constant rehearsal and reenactment; on the other hand, it may be the case that substance abusers are relatively fixated at this stage, and that explains both the ease at which they reenact it in their substance use, and the above-noted linkage between creativity and substance abuse.

The core self seems much more problematic for substance abusers. They seem to have very real confusion about boundaries, about ongoingness, about centeredness, and about solidity of self. The substance use is both an attempt to self-medicate this tendency of the core self to collapse into the emergent self and a cause of the fragility of the core self, which is disorganized by the substance use itself. This is well worth talking about in the therapy. Without using technical language, the therapist can talk about the shakiness of the patient's sense of self, his or her insecurity as to boundaries, going on being, centeredness, and solidity, and suggest that the substance use is an attempt to firm up the patient's sense of self, which tragically does the exact opposite, setting up a vicious circle. This interpretation, properly timed with the right patient, can be highly mutative.

Stern's subjective self is also a problem area for many substance abusers. They have great difficulty experiencing their own interiority, including their affects. If Stern is right, that affect is the experience that most makes for a sense of continuity, then it is not surprising that many substance abusers experience themselves as so discontinuous and fragmented.

Wurmser's notion of psychophobia also dovetails with the notion that substance abusers suffer deficiencies in their experience of Stern's subjective self. They externalize compulsively to compensate for the inner emptiness and inadequacy, or the relative paucity of content and arrested development of the subjective self. Once again, the treatment worsens the disease, and the self-medication with the usual concomitant acting out and externalization impoverishes the subjective self even more.

The notion of affect regression discussed above in the section on Krystal and Raskin also comes into play here, although Krystal and Raskin's notion of affect development is at odds with Stern's notion of affect constancy. With a relatively weak sense of subjective self, affect differentiation is bound to be fragile. Similarly, the addict's sense of the inner subjectivity, of the interiority, of others may also be impoverished. Having little contact with his or her inner world, the chances of bridging—through empathy—to someone else's inner world are not great. These deficiencies, difficulties, conflicts, and attempts at remediation through substance use can also usefully be discussed in therapy.

Therapy is essentially about revising the narrative self, helping patients tell a different story to themselves to account for their life. There are few more radical revisions in the narrative self than the change that comes about in the story that addicts tell themselves about the self before and after achieving sobriety. It almost seems to be the story about a different life. And this change in the narrative self is crucial if a sustained recovery is to become possible.

IV

Other Theories
of Addiction

The oldest (and still the most popular, no matter what people say) explanation of addiction is the theory of moral turpitude. This is the notion that substance abusers are bad people who do terrible things because they are evil. The treatment advocated by those who take the moral turpitude view of substance abuse is punishment, and the characteristic rehabilitation agency is prison. A lot of the rhetoric of the war on drugs is driven by a belief (acknowledged or unacknowledged) in the moral turpitude theory of addiction.

The moral turpitude theory brings to mind the story of the fundamentalist preacher who was giving a hell-and-brimstone sermon. As his preaching reached a crescendo, he bellowed out, "Tell me if anyone here is in favor of sin?" A little old lady in the back of the church stuck up her hand. "What? You're in favor of sin?" screamed the preacher. "Oh no," said the little old lady, "I thought you said gin." For her, sin and gin belonged to different categories, but this is not so for many of her fellow Americans.

Another major way of viewing drug addiction is to see it as alienation. This is the view of sociology. Substance abusers are social deviants, and social deviants are there for a reason. Society needs its deviants, if only to demarcate the normative, just as much as cops need robbers. The sociological approach is to try and understand what role deviancy plays in a culture, and what structural purpose it serves. Families may also need their deviants. Therefore, therapists should be alert to the role and structural function the addicted identified patient plays in the dynamics of the family or other system. It is always wise to ask, "Who benefits from the drug use, and how?"

Related to the theory of addiction and substance abuse as deviancy is the notion of *anomie* developed by the great sociologist Emile Durkheim (1897). Anomie, literally meaning without norms or standards, is a condition of marginality correlative with suicide, criminality, and addiction. The more one is an outsider, and the greater the social isolation, the higher the risk for all three of these conditions.

The third major model is the official one in our society, but not the one that the society really believes in or the prison would not be the predominant rehabilitation facility, and that is the disease model, discussed at length in several other places in this primer. Basically, the disease model, which is subscribed to by the American Psychological Association, the American Psychiatric Association, the American Medical Association, the National Association of Social Workers, and ambivalently by the courts, is the notion that addiction is a disease, usually meaning a genetically transmitted neurochemical predisposition, which causes users to metabolize drugs and react to drugs differently than other people, making them vulnerable to addiction.

The psychodynamic view of addiction is a variant on the disease model, in which the substance abuse is seen not as the disease, but rather as a symptom of an underlying disease process having to do with psychological deficit and conflict. Yet another major model is the self-medication model (also called the prosthesis model), in which the drug use is viewed as adaptive in one sense or another (or at least as an attempt at adaptation, however failed). The self-medication hypothesis (Khantzian 1981) holds that the drug is supplying some ego or self-need, for example, the ability to modulate anxiety, which the patient cannot supply. This is a variation on the psychodynamic model in which the substance abuse is seen as a symptom, but here the addiction is explicitly tied to specific ego and self deficits.

*What is the self-handicapping hypothesis of the
etiology of substance abuse?*

The self-handicapping hypothesis states that high-achieving substance abusers often have a dynamic as follows: at either a conscious or unconscious level, most usually unconscious, they protect themselves from failure by getting high when they face a challenging situation. It is a win-win situation for them. If they succeed at the task and the challenge in spite of being high, then, indeed, they are "supermen." If, on the other hand, they fail, then they are hardly personally inadequate in any way, since the reason they failed was that they were high. Thus, the user never risks testing his self, always hedging his bet by being high in a challenging situation. This is held by Steven Berglas (1987) to be a dynamic of male addiction. He holds that women use the premenstrual syndrome (PMS) in a similar way. If they succeed in spite of premenstrual tension then, indeed, they are magnificent creatures, and if they fail—well, of course, who wouldn't fail if they had to deal with PMS.

Berglas's theory of male self-handicapping by getting high to face a challenging situation (I don't see any reason why a woman couldn't do the same) implies an underlying deep insecurity. There is a psychological vulnerability that is then exacerbated by the drinking or drugging. That is so because the use of the drug, if that use continues for any length of time in order to self-handicap, inextricably leads to a decline in performance, which, in turn, leads to more insecurity and anxiety, and more use of the substance—and away we go, as in so many other dynamic models of addiction.

Self-handicapping certainly occurs, and, although it is not, in my opinion, a central dynamic in substance abuse, it can be usefully interpreted when the therapist has the sense that something like that is occurring: "Mr. Smith, you get high every time you're facing an audition because it protects you from failure—if you get the role in spite of your hangover, then you must be a good actor indeed, and if you don't get the role, then you can tell yourself it's because you're hung over. Thus, you protect yourself from exposure and risk but at an awful cost of decreasing your chances of succeeding. If you continue to set yourself up in this way, it is highly likely that your odds of success will go down, and that your substance abuse will go up." I have only occasionally made that interpretation, but I have found it quite mutative. Accordingly, I recommend it when it fits the situation.

What is the self-awareness model?

The self-awareness model is an explanation of the motivation of heavy drinking. It is based on the fact that one pharmacological effect of ethanol is impairment of cognitive functioning, including information storage, and that this impairment decreases self-awareness. Therefore, in situations in which self-awareness is painful, such as the aftermath of failure, drinking alcohol will be highly reinforcing. According to its author, Jay Hull (1981), empirical studies support the self-awareness hypothesis as one significant pathway to pathological drinking. It is easy to see how self-awareness obliviation could lead to a vicious cycle in which a failure results in drinking to blot out painful self-awareness, which, in turn, results in further failures "necessitating" more drinking ad infinitum until alcoholism develops.

What is the tension-reduction hypothesis?

The tension-reduction model originally applied exclusively to drinking, but has been generalized to account for other forms of substance abuse. It is congruent with popular beliefs and has the support of learning theory. Drive reduction, with anxiety or tension here conceptualized as a drive, is a highly reinforcing and powerful motivator. Early research (Conger 1956) seemed to support the notion that alcohol is tension reducing, but later research showed that this was not always the case. Tension reduction as a single-factor theory as to why people drink, or drink alcoholically, proved untenable. Whether or not ethanol is tension reducing is dependent on many factors: expectations, individual differences, dosage, whether blood alcohol levels are rising or falling, social setting, and stage of drinking career (there is evidence that alcohol actually increases tension in alcoholics, at least in experimental hospital settings). A further difficulty with the theory is that for many, the chief motivation for drinking is the anticipation of the initial euphoria (positive-affect motivation), not tension reduction (negative-affect motivation). Nevertheless, there is no question that ethanol and other drugs can be tension reducing, and that many drink or drug for that effect, whether or not their tension comes from prior use.

The difficulties with the tension-reduction hypothesis have led to a sophisticated reformulation of it known as the stress response dampening (SRD) theory (Sher 1987). It states that alcohol dampens the biological stress response and that that is highly reinforcing, increasing the likelihood that the individual will drink if stressed. This is particularly true if the person sees no alternative way of dealing with stress. Hence, the emphasis that most rehabs and outpatient treatment programs put on teaching coping skills in order to reduce stress has scientific support and makes a good deal of sense. Sher, who did not see his model as a univariate explanation of drinking behavior, reviews some possible biochemical pathways by which alcohol may dampen the adrenal-pituitary-hypothalamus stress response and concludes that—social-cognitive factors and the initial increase in heart rate notwithstanding—stress response dampening is a major motivating factor in both social and alcoholic drinking. Something similar may happen with other drugs at certain dosages in certain settings. The stress response dampening theory developed by Sher is essentially a physiological one, but one doesn't have to hold to the biological underpinning of the model to see that stress response dampening is, indeed, highly reinforcing and can lead to a vicious cycle in which the user becomes less able to cope with stress and more dependent on the drug, setting up a vicious cycle. The therapeutic implications in terms of teaching coping skills are clear—this is one place where a cognitive approach is most certainly appropriate and helpful.

What does learning theory tell us about substance abuse and its treatment?

There are three primary ways that human beings learn—through classical conditioning, operant conditioning, and modeling. Social learning is another term for modeling. There are a number of ways in which learning theory helps make sense of addiction. We know that rewards and punishments need to be associated with actions for them to increase or decrease the frequency of those actions. That is, reinforcement needs to be closely paired with an event if it is to be efficacious. A substance's first effects, such as tension reduction, anxiety modulation, disinhibition, and euphoria, are generally positively reinforcing. The punishments, such as cirrhosis, job loss, and self-hatred, are long delayed. Therefore, the connection between the negative consequences and the substance use is not established in the mind. This has therapeutic implications.

Aversion therapy is an example of a radical therapy derived from this learning theory principle. It says roughly, "Provide the punishment." In aversion therapy, alcoholics are given an open bar at which they can drink whatever they wish. However, they get a painful electric shock each time they drink. Aversion therapy has its advocates, and, although not as popular as it once was, is still occasionally used. Far more common is for the therapist to make the connection between the negative consequences and the substance use through interpretation and education. Given the realities of denial, this is often a hard sell. Nevertheless, it is always worth doing. As the therapist explores why the patient lost his last job, which may have to do with many things, the therapist keeps bringing it back to the substance use, and to the absences, ill health, and erratic performance secondary to that substance abuse.

The second learning theory principle, which is highly relevant to the dynamics and treatment of substance abuse, is the resistance to extinction of random patterns of reinforcement. If the pigeon pecking at the bar is reinforced with a food pellet the third time, the fortieth time, the forty-second time, the ninety-ninth time, and then not at all; the pigeon will go on pecking almost forever. Something very similar happens with substance abusers. Once their substance abuse was highly and fairly reliably reinforcing; this has long ceased to be the case. However, every once in a while the old magic is there, and the drinking or drugging is reinforced. Given this random pattern of reinforcement, it is perfectly rational to go on pecking the bar, or drinking at the bar, indefinitely, in the hope that there will be another reward. Participants at twelve-step meetings and substance abusing patients speak over and over about the euphoria of their first high. Twenty years later, they may still be searching for that euphoria, long since unavailable in glass or needle. This seems totally irrational and self-destructive behavior, but if we remember the principle of the power of random (or, as it is technically called, variable interval) intermittent reinforcement, it makes perfect sense.

A related notion has to do with the resistance to extinction of escape behavior. Drugs often provide cessation of pain, or escape from anxiety. This is, indeed, escape behavior and it is highly resistant to extinction. Even if the substance has long since ceased to provide such escape, the user goes on looking for it for a very long time.

Both classical and operant conditioning play a role in the creation of "triggers" or "drug signals," discussed below. Social learning theory teaches us both the importance of cognitive elements in addiction, namely, beliefs, expectations, and attitudes that profoundly affect the way in which people use drugs, and the even more powerful effect of the social surround. Modeling influences human beings vastly. That is, perhaps, one of the reasons why self-help groups work so well, as do other forms of group therapy. They provide models of health and models of sustained, happy sobriety, and these models being peers are readily identified with. Conversely, there are many models in our culture of substance use that glamorize it and make it seem cool or otherwise acceptable and attractive.

What are drink signals? Drug signals? Triggers?

A trigger is anything internal or external that elicits a desire to drink or drug. It may be five o'clock, it may be Friday night, it may be the sight of the boss, it may be a tense depression, it may be anxiety, it may be, and often is, friends who shared the highs, or it may be a Budweiser ad on TV Through stimulus generalization and classical conditioning, a vast network of drink or drug signals may come into being. For the most part, these are automatic, unconscious or, at least, unreflective responses. The therapist needs to make the drug or drink signal conscious and help the patient develop strategies—alternate behaviors—to cope with the trigger. This is most often done in group therapy, but can be done perfectly well in individual therapy. The therapist points out, for example, that whenever the user feels angry, he thinks of getting high. The therapy then continues with a discussion of what else the patient can do with his anger: verbalize it, process it, act on it, evaluate it, and perhaps come to the realization that it is inappropriate and excessive. What the twelve-step programs call the "people, places, and things" that trigger drug urges can largely be avoided, a discovery that comes as a surprise, a virtual revelation, to the user. The patient's growing realization of those things that elicit craving can lead to very fruitful discussions in group or individual therapy in which the patients themselves often come up with the alternate behavior or coping strategy. This eliciting and making conscious of triggers is one of the most effective therapeutic techniques we have to help people maintain sobriety.

What is the need-for-power theory?

The need-for-power theory, developed by David McClelland and his Harvard associates (1972), states that men drink in order to feel powerful. McClelland intends to refute the dependency conflict theory of addiction (or at least of alcohol addiction), but I don't think he succeeds. I think that drinking in order to feel powerful implies feeling power*less*, and in this powerless state one turns to substances in a counterdependent way in order to feel powerful. What it is all about is feelings of helplessness and worthlessness and the use of drugs to demonstrate the opposite. McClelland based his theory on the study of the themes and folk tales of many different cultures, and found that those cultures that told stories about personal, rather than altruistic (social) power were those cultures that had the highest rates of drunkenness. In Cambridge, he gave cocktail parties for Harvard graduate students at which they could drink all they wanted, provided they would tell stories in response to Thematic Apperception Test (TAT) cards. And, lo and behold, the stories the male students told when they were drunk were stories about personal power. The more they drank, the more obsessed with power they became, although those students who became drunkest were those whose stories reflected the most personal power themes to begin with.

As the women in McClelland's study drank they told stories whose themes were regarded as traditional feminine ones, that is, they were about makeup, clothes, and so forth. These female research subjects were graduate students at Harvard in the 1970s, and McClelland and his student Sharon Wilsnack (1973, 1974) hypothesized that these women pursuing traditionally masculine careers were intensely conflicted about their femininity and drank to resolve this conflict. They concluded that women drink to feel more feminine while men drink to feel more powerful.

What is the serotonin-deficiency hypothesis?

The serotonin-deficiency hypothesis of the etiology of alcoholism states that there is a robust correlation between low levels of serotonin and alcoholism and that that correlation is causal. If one is to believe the manufacturers of Prozac and similar drugs, there is an epidemic of serotonin deficiency such as the world has never seen, from which it logically follows that drugs that block the reuptake of serotonin should be taken by (more or less) everybody. I had a student in a substance abuse counseling class whose son was going to a highly competitive private school, who told the class that she was seriously thinking of putting her son on a selective serotonin reuptake inhibitor (SSRI) because so many of his classmates were medicated that he was at a competitive disadvantage, although he had no diagnosable psychiatric illness.

There is evidence that low levels of serotonin, which are associated with many emotional and behavioral disorders (particularly antisocial personality disorder), may indeed be etiological in alcoholism, and some patients who are prescribed SSRIs do lose (at least some of) their appetite for alcohol. In my experience, however, this is by no means a consistent reaction. Even with the same patient, the reduction of appetite for alcohol with the administration of SSRIs varies from highly significant to negligible across time. I suspect that if the drinking is a self-medication for painful depression, and the SSRI helps with the depression, then the drinking decreases. But if the person is drinking for other reasons, it does not work. The anecdotal reports in the clinical literature are rather similar for the use of these drugs for the treatment of other forms of substance abuse— sometimes they help, sometimes they don't. It is a hit-or-miss, trial-and-error, empirical business. Psychodynamic and cognitive treatments of the extremes of the personality dimensions, which Cloninger discusses (see below) are also efficacious. After all, there are millions of people in twelve-step programs who manifested all of the supposedly genetically determined traits correlative with alcoholism while they were drinking, and are now in recovery, working the AA steps with the social support of their groups, who do not manifest those behaviors. So simple genetic determination of these traits is clearly not the case. Neurochemistry sets the stage for the drama that is our life, but the play is still subject to the director's interpretation. It is worth noting that if a rodent that has some appetite for alcohol is bred with a rodent similarly inclined, and this process is continued for twelve generations, a race of rats is bred that has considerable appetite, even preference, for alcohol. If the rats are then put on Prozac, they do indeed lose their appetite for alcohol. So the scientifically best-supported conclusion about the serotonin-deficiency hypothesis of the etiology of alcoholism is that alcoholic rodents do well on SSRIs.

What is tri-dimensional personality theory and what is its relevance to addiction treatment?

Tri-dimensional personality theory was developed by C. Robert Cloninger and colleagues (1988) to account for vulnerability to addiction. Cloninger later looked upon it as a way of understanding personality variation in general. He postulates that there are three independently inherited dimensions of personality that reflect variation in underlying neurogenic systems. These systems, which involve neurological tracts in the brain that use differing neurotransmitters (the level of which is genetically determined) for synaptic transmission are postulated to mediate novel, appetive, and aversive stimuli. Although the three systems are independently inherited, they influence one another through negative feedback loops, so that the level of one affects the significance of the inherited level of the others. Cloninger does not suggest that personality is totally determined by genetically controlled neurotransmitter levels; on the contrary, he recognizes the influence of learning and environment on behavior and the expression of personality.

Cloninger's three dimensions are: novelty-seeking, harm-avoidance, and reward-dependence. He interprets the results of several longitudinal studies of drinking behavior, including the Oakland Growth Study (Jones 1968, 1971), and his own analysis of the data (Cloninger 1983) on adopted-out children of alcoholics in Sweden, as demonstrating two types of pre-alcoholic personality—antisocial (type 2) and passive-dependent (oral, type 1)—and he goes on to cite other data supporting this hypothesis. In terms of his three dimensions, type 1 (milieu-limited) alcoholics are characterized by low novelty-seeking, high harm-avoidance, and high reward-dependence. Type 2 (male-limited) alcoholics are characterized by high novelty-seeking, low harm-avoidance, and low reward-dependence. The neurotransmitters thought to be responsible for these characteristics are high levels of dopamine (mediating novelty-seeking), high levels of serotonin (mediating harm-avoidance), and low levels of norepinephrine (mediating reward-dependence). Cloninger is here not only looking for a neurochemical explanation of personality, but, I think, angling for a Nobel Prize (he just might get it). He has since elaborated his model into six dimensions, which seems to have less empirical support and is far more inferential.

Cloninger's model is intriguing. Unlike the serotonin-deficiency hypothesis (see above), which was derived primarily from findings of low platelet monoamine oxidase (MAO) levels in high-risk children of alcoholics, and which is unifactoral and hard to interpret because low platelet MAO is associated with a wide variety of psychopathologies, the tri-dimensional theory is sophisticated, multifactorial, and closely linked to drinking behaviors.

Cloninger and colleagues (1988) have attempted to apply his theory to predict alcoholism on the basis of childhood behaviors, these behaviors presumably being determined by the levels of serotonin, dopamine, and norepinephrine. High novelty-seeking and low harm-avoidance did indeed predict later difficulties with drinking, and, although the data is lacking, I am sure with substance use as well.

Cloninger's model tells us something about vulnerability to substance abuse that is worth knowing. The two types of antecedent vulnerability seem to be an externalizing defensive style involving much acting out, high novelty-seeking, low harm-avoidance, and at least mild antisocial tendencies (believing one is above the rules) including a kind of grandiose disregard for the ordinary limits that most people accept, which is clearly correlated with risk for substance abuse. The other behavior constellation, which he calls an oral personality constellation, consists of high levels of emotional discomfort (particularly tense depression), low novelty-seeking, high harm-avoidance, and high reward-dependence. These are the people-pleasing, insecure depressed, who all too readily self-medicate their misery with various drugs.

Cloninger is best known for his analysis of the data from the Swedish adopted-out study in which he found two patterns of hereditability, one limited to males and the other milieu limited, since it requires a heavy drinking environment to manifest itself whatever the genetic loading. His further discussion here is essentially an elaboration of the findings from the Swedish study.

As the culture changes its ways of understanding personality and character types, I wonder whether language to describe these character types will also change, and, instead of speaking of someone as being sanguine or melancholic (terms derived from the ancient humor theory), we will then say, "Sam is serotonic, and Sally is norepinephral."

What is the evolutionary perspective on drug addiction?

The new discipline of "Darwinian medicine" seeks evolutionary explanations for design characteristics that make organisms vulnerable to disease. Although highly speculative, the evolutionary perspective (Nesse and Berridge 1997) gives us a unique insight into the human propensity to addiction. Basically, the evolutionists argue that a built-in reward system that evolved as long ago as one billion years is still operating in modern man and that this system misreads the biological meaning of events consequent upon modern technological development. When this reward system evolved there were no drugs, so the effect of drugs on these systems was not factored in by the "invisible hand" of evolution. This is particularly true of the mu (µ) receptors, which are involved in dopaminergic brain circuits and also serve as opioid receptors. Stimulation of these receptors gives the brain a "fitness benefit" (as in survival of the fittest) signal. It is postulated that all addictive drugs affect receptors in the midbrain. These midbrain circuits misjudge the fitness benefit of drugs, which did not exist when these neural mechanisms evolved, so modern man is predisposed to get into trouble with drugs. The brain signals the organism to pursue the nonexistent fitness benefit even after subjective pleasure in the drug has long ceased. Darwinian medicine theorists see "process addictions," that is, nonchemical ones, as resting on similar mechanisms and postulate that such phenomena as "video addiction" result from misread fitness benefit signals. This, of course, does not explain why one person rather than another gets hooked.

> *What does John Bradshaw teach us about substance abuse and its treatment?*

John Bradshaw, the enormously popular, evangelical ex-priest, is by far the best of the pop psychologists writing on substance abuse. He is extremely insightful in terms of being in empathic contact with the pain of addiction and the defenses against that pain—chemical, behavioral, and psychodynamic. Bradshaw's flaws are those of most popularizers; he is overly simplistic, unifactoral, and repetitious. But he has something important to say.

Bradshaw's (1988) basic theory of the psychodynamics of substance abuse is that it is the product of the repression, anesthetizing, and acting out of what he calls *toxic shame*. Toxic shame, according to Bradshaw, is a product of *poisonous pedagogy*, that is, child-rearing methods in which children are systematically shamed. Bradshaw is on to something important here. It is true that when children are persistently mistreated, they not only have all of the feelings of rage, self-blame, and vulnerability to depression that one would expect, but they are also *ashamed* of having been mistreated.

If you have been treated like a piece of shit, you don't want anyone to know it, including yourself. Substance abuse is a very good answer, at one level, to a history of shaming and/or overt abuse—physical or sexual. It is a way of enacting a lot of rage and externalizing it, with the substance use often being substance use *at* somebody. It is a manic defense against the underlying pain, and it anesthetizes that pain. Unfortunately, in the long run, the shame avoider reexperiences his or her shame, sometimes exponentially increased.

Bradshaw views addiction very broadly, so broadly, in fact, that his notion of it encompasses, as far as I can see, almost everything. I think that this is a flaw in his theory, a flaw insofar as he doesn't make distinctions between distracting rituals we all probably have and pathological forms of compulsion and substance abuse. On that preachy side he is reminiscent of the seventeenth-century philosopher Blaise Pascal (1670) who talked about "busyness" as a distraction from ontological anxiety, from the realization that one is ultimately alone and is going to die, that one has limitations and must ultimately experience the attendant dread intrinsic to the human condition. Pascal's writings are very much in the spirit of Bradshaw, whose treatment is powerfully focused on bringing people back into contact with the pain and the shame intrinsic to life. Bradshaw strives to help patients end the distractions of compulsive relationships, compulsive behaviors, substance abuse. One way of doing this is to get in contact with what Bradshaw calls "the child within" or "inner child," whom the patient then tries to heal with acceptance and love. Bradshaw's ultimate answer is a religious one, or, as he would say, a spiritual one, involving a coming into awareness of some sort of protective and loving force in the universe, much like the twelve-steps' higher power. For those capable of and interested in that kind of experience, it can indeed be extraordinarily healing.

Bradshaw's treatments tend to be short-term workshops, which, much like the encounter movement of the 1970s' marathon weekends, produce wonderful short-term results. People go to such workshops and leave feeling glowing and up, but the long-term carry-through is doubtful. That doesn't make such short-term intense experience any less valuable— orgasms are short-lived also, yet few of us would wish to relinquish them. Bradshaw, on the popular level, like Wurmser (1981) on the scientific level, puts shame on the map as a key emotion in the psychodynamics of substance abuse. They are both right.

What is cognitive dissonance and what does it tell us about the dynamics of addiction?

Cognitive dissonance is a theory of Leon Festinger's (1957) that states that discrepancies between expectations and reality (both experienced as cognitive structures) are painful. Although the theory uses the word *cognitive*, it is really an affective theory about pain and reduction of pain. It postulates that people distort either the outcome or the expectation in order to reduce cognitive dissonance.

Festinger's original example concerned a cult that predicted the end of the world, and when the end of the world didn't come on the predicted date, before which the cult members had divested themselves of their possessions and put themselves in an impossible economic position, one would think that they would have repudiated the cult and its belief system and its leader. But they didn't. They had lost a great deal, and the failure of their leader's prophecy had to be explained away. Rather than devalue him, they simply found ways to explain away the failure of the world to end on the predicted date. According to Festinger, their far-fetched "explanations" served to reduce the pain of the cognitive dissonance between expectation and reality. What psychologists refer to as the "severity of initiation" phenomenon works in a similar way. When people go through a rigorous boot camp or other initiation experience, they come to believe that being a member of, for example, the Marine Corps, is a wonderful thing. This justifies the pain of having gone through the initiation rite of basic training. Equating the severity of initiation with the value of group membership is a form of cognitive dissonance reduction. In summary, Festinger's theory postulates that cognitive dissonance is so painful that people will do and believe irrational things in order to reduce that dissonance. It seems to me that a similar dynamic is at work in substance abuse and that the drug is invested with all sorts of magic to reduce the cognitive dissonance between devastatingly negative consequences and scant pleasure in its use.

As the addiction progresses and as the addictive career unfolds, the biphasic nature of the drug's effect leads to a diminution of pleasure and an enormous increase in the pain associated with the use of the drug. Yet, at the very same time, when the negative consequences of drug use seem overwhelming and undeniable, users will routinely focus on the great benefits and pleasures supposedly derived from their use of the substance. It is as if they were saying, "I can't stand the cognitive dissonance of believing all this pain is really getting me nothing, so I have to glorify the substance I am using and idealize what effects it has on me." There is certainly an idealizing transference going on there, with many levels of meaning, and yet, as far as I know, no one has tried to explain in terms of cognitive dissonance theory this very common phenomenon of abusers holding on to the alleged wonderfulness of their drug use, even as the world is falling down around them. Denial is, in part, a way of dealing with the pain of cognitive dissonance. It's a dynamic that makes sense, is interpretable, and can be heard by patients.

I sometimes compare the patient's continuing use to the losing gambler who keeps doubling his bet in the hope of recouping his losses. That, too, is a way of reducing cognitive dissonance. More usually I say to the addicted patient, "Your shooting up is costing you so much [which I spell out in terms of health, economic loss, damaged relationships, and so on] that you have to believe heroin is the best thing life has to offer or else face the pain of having been taken in by it. And that's just too damn awful to even think about." Using drugs to blot out the pain of the cognitive dissonance their previous use has induced is another form of the addictive vicious cycle in which the addict uses because he uses.

What is Levin's theory of management?

My theory of management states that employers will have a highly productive work force if they hire alcoholics and other substance abusers while their addictions are at an early stage, and fire them when they deteriorate—robber baron capitalism at its worst, perhaps, but definitely a formula for a crackerjack work force. The reason for this is that most alcoholics and substance abusers (there are exceptions) are driven by guilt and fear of discovery. They know at some level that their substance use reduces their efficiency and makes it harder for them to perform. Sometimes, it is hard or even impossible to merely get to work. Additionally, they feel guilty about all sorts of other things, and have great problems maintaining a reasonably constant and satisfactory level of self-esteem. At some level, conscious or unconscious, they think they are really awful people. Therefore, they must overcompensate to prove that the opposite is true. Further, being a successful—or even a supersuccessful—and reliable worker serves to maintain their denial: "If I'm such a crackerjack worker and good provider, I can't possibly have a problem with Scotch or Tijuana Gold."

So for a long period, depending on the drug and the person, potential addicts (currently substance abusers) make ideal employees. They are driven to prove that there is nothing wrong with them and they will work their asses off to prove it. At this stage, the canny manager will get much mileage from them. As their disease progresses (from a disease model point of view) or as their substance use escalates (looking at it descriptively without any particular theory about why that is happening), their performance also declines—eventually markedly. This is the point for management to dismiss them in this strangely exploitative drama.

My theory of management might be commended not only by Adam Smith but also by Karl Marx. From a Marxist point of view, the capitalist must compete to the very utmost and exploit his workers to the maximum, lest his competitors gain an advantage in the ruthless warfare in the market, and drive him into bankruptcy and absorption by a bigger shark. Marx would say that the capitalist has no choice but to exploit the substance abuser's guilt before discarding him on the dustbin of history. I have sometimes explained my theory of management to a patient. In some cases it has provoked an "Aha" experience, which has sometimes led the patient to abstinence, not wishing to be exploited, and the realization that he was working himself to death to try to prove that there was nothing wrong with him. This is not an interpretation of wide applicability but sometimes it fits and is worth a try.

These days, many businesses, labor unions, and government agencies have employee assistance programs (EAPs), which are short-term counseling and referral resources within the organization intended to salvage workers with substance abuse problems. That, of course, is not only more humane than my management approach but is actually good business, because by the time an employee with a substance abuse problem comes to the attention of supervision he or she has long declined in performance, and only now can the employer have a chance to recoup what essentially has been a loss, by rehabilitating the worker.

I have known cases, which unfortunately might persuade management that the EAP approach is not good business, in which the alcoholic or addict became sober, realized that he or she was working compulsively to compensate and to prove self-worth, and ceased doing so. This is not as uncommon as it might seem. Many workers become sober and discover that they really don't like what they were doing, and that they were staying only because they were so shaky that they were fearful that no one else would want them (which probably had some reality behind it), and now in sobriety move on to something else.

For this reason, vocational counseling is often an important component in the rehabilitation of substance abusers. A primary therapist can serve in the role of rehabilitation and vocational counselor, or can refer the patient to a specialist. In either case, this is an area needing attention if any sort of harmonious sobriety is to be attained.

What is stage theory?

Stage theory holds that people change in a fairly determinative way, including the change from addiction to sobriety. Prochaska and colleagues (1992) describe five stages of change: precontemplation, contemplation, preparation, action, and maintenance.

In the first stage, precontemplation, the pleasurable effects of using the drug predominate and the user does not even entertain the thought of quitting. Why should he? In the next stage, contemplation, the adverse consequences have become too insistent to be completely ignored and the thought of stopping, or at least cutting back, is now allowed to enter consciousness. Although no action, as yet, is actually contemplated, it is at least a possibility. Retaining patients in the precontemplative stage is extremely difficult. They enjoy their drinking or drugging, and are not yet seriously considering stopping or changing it. The best the therapist can do is to recognize where the patient is, and not get into a power struggle. However, in the contemplative stage, the pleasure/pain ratio is changed, and the patient is almost beginning to consider behavioral change and fleetingly may be seriously considering it. There is, however, intense ambivalence. The therapist must acknowledge and reflect back the ambivalence and minimize his or her countertransferential frustration and rage by understanding where the patient is at. In the preparation stage, the patient actually considers a concrete plan of action, but is not yet ready to carry it out. Finally, the action stage is reached and change occurs.

Unlike the twelve-step model, which envisions "hitting bottom" or "surrender" as sudden moments of illumination, the stages-of-change model elucidates and articulates a long developmental process for which it offers empirical evidence, which precedes the eventual action. The model emphasizes that reaching the action stage will not lead to any permanent change. Rather, the patient must institute certain changes in lifestyle, in attitudes, and in self-awareness, all of which constitute the maintenance stage. Without the maintenance stage there is no recovery. Recycling is by far the most common outcome of having reached the action stage without having built in any kind of maintenance into one's life in the form of participation in a self-help group or a therapy group, or otherwise working on one's self.

The stages-of-change literature, with its emphasis on maintenance, is reminiscent of Bill Wilson's distinction between two kinds of conversion experience, which he borrowed from William James's (1902) *The Varieties of Religious Experience*, in which James speaks of the "Damascus experience," the sudden moment of insight that happened to Paul on the road to Damascus, and what Wilson, following James, called the "educational conversion experience," which is the ongoing accretion of insight enabled by a structure such as that provided by a therapy that is ongoing. It requires a considerable amount of time for the internalization of insight and psychic structure. The twelve-steps view is that such internalization is never complete and that outside reinforcement is always needed in the form of ongoing, open-ended participation in the program. John Mack (1981), in his notion that "self-governance," which he sees as a superego function, is always imperfectly internalized and reliant upon the social surround, is very much on the same track. Similarly, Freud (1937), in his great essay, "Analysis Terminable and Interminable," holds that the analyst should return to analysis periodically throughout his life. All hold that action requires maintenance.

The chief clinical utility of the stages-of-change model is the guidance it gives the therapist in knowing what to look for and what to expect in substance abuse treatment. In fact, it is especially helpful to the therapist in dealing with his or her countertransference. If the therapist understands where the patient is along the stages-of-change continuum, without taking it too concretely, then the therapist will not have unrealistic expectations that set up frustration and countertransferential rage, which all too easily lead to retaliation against the patient in the form of devaluation rationalized as therapeutic confrontation.

What do Gemeinschaft *and* Gesellschaft *have to do with the social and psychological dynamics of addiction?*

Gemeinschaft and *Gesellschaft*, usually rendered in English as community and society, are the two poles of a dichotomous analysis of the way in which cultures operate; they were elaborated by the nineteenth-century sociologist Ferdinand Toennies (1887). Toennies was referring to the difference between the social organization of the preindustrial, prebureaucratized structure of the village and of the *volk*, which is *Gemeinschaft*, and the relatively impersonal, universalized, and abstract values and ways of relating of the modern business, educational, and industrial organization, which is *Gesellschaft*. It would seem that substance abusers, on the whole, fit much better into a *Gemeinschaft* type of organization and way of relating, a form of organization characterized more by emotion than by reason. Another way of saying this is that alcoholics and other substance abusers seem strongly drawn toward the personal, the particularistic, the diffuse, the concrete, and the nonhierarchical. If this is the case, it makes it extremely difficult for them to fit in and do well in the *Gesellschaftlich* contemporary world.

The American sociologist Talcott Parsons (1954) elaborated Toennies's dichotomy, between the abstract values of the secondary group and the personal values of the primary group, into a complex analysis of social systems. In that analysis, Parsons teases out such abstract components of *Gesellschaft* as rationality, delayed gratification, and narrowness of focus, which he later elaborated into what he called pattern variables, whose dichotomous values reflected Toennies's dichotomy. Parsons spoke of universalism, affective neutrality (meaning the ability to delay gratification and to stay with affect), and specificity (meaning having firm boundaries). It would seem from the empirical psychological literature on the clinical addictive personality that it is precisely this sort of universalism, affective neutrality, and specificity that substance abusers have such a difficult time with. Therefore, they are drawn to social organizations like the "bottle gang" and the "drug clique" in an attempt to find a more *Gemeinschaftlich* environment.

Substance abusers are drawn toward what sociologists call "primary group relationships," corresponding to what psychodynamic theorists call the symbiosis of early stages of development, which both predisposes abusers to seek out the kinds of relationships and organizations in which drinking and drugging take place, and simultaneously makes it difficult for them to operate in the impersonal modern world. The sociologists were speaking of a cause of social strain that they saw as characteristic of twentieth-century industrial societies in general. Here, I am speculating that substance abusers, or at least a substantial minority of them, are particularly afflicted with difficulty negotiating this cultural shift. It is of some interest to note that the twelve-step organizations are about as *Gemeinschaftlich* as one can get. It is also worth noting that at the end of the addictive cycle, the relationship between the addict and the substance to which he or she is addicted is at the *Gemeinschaft* end point of the *Gemeinschaft* and *Gesellschaft* continuum. The feelings of closeness, of merger, of dedifferentiation, the absence of hierarchy, are all epitomized in the symbiosis between user and used. If this analysis is correct, then helping substance abusers move toward impersonality, rationality, universality, and better-defined boundaries will reduce their need to turn to substances and the social organizations in which they are used as a way of compensating for the inability to deal in that more abstract adult world we fortunately (or unfortunately) have to live in.

My dissertation research was precisely on this problem (Levin 1981). In it I demonstrated that men entering AA, that is, those at an end point of an addictive career, epitomized the *Gemeinschaft* values and ways of being in the world. However, those who remained in AA changed over the years, as demonstrated by a regression analysis of the variables that I measured, which were those that Parsons derived from Toennies's theory and showed a significant move toward the *Gesellschaft* end of the continuum. In a small way, this is empirical support for the speculations offered in this section.

What are gateway drugs?

Gateway drugs are the drugs that have been shown to regularly precede the so-called hard drugs. Such an order of use has been demonstrated by many researchers, most notably Kandel (1975, Kandel et al. 1992). Gateway drug research has demonstrated that people who later become addicted to heroin, cocaine, and other hard drugs started out smoking cigarettes, that they only later started drinking wine and beer, then progressed to drinking hard liquor, which was followed by their smoking marijuana. The evidence for this progression is fairly clear and well established.

However, the converse is not true—all cigarette smokers do not become heroin addicts; many simply die of lung cancer. Nor do all, or anywhere near all, pot smokers end up mainlining heroin. Nevertheless, Kandel's research, in spite of its rather moralizing tone, is important, particularly in terms of educating and working with adolescents. Her data also strongly show that the earlier the youngster uses drugs, including alcohol and tobacco, the more likely he or she is to develop a major addiction in adulthood. Another interesting finding is that maternal smoking was found to be highly correlated with addictive outcomes in the children. It is not clear whether that is an intrauterine, a genetic, or object-relational causal phenomenon.

What is enabling?

Enabling is the conscious or (usually) unconscious process of helping the addict by making excuses, by supporting, by providing money, by providing shelter, by covering for, and so forth. Enabling is usually seen to be a psychodynamic process based on denial and an unconscious need to control and to keep the user using. In my experience this is not necessarily true. It describes some enabling that is, indeed, a psychodynamic process, but other enabling is the result of ignorance.

Therefore, the therapist should start with didactic interventions explaining the detrimental effect of the enabling. Only then will the therapist clearly see a more pernicious form of enabling if indeed that exists.

Enablers give many excuses: "How can I let him starve if I love him?" "I can't let that happen to him," and wet handkerchiefs are common. If, despite the therapist's didactic and educational interventions aimed at eliminating the enabling, it continues anyway, then something else is going on. Persistent enabling may be driven by guilt, shame, the need to control, or an accurate perception that the user will die without the support, even if the support is also killing him. In the last situation, the user has to be hospitalized as a lifesaving procedure. This is not an uncommon solution, and overzealous therapists who go after the enabling in a confrontational manner may be barking up the wrong tree when they try to persuade the parents or the spouse to withdraw support from an addict who is going to die without that support. Each situation has to be addressed very carefully, but usually the enabling is damaging and needs to be stopped. In cases in which the enabling is psychodynamically driven, the therapist should look for the payoff for the other members of the user's system.

The story comes to mind of the man who goes to the psychiatrist and says, "Doctor, my son believes he's a chicken," to which the psychiatrist replies, "Well, that's the sort of delusion we psychiatrists do rather well with. If you and your son come back, I'm pretty sure I can cure him." A month passes and the father hasn't returned, so the psychiatrist calls him and says, "Mr. Smith, I thought you and your son were coming back so I could treat his delusion that he is a chicken," to which the father replies, "Well, Doctor, we thought it over and decided we need the eggs." In many substance abusing families there is a decision that they need the eggs.

> *Could you comment on gender differences in the*
> *prevalence and etiology of addiction?*

Women are more likely to be addicted to food. In all the other addictions, men predominate. However, if one includes codependency, whatever that may be, or what Karen Horney (1945) called *morbid dependency*, as an addiction, then clearly women predominate in the addict population. In the case of alcoholism, the ratio of male to female alcoholics is roughly two to one, while in the case of other drug addictions (with the possible exception of crack), the gender differential is even greater in favor of males. But in absolute numbers, millions of women are alcoholics and addicts. So even though proportionately they are a minority, female addiction constitutes a major social and personal pathology. It affects an enormous number of people.

Women suffer from addictions more than men, both because of the social stigma and because of the physical effects. For example, women are much more prone to cirrhosis and to neurological damage from alcohol even on lower dosages consumed for shorter periods of time. The same is roughly true of the other drugs of abuse. Psychodynamically, the main difference seems to lie in more acting out and externalizing defenses and dynamics in men, and more self-medication of depression and low self-esteem in women. But these data need to be interpreted cautiously, and therapists should not allow any theory or generalization from the research literature to take precedence over observation of the individual patient.

Yifrah Kaminer (1994) of the University of Connecticut, who specializes in adolescent substance abuse, feels strongly that antisocial tendencies in women (in his case, in adolescent girls) are radically underdiagnosed because of the male bias that women are sugar and spice and everything nice. Men are simply too threatened by antisocial behavior in women, and do not see it when it is there. This is an interesting notion. I do not know how much data Kaminer has to support it, but he is a major researcher in the field and seems to feel rather confident about the underdiagnosis of antisocial tendencies in women. Mutatis mutandis, the same is true of underdiagnosis of depression in men who have a lot of externalizing and acting out defenses going for them. Therefore, with male patients therapists need to look for the depression underlying their various manic and acting out defenses.

Howard T. Blane, in his classic book *The Personality of the Alcoholic: Guises of Dependency* (1961), argues that addiction in men is essentially driven by a counterdependent dynamic in which they use substances rather than people to meet their dependency needs, which at an unconscious level are denied; while addiction in women is driven by an attempt to raise self-esteem. (Blane's analysis of male drinking is discussed in more detail on p. 103). In Blane's view, women are much more likely to self-medicate depression. There is some research support for his position on this. Clinical experience also supports Blane. Male addicts do tend, at least overtly, to be more counterdependent, and female addicts do tend to self-medicate depression and desperately try to raise their self-esteem. However, there is no dearth of counterdependent substance-abusing women, and all substance abusers suffer from low self-esteem; to some degree, their use is driven by an attempt to raise it. Gender differences are certainly significant in both understanding and treating addiction; nevertheless, both men and women are people, for better or worse, and people have an amazing amount in common. The therapist needs to be sensitive to gender differences, yet at the same time to be cognizant of the universality of all of the dynamics across gender, across class, and across ethnicity.

> *Would you comment on special populations and how*
> *membership in one relates to substance abuse?*

In the substance abuse literature, "special populations" refers to children, adolescents, women, minorities, the physically disabled, the dual-diagnosed, and the elderly. The special-populations literature is rather uninformative, probably because the research in this area is in its infancy. However, researchers have found out some extremely important things. The most important of these is that addiction and substance abuse exists and is quite prevalent in all of these populations, so the therapist must be alert to the possible existence of these conditions where one might not expect to find them.

Drug addiction in children is unhappily not all that uncommon. Over the years I have taught many aspiring substance abuse counselors who worked in the New York City public schools, at the elementary or junior high school level, and who reported students coming to class high, or becoming high during the lunch hour. Adolescent substance abuse is a well-known phenomenon and notoriously difficult to treat. Apparently, the key, according to experts in the field, is to treat the comorbidity, particularly the depression, often accompanying adolescent substance abuse. Substance abusing adolescents who are comorbid for depression have a much better outcome than those who are not, probably because depression is so painful that it keeps them in treatment.

The physically disabled have very high rates of substance abuse, particularly alcoholism, both as cause and effect. That is, many became disabled because of accidents while they were high, and many disabled people become physically addicted because their disabilities are so difficult to deal with.

The mentally ill are also highly vulnerable to substance abuse, and it is only in recent years that this phenomenon is being recognized and addressed. Substance abuse, particularly of alcohol, is also fairly common in higher functioning retarded populations.

Use of alcohol and drugs among minority populations differs somewhat from that of the white middle-class population, but the epidemiological data indicate that it is not all that different. The psychodynamics of minority substance use are also not all that different, but cultural factors are powerful, and the therapist needs to be sensitive to cultural differences. For example, Hispanic males have a tradition of "machismo" drinking in which their very masculinity is associated with heavy drinking, a phenomenon not unknown in Anglo culture, but not to the same degree and extent. If the therapist is not aware of that meaning for the Hispanic male substance abuser, the therapy is going to have a very difficult time getting anywhere at all.

It is certainly true that sensitivity to culture, to social class, and to gender, in terms of the kinds of problems, strengths, experiences, and values that membership in these cultures, classes, and genders entails, and to substance use and abuse is necessary background for the therapist. However, in my opinion this has been overemphasized in recent years and the current, politically correct tendency is to ignore the commonalities found in substance abusers. As Harry Stack Sullivan said, "Everyone is much more simply human than otherwise."

Epidemiologically, poverty, Jewishness, religiosity, living in a rural area, and advanced age are all negatively associated with alcoholism. Nevertheless, if you stay in the field long enough, you are going to meet a poor orthodox Jewish lady from rural Arkansas who is highly religious and who drinks two quarts of bourbon a day. Patients use age, gender, ethnicity, and religion as reasons why they cannot possibly be addicted. They tell their therapists that after all is said and done, "I'm too young to be alcoholic," "Jews don't drink very much," "In my Protestant denomination there are no drug users," and so on. The therapist needs to be alert to these kinds of rationalizations and ways of bolstering denial.

Substance abuse, particularly alcoholism, in the elderly had been neglected until recent years, yet is extremely common. Drinkers' livers age along with the rest of them, and late-onset alcoholism can be fatal rather quickly. When people who are lifestyle drinkers retire from employment, they lose the structure that they had and begin to suffer some of the narcissistic injuries ineluctably concomitant with later life. They might escalate their drinking in a futile attempt to deal with loss—with disastrous consequences. Addiction to prescription drugs, particularly to the benzodiazepines, such as Valium and Xanax, is also very common in this population.

Therapists treating the elderly patient may very well think of their own parents, who are the very opposite of drug addicted, and in that countertransference miss the patient's problem. There may be a counteridealization going on here.

One clue to substance abuse, particularly alcoholism, in the elderly, but not only in the elderly, is depression that does not remit with suitable treatment—psychodynamic, cognitive, and/or psychopharmacological. Such depressions are very often caused by secretive drinking. All the therapeutic work is undone by the substance use. This is a difficult diagnosis to make with a cagey patient who is socially functional, but the therapist needs to be suspicious in that circumstance. There are depressions that are simply very treatment resistant and have nothing to do with substance abuse, but more often than not substance use is the reason the patient is not getting well. Again, this applies not only to elderly patients.

To sum up the import of the special-populations literature, therapists need to be alert to the possibility of substance use across the life span in both genders, in all ethnic and racial and religious groups, and whatever the epidemiological differences—they are there and they are real—any particular person of any demographic characteristic may be addicted or may be substance abusing. Further, therapists need to be sensitive to ethnic, cultural, gender, and age differentials in working with patients. But this is merely to say that therapists need empathy and therapeutic tact, which has always been the case, if they are to be effective therapists.

What is the relationship among attention deficit disorder (ADD),
hyperactivity, and substance abuse?

Tarter and Alterman (1989) found that childhood hyperactivity and attention deficit disorder are highly correlated with adult alcoholism and substance use. Apparently, the substance use is an attempt at self-cure. If the substance-abusing patient suffers from adult ADD and hyperactivity (which is not always the case since these conditions are sometimes outgrown at adolescence), and the substance abuse ceases, the patient may have a very hard time with distractibility and difficulties with learning. This raises the question of whether to medicate the ADD with the amphetamine Ritalin. This is a difficult decision and carries some risk of setting up the patient for a slip. If the patient has long believed that one drug is good, then another drug must be better. Clinicians working in the field maintain that the chances of a slip from the difficulty of trying to function with the ADD are greater than the risk of going back to illegal drugs merely because the patient is taking a medicinal drug. In my limited clinical experience, this seems to be true. The difficulty I have seen in adult ADDs who were in recovery is not so much that they have slipped, even if they were previously stimulant users, when they went on therapeutic doses of psychostimulant drugs, as that the drug treatment is not all that effective. I have not seen any great changes in my adult ADD patients who have tried medication, but my sample size is small. Pharmacological treatment is worth a try if a recovering patient is having serious difficulty with distractibility.

More important psychotherapeutically is to explore the secondary overlay of the ADD and hyperactivity in the patient's childhood, which often has caused the patient great pain in the form of difficulties in school and difficulties in relationships, and which may have driven him (or her) into a deviant and drug subculture, where his deviancy was inconsequential and he found acceptance. Helping the patient work that through and come to an understanding of the effect of ADD on his life will result, one hopes, in the patient developing some kind of self-compassion (in contradistinction to self-pity) about how difficult coping was and how natural it was that he found a drug that at least gave the illusion of improving things. This can be highly therapeutic, making sense of the patient's experience without serving as a rationalization for continuing use of the "wrong" drugs. In this way, exploring the evidence for ADD in the patient's childhood can very much aid in the patient having a satisfying recovery. Such an investigation of a history of an unconscious attempt at self-medication also provides a cognitive structure that makes sense of a chaotic and painful experience (namely the addicted life), and that cognitive structure reduces anxiety and gives the patient a feeling of self-understanding, which raises self-esteem.

What does Ralph Tarter's research tell us about the etiology and dynamics of substance abuse?

In addition to his highly salient discovery of the connection between ADD and addiction, Tarter is gathering evidence that the children of alcoholics and other substance abusers are different from an early age. In ongoing research he has shown that from as young as two years these children are more likely to manifest "difficult temperament," cognitive and learning problems other than ADD, social difficulties, and, perhaps most important, what Tarter calls "dysregulation," meaning difficulty in regulating affect. In a complex multivariate developmental model he conceptualizes these characteristics as resulting from a constitutional-environmental interaction. He sees a particularly unfortunate outlook for the difficult temperament (which he conceives of as constitutional) child raised by one or more difficult temperament parents.

Tarter (1991) sees the matrix of addiction as residing in genetic endowment, but the outcome of the effect of that endowment is highly influenced by the environment. Therefore, although he believes he has demonstrated that vulnerability to addiction resides in characteristics such as dysregulation, which have a heavy genetic loading and which he has shown to be more prevalent in the children of addicts, he emphasizes early intervention. Tarter sounds like a genetic determinist, but he is not. He believes that very little is hard-wired, so that addiction can be prevented if highrisk children get the help they need early enough.

Do drugs help people feel alive?

Feelings of aliveness are less than optimal in many substance abusers. Such inner deadness is usually predicated on emotional repression, but derepression is too frightening for the patient to risk it and, in most cases, would not have been possible without psychotherapeutic help. So the patient turns to drugs, particularly "up" drugs like cocaine, amphetamine, crystal meth, and crack, in a desperate attempt to feel alive. As in so many other attempts at self-cure through substance abuse, a vicious cycle is set up and the very treatment of the aridity, woodenness, and deadness leads to more and deeper feelings of deadness, necessitating more use of the drug. The patient's enhanced feelings of deadness are driven both pharmacologically and psychodynamically by the failed attempt at self-cure.

One of the most rewarding aspects of working with substance abusers is watching them come alive after a long period of deadness. That happens for most patients spontaneously in recovery, as they stay clean and begin to discover possibilities for themselves. But it isn't an altogether spontaneous process. The derepression leading to contact with the affective life, and the inner life of fantasy in the course of the therapy, enables that aliveness and intensifies it.

Leon Wurmser (1978) speaks of "psychophobia," a fear of the inner world of affect and fantasy, as a powerful dynamic in substance abuse, which is, by definition, an externalizing lifestyle. Wurmser points out that the patient's psychophobia is reinforced by our culture's psychophobia. Psychophobia contributes to and is etiological in feelings of deadness.

Donald Winnicott (1960) speaks of the "true self" and the "false self," the false self or persona allowing the true self, which is affective, messy, asocial, and egocentric, among other things, to go into hiding. The true self went into hiding because it was not welcomed nor did it feel safe. Since feelings of aliveness reside in the true self, the person who is living as a false self—however socially, academically, and vocationally successful—is essentially experientially dead. The next step is self-medication for the dead false self, which results in a parody of the vitality of the true self and a mere simulacrum of aliveness. The only way out of this trap is to get in touch with the true self, which cannot happen as long as the substance abuse continues. Putting the patient in touch with his or her true self is the business (or at least a very important part of the business) of therapy.

What is people pleasing?

People pleasing is a twelve-step term referring to a manifestation of what Winnicott (1960) calls the *false self* (see above). People pleasing is driven by insecurity and is characteristic of many substance abusers who try to jolly everyone, including the therapist, out of a pathological need to be liked by everyone. The underlying dynamic here is low self-esteem and self-hatred. Treatment needs to be focused on uncovering the source of the self-hatred and low self-esteem, if it is antecedent to the drug addiction, which it usually is. There are at least two layers that must be worked through: the self-hatred consequent on the substance abuse; and the self-hatred stemming from feelings of wanting to kill the father (oedipal guilt), or feelings of worthlessness arising from not being loved by parents, or other early experiences.

> *What is the relationship between posttraumatic stress disorder*
> *(PTSD) and addiction?*

Addiction, substance abuse, and posttraumatic stress disorder (PTSD) are highly correlated. Although it is not the case that most substance abusers suffer from PTSD (in fact, many do), drug and alcohol abuse is highly consequent upon PTSD. That is, many self-medicate the pain of PTSD with alcohol and drugs. Research has shown (van der Kolk et al. 1996) that childhood sexual and physical abuse, which are traumatic, are highly correlated with substance abuse in the parents, and that this childhood abuse leads to vulnerability to substance abuse in adolescence and adulthood.

We also know that trauma is encoded, not only in terms of repressed memory, but also in terms of neurochemical vulnerability (Kramer 1993). This means that the trauma leaves the nervous system more vulnerable to anxiety, depression, and other negative affect. All of these conditions are commonly self-medicated by the use of various substances. These facts make it apparent that early, severe, acute, and chronic traumatization fertilizes the ground for and plants the nascent seeds of substance abuse. Unfortunately, they frequently sprout.

As in all dual-diagnosis situations, the therapist treating substance abusers who suffer PTSD will not get very far unless both conditions are addressed. Authorities in the field uniformly believe that the substance use must be halted before the PTSD can be effectively treated. The situation is complicated by the frequency of severe trauma *during* the substance abuse so that the therapist (and the patient) has to deal with layer upon layer of trauma—the original traumas antecedent to the substance abuse, and the secondary traumas consequent upon it. Once the substance use is brought under control, then the original trauma needs to be explored, uncovered, and worked through, and the patient taught coping strategies and skills to deal with the residuals of the trauma, for example, compulsively repetitious memories of the trauma, which are intrusive and lead to substance use or intolerable psychic pain. The treatment of PTSD seems to be a very delicate balancing act between retrieving memories and helping patients work them through, and helping patients control and put aside those memories. So there is a place for derepression and a place for suppression in the treatment of PTSD (van der Kolk et al. 1996). There are those memories that are usefully surfaced and worked through, and there are others that are compulsively reexperienced with no learning occurring, which the therapist needs to help the patient control and, indeed, stop.

> *Could you give an example of a posttraumatic stress*
> *disorder–substance abuse dual-diagnosis case?*

Sam came for treatment for a drinking problem. An engineer on a research project, he had no trouble functioning at work and felt no desire to drink during the working day, but each night as he drove home, his car seemingly drove itself to the beer distributor where he bought a case of beer, returned to his home, and drank until he collapsed. He hated himself for his "weakness." Our early sessions were entirely about his current drinking. Only later did he tell me that he had had a period of recovery lasting eight years, during the early part of which he had attended AA and simply did not drink, and had been a reasonably happy fellow. Then the Gulf War broke out and the patient became obsessed with body bags. One night, in his rural home, he saw the "gooks" coming out of the trees, reviving his experience in Vietnam in which he had killed and seen buddies killed, an experience he had never talked about. Soon after he started obsessing about body bags, he started drinking again. Each day as he drove home from work he would see, in his peripheral vision, shadows that he thought might be Vietcong about to fire upon him. It is hardly surprising that the car infallibly found the beer distributor.

The therapy went nowhere. The patient would begin to recount his traumatization in Vietnam, would pull back from it saying, "I don't like to tell war stories, nobody wants to hear them." I would say, "I want to hear them," but with little effect. Finally, I said to Sam, "There's a drug, Antabuse, which has no effect unless you drink, in which case you become very ill. As long as you take the pill, you can't drink the beer. Would you be willing to try it?" Sam, who was very depressed because of his "weakness," jumped at the idea, expressing great rage at a previous therapist for not recommending Antabuse. He went on it, stopped drinking, and his depression lifted. His depression had been driven by both self-hatred and the (depressive) pharmacology of ethanol.

Antabuse was a very risky treatment because Sam might have decompensated and had an overt psychotic break when he was home alone without his self-tranquilizing beer. Fortunately, that did not happen. The psychiatrist who put him on Antabuse had explored the use of other medications, especially antidepressants, but Sam had refused them. Now, with his drinking under control, Sam and I had a chance to work on the PTSD. Unfortunately, his employer closed the facility he was working at and he had to transfer to another state before we really had much opportunity to work through his Vietnam experiences. We did, however, get far enough for it to be clear that guilt was a major factor in this man's psychodynamics. He experienced himself as a murderer and found all kinds of ways of punishing himself, including alienating himself from his now-grown children, which caused him enormous pain. He suffered generalized feelings of unworthiness. If Sam had not stopped drinking, there would have been no possibility of working through any of this. I strongly recommended that he reenter therapy in his new community, and, although I have not heard from him again, it seemed likely that he would do so.

> *Could you give an example of a PTSD/substance abuse case in which the trauma occurred in childhood?*

Sally came to me for treatment of a posttraumatic stress reaction. She had been in an automobile accident in which her face was badly scarred. She was deeply depressed. She later had successful plastic surgery, but when I first saw her, she had no way of knowing she would get such a good result. Her accident was merely the latest of a long series of traumas dating back to early childhood. Sally turned out to be a case of acute and chronic trauma.

Sally was young and very appealing. She had been referred by her attorney, who had not mentioned alcohol, so I was surprised when she told me that she had been alcoholic since the age of 12 and that she hit bottom four years ago at the age of 25. I asked her to tell me about her drinking and what led her to hit bottom.

I come from an alcoholic family. Both my parents died of alcoholism. My father deserted us when I was 4. I remember the last time I saw him. We were eating in a diner and I was spilling my food. He screamed, "You're disgusting," and ran out. I've always felt that he left because I was so disgusting. I feel like a pig; I'm a compulsive overeater. I know in my head that he didn't leave because of the way I ate, but I don't know it in my heart. I still believe it.

Things got worse after Dad left. My mother drank more and more and we had very little money. Sometimes there was no toilet paper in the house, but there was always beer. Later we moved to my grandfather's. He was rich, but he grabbed my thing when my mother wasn't around. I think he was senile but he drank too, so maybe that was it. After I grew up, my mother told me she had known what he was doing to me, but was afraid to do anything about it because he would have thrown us out. She was drunk when she told me that. Why did she have to tell me? I hate her for letting it happen and I hate her for telling me that she let it happen. How could a mother do that? I have a daughter. I'd cut off his balls if a man did that to my daughter. My grandfather got more senile and I don't know exactly what happened after that. My mother was like two people. When she was sober, she was wonderful—beautiful and interested in me, but very snobby and uptight. Then, I didn't think she was a snob, I thought that she was a great lady—perfectly dressed and so elegant. I loved her so much. Then there was mother when she was drunk, sloppy, and falling down. She'd sit with her legs spread with no panties and you could see everything. She'd curse and then try to play the great lady again, "Oh my dear," and all that shit. I hated her then.

I started having sex play with the neighborhood kids. Mostly with the boys, but sometimes with the girls, too. Do you think I'm a lesbian? I loved sex—it felt so good and it made me feel good about myself. Somebody wanted me. I must have felt guilty underneath. Later I hated myself and all that sex play had something to do with it. I was raised a strict Catholic. Once I was naked—I had just gotten out of the tub and I did an imitation of the Virgin Mary—I was about 6—and my mother really whaled my ass with a ruler.

When I was about 10, my mother met my stepfather. Eddy was a complete asshole. He drank all the time, too. Mother dropped me; she was more interested in drinking with Eddy. I started getting in trouble in school—at 11 I got fucked for the first time. And I mean I got fucked, not made love to, by some 20-year-old pervert. Can you imagine an 11-year-old getting fucked? I loved it, or thought I did. I hung out with all the older boys. They had cars and liquor. I can't tell you how many men I had. Big ones, small ones, white ones, black ones. And you know, I was never sober once. Every one of those guys had something to get high on—beer, pot, hard stuff. I loved booze from the first time I tasted it. It was even better than sex. I drank a lot. Any boy or man who gave me something to drink could have me. Sometimes I really liked it, but mostly I wasn't really there. I think I was really turned on by myself. My mother and stepfather raised hell when they weren't too drunk to care and finally my mother had me put away. Can you imagine that? What kind of fucking mother would put a kid in the places she put me in? For God's sake, one place had bars and I was locked in. I hate her for doing that. Mental hospitals, homes for delinquent girls, the House of the Good Shepherd, the whole ball of wax. Finally I got out and met Calvin.

What a bastard he was. Oh! I forgot to tell you that when I was 15 I was team banged. They beat me, too, but not as hard as Calvin did later. Oh yeah, Calvin beat me all the time. I must have been crazy but I loved him. He took me away from my hometown and my mother didn't bother me anymore. He sort of made a prisoner out of me—if I even went to the grocery store without his permission, he beat me. He always had beer and weed and other stuff and I stayed high most of the time. He's the father of my child. When I went into labor, he was stoned. He slapped me and called me a rotten whore. He wouldn't go to the hospital with me. Do you know what it's like for a 16-year-old kid to have a baby alone? Forget it!

I never cheated on Calvin, but he never stopped accusing me of being with other men and hitting me. Sometimes he hit me with a wooden plank. I think I thought I deserved it, that I needed to be punished for all the things I had done. I needed Calvin to beat me. As long as he supplied drugs and alcohol, I would have stayed. It was the way he acted around the baby that made me leave. One day when the baby was about 2, I ran away when he wasn't home. I couldn't stand his insane jealousy anymore; he was even jealous of the baby. A guy crazy enough to be jealous of his own kid; that's sick. Something in me said, "Enough, you've been punished enough." Of course, I kept drinking. There wasn't any more sex, just falling-down drunk every day. I went on welfare and sometimes I worked off the books. I was sort of dead. That went on for a few years and I hated myself more and more. I tried to be a good mother and I don't think I did too badly, but God was I depressed.

My stepfather was dead by then and my mother was far gone. My brother was in the program—AA, that is. I thought he was a jerk, a real ass, an uptight loser. Who else would join those holy rollers? What I couldn't figure out was how such a raving asshole could be happy, and the damn jerk *was* happy. Even *I* could see that. He did something really smart; he didn't lecture me. In fact, he never even mentioned my drinking. Damn good thing he didn't because the way I rebelled against everything and everybody I would never have listened. What he did do was tell me what had happened to him—ran his story, as they say in AA. I didn't want to hear that shit, but I heard it in spite of myself. I was getting worse; I was terrified Calvin would come back and kill me. I guess I thought that he should, because of the way I was living, but I didn't know that then, I was just scared. I was getting sicker and sicker from drinking. It got to the point where I couldn't stand any more. If it wasn't for my daughter, I would have killed myself.

I don't know why, but one day I asked my brother to take me to an AA meeting. I think it was the guilt—once I didn't have Calvin to beat me, I couldn't stand the guilt. I knew, I mean I *really knew* what it is like to have alcoholic parents. I loved my daughter—she has such a sick fuck for a father, so I wanted her to have at least one parent with her head screwed on straight. So I went to that fucking meeting. I loved it, I mean I *loved* it like I never loved anything. For Christ's sake, I even identified with the coffee cups. When I do something I do it. I went all the way—the whole nine yards. I was sick—sick, sick, sick—from my crotch to my toes, not to mention my head. I was so scared; I hadn't had a sober day in years, but I've made it a day at a time. I still can't stand the guilt and the rage; you wouldn't believe how angry I get, and the crying, I cry all the fucking time, but I don't drink, I don't drug, and I don't care if my ass falls off, I'm not going to. At least not today.

I didn't want to be like my mother. I *won't* be like her. She's dead now. I couldn't stand it when she died—she died from her drinking. She had an accident drunk, it was kind of a suicide. I knew she was dead, but I didn't know it. I couldn't let her go—not the awful way it was—if she was sober and I was sober, I could have let her die; but she wasn't. So I knew, but I didn't know she was dead. I never accepted it; she couldn't forgive me dead; nor I her. Then one day, I went to the cemetery. I looked at her grave for a long time. I couldn't believe she was dead; I started screaming, "Move the fucking grass! Move the fucking grass, Mother!" I screamed and screamed but she didn't move the fucking grass and I finally knew she was gone. I went to my home-group meeting hysterical. All I said was she couldn't move the fucking grass and I cried the rest of the meeting. Nobody said a word, they just let me be, they didn't try to take away my pain, and I didn't want or need anybody to take it away. What I needed was somebody to be with me in that pain, and they were.

I love the fucking program and all the crazy screwed up people there. They're like me; I'm crazy too, but I'm sober. For God's sake can you imagine what it would have been like if I was drinking when she died? Thank God, I wasn't. I hate her—I love her—I still can't let go of her although I know she's dead. I hate alcohol. I hate drinking. Look what it did to her, to my father, to me. How did I get sober? I don't really know—I sort of had two bottoms—a being-beaten bottom and an alcohol bottom. In that first bottom, I sort of saw myself and saw I couldn't go on exposing my daughter to that stuff; the second was luck or something. No, not exactly luck, or not only luck. It had something to do with willingness—I became willing to go to that meeting. Maybe I had just had enough. I didn't want any more pain for me or for the baby; she's not a baby anymore. They say, "Why me?" in the program. When you're drinking you have the "Poor me's," so you're always asking, "Why me?" If you recover, you ask if differently. I don't know why me. The way I lived, I should be dead, but I'm not. I don't know if I deserve it or not, but I'll take it.

What does learned helplessness have to do with substance abuse?

Learned helplessness is a concept developed by Martin Seligman (1975, Seligman and Maier 1967), a psychologist at the University of Pennsylvania, that serves as a paradigm for some types of human apathy, hopelessness, and depression. Seligman conducted an experiment in which he first trained dogs to escape from a noxious stimulus, namely an electrified floor, by jumping over a barrier to a safe place. He then electrified the floor of the escape section of the experimental apparatus. The dogs now could not escape the shock. After a few trials of jumping back and forth across the barrier, they gave up and simply lay whimpering on the floor. Seligman now, once again, changed the conditions, and ceased to electrify the escape chamber so that the dogs now could really escape the shock they received. None of them even tried. They had learned that they were helpless, hence the label—learned helplessness—and they acted accordingly, simply lying on the electrified floor and whimpering even though they could readily jump the barrier and escape.

Seligman postulated that human beings do something very similar and that, given analogous conditions, they learn that no action is efficacious and stop trying. Seligman then took the dogs and literally dragged them over the barrier to the nonshock floor. One would think that once the dogs had discovered that they were able to escape, they would quickly relearn the escape behavior they had once demonstrated and jump over the barrier when they were shocked. That did not happen. It took at least ten trials in which the experimenter dragged the dog across the barrier to the safe condition before the dogs would jump.

Seligman's paradigm has several implications for substance abuse treatment. Many substance abusers grew up in situations not unlike the situation of Seligman's dogs. Living in homes with alcoholic, drug-abusing, and abusive parents, they learned that action was futile. Many gave up. Of course, this is not an accurate description of the childhood of the majority of substance abusers. Nevertheless, it is a close analogy to the situations of a substantial minority. As adolescents, these proto-addicts discovered drugs and found that drugs assuaged their pain and sense of futility. In a sense, their use of drugs was an attempt to overcome their learned helplessness. Taking a drug is at least an action, an attempt to do something on one's behalf, however mistakenly.

Further, many substance abusers have made numerous attempts to control their addiction. A substantial minority have attempted abstinence many times. They always failed. Hence, they too suffer from learned helplessness, in this case helplessness and hopelessness about the possibility of overcoming their addiction.

The second part of Seligman's experiment in which he repeatedly dragged the dogs over the barrier before they learned that they could do something efficacious, applies quite directly to the therapy of substance abusers. The clinical implication is clear. Namely, that the therapist must be very active, and not at all neutral, as he or she drags the dog repeatedly across the barrier until the dog realizes that escape is possible—that action is not futile and that it can have a positive outcome. Therefore, the substance abuse therapist must be active, must take a positive stand for sobriety, and must expect a considerable period of frustration to which he or she must respond with persistence. If the patient has no hope, then the patient has to borrow the therapist's hope. The hope of the therapist that recovery is possible and potentially satisfying is realistic.

What does Aristotle teach us about addiction and its treatment?

In his *Nicomachean Ethics* (325 B.C.), Aristotle, in one of the more flattering philosophical assessments of human beings, states: "Man by his nature desires to know." If Aristotle is correct, substance abusers, like other human beings, no matter how deep their denial and how distorted their thinking, have somewhere within them the desire to know. It is this desire to know that makes treatment possible.

There are clinical implications of Aristotle's attribution of an innate drive to knowledge in human beings. It suggests that didactic and educational interventions, as long as they do not lead to sterile intellectualization, may be highly mutative in the treatment of substance abuse. That is, the therapist needs to do a good deal of teaching about the nature of substance abuse, the reasons for viewing it as a disease, the effects of the drug on mind and body, and whatever else is relevant and can be heard by the patient that the therapist may know about substance use and its effect.

Knowledge provides structure, it makes sense out of chaos, it suggests possibilities for rational control, it can give comfort even when unwelcome. All of this suggests that didactic interventions have a particular place in the therapy of substance abuse that they may not have in other forms of psychotherapy.

What does Copernicus have to do with substance abuse treatment?

Nicolaus Copernicus, the sixteenth-century astronomer, suggested that the solar system was better accounted for by assuming that the earth revolved around the sun than that the sun revolved around the earth. As I learned from Harry, a dual-diagnosis, anxiety-disordered, alcoholic patient, this paradigmatic shift from a geocentric to a heliocentric conceptualization of the solar system is a powerful metaphor for a radical shift in self-perception. Harry came to me for psychotherapy some years after he achieved stable sobriety. Although sober, he continued to struggle with disabling anxiety. He found particularly helpful my interpretations concerning his fear of losing control of repressed rage and of his self-punitive identification with his father's fatal heart attack, which his anxiety symptoms mimicked. It was a successful therapy. In the termination phase, he said:

> The most helpful single thing I got from you is the idea that the irrational might be rational, that my anxiety attacks, which seemed like lightning bolts of divine wrath, have a cause, and that I have some-thing to do with that cause. The anxiety, which seemed external, some-thing that happened to me, became *my* anxiety. As I came to own the cause of the anxiety, to make it mine, I also came to see that I might be able to do something about it, to control it. After one of our ses-sions, I had a severe attack. In our next session, you offered me ex-planations of what happened that made sense to me. Although what you said caused me pain, I felt enormous relief. I still have anxiety attacks, but they don't have the same quality of abject terror. Now I can look for the cause—the reason inside me. It was not so much what you said, but that it made sense that allowed me to make what I call my *Copernican revolution.*

What Harry called his Copernican revolution, that is, his assuming responsibility for and internalizing his symptoms, hitherto experienced as externally caused, can also be understood as a shift from an external to an internal "locus of control," something we know tends to occur in recovery from substance abuse. It is one of the most mutative effects of successful therapy.

It is of some interest that the geocentric system was shored up with progressively more fantastic "epicycles" as it became less and less able to make sense of the new observations made possible by the invention of the telescope. This is precisely analogous to the progressively more fantastic rationalizations and projections of the substance abuser attempting to make sense of what is happening to him or her. The Copernican revolution in this case is relinquishing denial and realizing how powerfully the use is affecting one's life.

It is also of some interest that Freud cited Copernicus's paradigm as one of three narcissistic wounds science had inflicted on humankind (the others having been inflicted by Darwin and by Freud himself). This suggests that paradoxical as it may seem, moving toward internal loss of control is a move away from pathological narcissism.

What does Kurt Goldstein teach us about substance abuse and its treatment?

Kurt Goldstein was great neurologist who made his reputation working with brain-damaged soldiers in World War I. What Goldstein came to see was that the seemingly bizarre behavior and symptoms of those injured veterans made perfect sense if they were viewed from a holistic perspective, which tried to understand the organism's struggle to adapt to impairment. "Symptoms are consequences of the sick organism's struggle with the demands of the task confronting it. In other words, symptoms are forms of behavior by which the individual tries, in spite of his defect, to come to terms in the best way with the inner and outer world" (Goldstein 1952, p. 771). It is the therapist's job to creatively perceive seemingly bizarre pathological behavior as the outward manifestation of a holistic reordering of the remaining potentialities to function. This has direct relevance to substance abuse treatment in two ways: substance abusers, particularly alcoholics, suffer some degree of organic brain syndrome with which they must come to terms as best they can; and the substance abuse itself can be understood as the organism's attempt to come to terms, in spite of the defect, with the internal and external world. This resonates with the work of Gedo (pp. 71–74), Krystal and Raskin (pp. 90–92), and Khantzian (pp. 95–98).

Goldstein also wrote of the loss of the "abstract attitude" in organicity. The organically impaired patient can only function in the "concrete attitude." Substance abuse patients suffer, transiently, one hopes, the loss of the abstract attitude. The therapist must keep in mind the patient's impairment of the ability to abstract in formulating interventions, and must be simple, clear, particular, concrete, and redundant in order to be heard and understood, particularly with active users and early sobriety patients.

Goldstein saw pathology as regression or *dissolution* to more archaic (primitive) modes of functioning. He borrowed the notion of dissolution (in contradistinction to evolution) from the brilliant nineteenth-century neurologist Hughlings Jackson (Lassek 1970) who also influenced Freud and Freud's notions about regression. Substance abuse can be understood as dissolution (regression) to a more primitive level of organization and functioning in the face of deficit and the organism's attempt to adapt to it.

Goldstein (1939, 1940) discriminated between *neurotic anxiety* caused by internal conflict, which is best treated by interpretation, and *catastrophic anxiety*, which comes from the patient's incapacity to function in a given situation. The patient passively avoids tasks he cannot perform and develops "preferred conditions," for example, substance use, to achieve the best functioning possible. Interpretation makes things worse; rather, the therapist must support the defense.

Viewed externally, the patient's preferred conditions appear rigid, compulsive, uncooperative, or bizarre. Viewed phenomenologically, the preferred condition is the organism's attempt at self-actualization in the face of deficit. This perspective—understanding the substance abuse as avoidance of catastrophic anxiety—reduces negative countertransference and helps the therapist deal with the substance abuser's apparent irrationality.

V

Treatment Techniques in Substance Abuse Therapy

> *What are the stages of substance abuse treatment?*

Diagnosis, confrontation, education, and working through.

> *Are dynamic techniques useful in substance abuse treatment?*

Yes. No matter what the style of treatment, the therapist must always be aware of transference both to the therapist and to the substance. It is no less vital that the therapist be aware of his or her countertransference. The dynamic techniques of confrontation, clarification, and interpretation can be extremely useful in substance abuse treatment, particularly after abstinence has been established. Even in cases in which a therapist is working in another tradition, such as the cognitive tradition, an understanding of dynamics may make all of the difference even if no interpretations are offered. Generally speaking, dynamic approaches are most useful late in the treatment, after either control or abstinence has been established. But there are exceptions in which working through the dynamic conflicts leads to control or abstinence. This contradicts the current conventional wisdom that holds that you have to stop the addiction before you worry about what its causes may be. By and large, that is true. Nevertheless, there is something very strange about saying that substance abuse is a disease that we can only treat once it has been cured, that is, once the patient is abstinent. This is the policy of many agencies and it makes very little sense. That policy and that attitude came into being as a result of dynamically oriented therapists working analytically while ignoring the pharmacological regression induced by the various drugs of abuse leading to long and futile treatments. I believe that few people work that way today and the criticism is antiquated and that the pendulum has swung so far to the other side that insight is ignored as a means of promoting abstinence or control. Yet insight may be very much needed.

Are cognitive techniques useful in substance abuse treatment?

They certainly are. A great deal of substance abuse therapy is cognitive therapy. There is much emphasis on the changing of attitude and the modification of irrational or incorrect beliefs. For example, many drinkers passionately feel that they cannot do without alcohol because they are so terribly depressed. They simply could not stand the depression if they couldn't get some relief by drinking. The cognitive therapist would explain that alcohol is a central nervous system depressant that may give some temporary relief from the depression because it is an anesthetic, but that it is actually making the depression worse on a physiological level. That type of cognitive intervention is often called a *didactic intervention* and there is a great deal of didactic and educational work that needs to be done in substance abuse treatment. That didactic work in no way vitiates the possibility of doing dynamic or interpretive or insight work. In fact, the two go hand in hand and the didactic educational work often greatly strengthens the therapeutic alliance and the contextual transference, in effect creating a holding environment in which the patient feels understood and this allows other work to proceed.

There are other kinds of cognitive interventions that are also extremely useful. Especially salient are those that enable increasing levels of self-efficacy, that is, those that convince the patient that he can act in his or her own behalf and those that induce attitudinal change. Many of the twelve-step slogans are in essence cognitive therapeutic mechanisms. For example, the notion that alcoholism or addiction is "self-will run riot," speaks to pathological narcissism, not in a way of enabling insight or working through or looking at the genetic determinants of such narcissism, but in a very directive didactic kind of appeal to the abuser to get some perspective on his or her behavior and set aside some of the willfulness.

When is confrontation of denial necessary?

Twelve-step programs say that addiction is the disease of denial. There is a good deal of truth in that. People in the midst of substance abuse or dependence inevitably minimize the effect of that use or dependence upon themselves and engage in an active psychodynamic defense of denial. This denial is in protection of the addiction, which at both conscious and un-conscious levels is experienced as necessary to survival and to the mainte-nance of self-esteem. Anything that threatens the substance use or the very integrity of the self is not to be tolerated. Peter Hartocollis (1968) believes that the denial of the substance abuser is denial not only of the pernicious-ness of the substance use, but also of the need for help, and that the denial is part of a kind of pseudo–self-sufficiency. This is very much on target. Leon Wurmser (1978), on the other hand, although he would not disagree with Hartocollis, has a quite different understanding of denial, as denial of the entire inner world of fantasy, wish, drive, and indeed of the unconscious. So denial is not only denial of the perniciousness of the substance use, it is a form of what Wurmser calls *psychophobia*, a psychophobia that is en-demic in our culture and results in the search for external solutions to in-ternal problems, which is exactly what the substance abuser does, turning to the substance of abuse to solve an inner dilemma. The implication of all these views of denial is that the therapist has to be very active in confront-ing the denial because the patient will not get there on his or her own and that the denial needs to be interpreted on all three of these levels: (1) denial or minimization of the damage the use is causing; (2) denial of the fear of turning to people for help because that is too scary and has resulted in using drugs as helpers; and (3) denial that there are internal problems that need to be worked on. Denial of the existence of internal problems leads to the use of external solutions, the "solution" being use of the drug rationalized, for example, "I can't stop drinking because of my depression."

Could you give an example of denial?

John had received his fourth DWI (arrest for driving while intoxicated). He was in therapy much against his will.

It wasn't my fault. It was my girlfriend. If the bitch hadn't dumped me, I would never have taken that drink—not that I was drunk or anything. It was my sister's fault. She's a social worker and social workers have a bug up their asses about drinking. She told Susan to drop me because I'm a loser. Fuck her! Anyway, I was in the mall— it was Christmas time and the place was filled with couples holding hands and snuggling up. I couldn't take it. Susan had just told me to buzz off just because I had a few drinks that week and my sister, the cunt, didn't like it. She got Susan stirred up and the two of them really fucked me! Anyway I was really upset watching all those lovey-dovey couples, so I just had a few—to take the edge off—I was in pain, man—but nothing to interfere with my driving. The drinks— only four or five beers—oh, yeah, and a shot—worked. No getting sloppy or anything, and I felt pretty good when I got in the car. Then the first thing I knew—flashing lights. I was driving fine. It was the fucking mechanic! He didn't fix my taillight and it was out. But if it wasn't for Susan, I would never have drunk. She did it to me! Anyway, the cop stopped me because of the taillight, not because of my driving. He said I was weaving, but I wasn't. He was off his gourd— a real prick! Then he took out the fucking Breathalyzer. In the old days cops never took a reading on the Breathalyzer. They just told you to sleep it off and then drive home. At the worst, they took your keys. [I wondered how John had gotten his first three DWIs if the cops in the "good old days" never read the Breathalyzer.] Well, this prick nailed me! Any other cop would have let me go—Christmas and all. If that cop wasn't such a prick, I wouldn't be here!

My association was to my great-grandmother who was something of a family legend. Living in the age of robber-baron capitalists, she was in her own small way a robber baroness. She owned a series of corner grocery stores, which had a way of closing in one place and reopening down the street when the creditors closed in, in Philadelphia's equivalent of New York's Lower East Side. One day "Bubbe" (grandmother) came home in a rage:

"Mrs. Kaplan—'*chalearye zol sie nehen*'—the plague should take her—better never set foot in my store again!"

"Bubbe, what happened? Why are you so angry at Mrs. Kaplan?"

"The nerve, nothing like this ever happened to me before. Mrs. Kaplan—she should only drop dead—learned to read the scale!"

So great-grandmother became an honest woman in spite of herself. Like Mrs. Kaplan, the cops had learned to read the scale, and John was no happier than Bubbe. Given the near psychotic (not to say sociopathic) nature of his denial (which unfortunately is not all that uncommon), John's prognosis was poor, and he left therapy after a few sessions.

When do I confront?

This is perhaps the key question in substance abuse treatment. There are those who maintain that confrontation must come very early; others work with patients a very long time before they confront the addiction. Wisdom, as it so often does, lies somewhere in the middle. One must also be sensitive to where the patient is at. There are situations in which the confrontation should be in the first session.

A substance abuse counselor, who himself was in recovery, had relapsed. He attended a lecture of mine, and then called and asked for an immediate appointment. He drove a long distance to get to my office, insisting he had to see me immediately. When he entered, he was in appalling condition, bouncing off the walls. I said to him after five minutes: "I cannot treat you in this condition. You must enter a hospital to be detoxified, and then a rehabilitation program, and then we can work together." He heard me, perhaps because he liked what I had said in the lecture so much that he had sought me out, or because he was so ill that he was desperate. He entered a detoxification program and subsequently rehabilitation, and lived for a number of months in a halfway house. He then returned to the city, called me, and settled down into a 5-year, highly fruitful psychotherapy.

Tom, an English professor, had been in analysis for fourteen years. He terminated what was considered by both analyst and patient to be a successful analysis, yet continued to drink. When a number of years after his termination he called his analyst, saying that he was really in trouble with alcohol, she referred him to me. We spoke a great deal about his situation. I suggested to him that his alcohol use had an awful lot to do with his anxiety, his depression, and his marital problems. I suggested an experiment in which he stopped drinking to see what effect it might have on his life, making it clear that he could always return to drinking if there was no improvement. The patient stopped drinking for exactly one year, which he agreed to do as his "experiment," the length of time being determined by him. He followed his contract; he did not drink for a year and hated every minute of it, and hated me for every minute of that year for having suggested it. He vigorously maintained that there was no improvement whatsoever in any aspect of his life. He indeed made sure that was the case. One year and one day after our initial session he resumed drinking with a vengeance. I continued to see him for several years while he was drinking, since he was functional, had no major physical symptoms, and was no danger to himself or to anyone else, hoping to build a relationship and have enough saliency to be heard when I connected his various difficulties with his drinking, as I repeatedly did for a long time with little manifest effect.

The patient always gave me a Christmas gift. The first year it was a recording of Schubert's *Winterreise* (*Winter Journey*), a haunting depiction of loneliness, alienation, and death. The second Christ-

mas he gave me Richard Strauss's *Four Last Songs*, the moving fare-
well of a man in his mid-80s. The third Christmas he brought in a jar
of rotting, stinking pickles—in other words, he gave me a gift of shit.
Shortly thereafter he quit drinking. His last Christmas present was a
last act of defiance. Tom had developed various physical symptoms
including swelling in his scrotum, which deeply frightened him and
had much to do with his throwing in the towel and deciding that alcohol was not for him. However, our two years of struggle during
Tom's phase of negative transference were not inconsequential. On
the contrary, my repeated interpretations that his various marital difficulties, depression, anxiety, and so forth were intimately connected
to his drinking were heard, however much denied, and eventually led
to his decision to stop drinking. Tom subsequently became one of the
most devoted of AA members and has since experienced many years
of satisfying sobriety.

Is abstinence necessary?

This is perhaps the most vexing question in substance abuse treatment. I think the proof is in the pudding. If one can establish control over
one's drug use and the abuse was essentially a symptomatic or reactive phenomenon, then indeed abstinence is not necessary. However, for those who
have developed a full-blown dependence or addiction, this is extremely un-
likely to be the case. The more symptomatic an abuser is, and the more
psychological, emotional, psychodynamic, psychiatric, interpersonal, educational, vocational, and medical consequences of the use the patient has
experienced, the least likely it is that he or she can safely return to social,
casual, or recreational use. In my experience, most patients come to see
sobriety as a highly positive, rather than a deprivation, state. But there is
certainly a painful transition to sobriety.

There is another class of patients that would clearly do best abstain-
ing, but these patients are unwilling to so. They are neither in stable recovery nor able to return to asymptomatic social use, and yet they continue to
use. Traditional substance abuse counseling terminates with these patients.

I believe it is better to approach the decision to terminate on a case-by-case basis, and to evaluate whether or not the therapy is helping. Sometimes less is definitely more. For a cocaine addict who was using cocaine three times a week, embezzling from his employer and living in fear and paranoia, to have moved to a position where he has an occasional spree is clearly a worthwhile improvement. For whatever reasons, that cocaine user may be unwilling to give up his three-times-a-year cocaine high. If the therapy is helping that person restrict his use to three times a year instead of three times a week, it is clearly a worthwhile treatment, however strongly the therapist may believe that abstinence would be the wiser course for the patient. So a therapy may be conceived of as successful without abstinence. Having said that, I would emphasize that for most seriously involved drug users, abstinence is clearly the preferable and in many cases the only possible path to sustained improvement and health.

What is the abstinence violation effect (AVE)?

The abstinence violation effect is a notion developed by Alan Marlatt (Marlatt and Gordon 1985), a cognitive behaviorist and a critic of the disease concept. He maintains that many substance abusers who have been taught the disease concept, particularly in twelve-step programs, come to believe that they have lost control. They therefore expect that if they slip, that is, pick up a drink or drug, that they will continue to drink or drug; that is, they believe they will lose control. In effect it becomes a self-fulfilling prophecy. Marlatt and his followers want to teach, on the contrary, that slips have reasons that can be explored, that there is nothing mysterious about them, and that there is nothing inevitable about continuing to drug or drink once one has a slip. They further teach that the abstinence violation effect is totally one of expectancy, and that it has no reality aside from its psychic component.

I believe that Marlatt misunderstands what twelve-step programs teach and believe, at least in this regard. In my experience, twelve-step groups, although extremely tolerant of slips, urge members to return as soon as possible and try to minimize the guilt associated with the slip so that the member does not continue to use in order to obliterate the guilt felt over the slip. Twelve-step programs in no way suggest that one who has slipped cannot stop quickly and return to the program. What twelve-step really teaches is that it is very dangerous to experiment, because a slip may be difficult to recover from. And it is true that patients may indeed get into very serious trouble if they are true alcohol or drug addicts and they use. I think that is factual and realistic, and does not imply what Marlatt thinks it does. Be that as it may, it is important for the therapist to convey to the user, if abstinence is the goal, that slips are extremely dangerous, but that if he or she has a slip, something should and can be done about it as soon as possible, and that there is no inevitability that the patient will continue to use until disaster occurs. Once stable sobriety has been reestablished, the patient and the therapist "analyze" the slip to understand it and to strategize ways to prevent the slip from reoccurring.

What is the least-harm approach?

Least harm is the notion that any therapy that reduces the harm people are doing to themselves or to others is worthwhile doing. On a social-political level, this could be a needle-exchange program to provide clean, HIV-free needles to heroin addicts, both for their personal benefit and to halt the spread of disease. On the individual level, this could be a therapist helping a patient minimize his or her drug use. The wisdom of least harm or the lack thereof is clearly a value judgment. Some therapists enthusiastically engage in least-harm treatments. Others who are more committed to the disease model, and more influenced by twelve-step programs, have scant interest in least-harm outcomes.

How does one work with twelve-step programs?

Twelve-step programs are a valuable ancillary therapy, which for many patients makes the difference between recovery and lack of recovery. They provide ongoing, continuous support. There are so many meetings held in a large city that one could go to AA meetings around the clock seven days a week, a level of support a therapist clearly cannot provide. The therapist must examine his or her own feelings about, and countertransference to, twelve-step programs. The programs bring out many different feelings from revulsion to admiration, and sometimes both of those feelings in the same person. There is a kind of anti-intellectualism in twelve-step programs that is deeply offensive to many therapists, as manifest in the slogan KISS, which stands for "Keep it simple, stupid," and in another slogan, "Utilize, don't analyze." The thrust is emotional and evangelical rather than rational. But the twelve-step programs are also wonderful. They provide a very high level of support. They are extremely effective in deliquescing guilt. They are extremely effective in dealing with counterdependency and making healthy interpersonal dependency an acceptable alternative to dependence on drugs. They offer fellowship, companionship, friendship, and all of the conflicts and difficulties inherent in any human organization or human relationship.

The therapist needs to listen extremely carefully to what patients say about their involvement in twelve-step programs. One of the limitations of twelve-step programs is that they allow very little room for negative transference. Such slogans as "Principles before personalities" and "The program is always right" tend to make for suppression or repression of negative transference to AA, NA, OA, or the other twelve-step programs. It is extremely therapeutic for the patient to have a place to express that negative transference in his or her therapeutic sessions. The overzealous therapist who hears that as denial and immediately moves in, perhaps argumentatively, to defend the twelve-step program is cutting the patient off and may actually drive the patient out of the program, while allowing for expression of negative feelings toward AA may allow the patient to continue his or her affiliation.

There was in Manhattan for many years, a gentleman known as "Negative Mike" who went to many AA meetings. These meetings tended to be extremely upbeat and Pollyannaish and at some point Mike would put up his hand and say, "We're all doomed, there's no hope for anyone in this room." Negative Mike, who was a semi–street person, probably an ambulatory schizophrenic, and no doubt looking for attention, provided an extremely valuable service to his fellow twelve-step members. He articulated the flip side of their enthusiasm for the program—the shadow negativism that the program tends to squash. Therapy allows twelve-step members to express their inner "Negative Mike."

What is a sponsor?

Sponsors are more experienced members of the various twelve-step programs who act as mentors to "pigeons," that is, new members. All members are urged to have a sponsor. Sponsors are supposed to share their "faith, hope, and experience" with newcomers and not be preachy or directive. But very often that is not the case. In very early recovery, a high degree of direction may be welcomed by the newly sober member who is confused and disoriented, as is inevitable in early recovery, but that direction soon comes to be resented because it is controlling and infantilizing. In many sponsor/sponsee relationships the sponsor has rampant and totally unconscious countertransferential involvement with the sponsee and is often enacting power and control scenarios of his or her own. (*Sponsee* is AA-ese for one who is sponsored.) As therapists listen to some of these disturbed sponsor/sponsee relationships, they are in a very difficult position. The relationship with the sponsor, who has experience in and knowledge of the program, may be a lifeline for the patient, yet it may be highly destructive. The therapist can say, "Your relationship with your sponsor isn't a marriage. If it isn't working, get someone else." Yet therapists also need to be sensitive to the fact that the patient's transference to the sponsor may lead to distortion in the patient's perception of the sponsor, and that transference can be acted out in various destructive ways, including "picking up" (i.e., using drugs again), and/or enacted without insight. Sometimes it is helpful for therapists to comment on that, perhaps telling the patient, "You are finding reasons to dislike your sponsor so you can leave the program and return to drugs."

Therapists also have their feelings about the sponsor who more often than not is antitherapist or at least not very enthusiastic about therapy. This has changed in the last few years as the twelve-step programs have become

more positive toward psychotherapy, but the older attitudes persist. Competitive and angry feelings can be set up in the therapist vis-à-vis the sponsor, and it takes a high degree of self-awareness and sensitivity to support patients in relationships with their sponsors, while allowing them to express their dissatisfactions or presenting to them the possibility of withdrawing from the sponsor/sponsee relationship and switching sponsors if that seems to be in their interest.

There is a high incidence of severe narcissistic injury in sponsor/sponsee relationships. Sponsors let sponsees down; they abandon them, or they prefer other sponsees, which can be devastating for the patient. Therapists need to be alert to these narcissistic injuries, and to help patients experience them rather than act them out, and to help them work through their feelings.

> *What is the surrender experience?*

Surrender is a twelve-step notion that involves admitting one's powerlessness over one's addiction, and reaching out to the group, or perhaps to the therapist, or for some to the "Higher Power" for help. This is a Zen maneuver, because the very admission of powerlessness empowers the user. The powerlessness the addict admits to, and the concomitant relinquishing of control, the letting go, is the letting go of an illusion, a grandiose delusion of the ability to control substance use and, indeed, the universe. With the relinquishing of this illusion, real control and realistic power become possible.

> *Is surrender necessary for recovery, as the twelve-step
> people would tell us?*

People recover in many different ways, and surrender need not be part of the experience. However, for those who experience it, surrender is extraordinarily liberating. This form of hitting bottom, painful as it may be, frees the addict from the need to attempt to exercise omnipotent control over self, substance, and world, and frees his or her energies to pursue more realistic goals. It also frees the abuser from the obsession with the drug or the compulsive activity. Perhaps not consistently, there will be moments in which the old pleasures seem highly attractive, but for someone who has truly had this kind of experience, things *are* changed. There is a shift in existential stance, and one will never be quite the same again. It is a knowing, in depth, that there are some shows that one cannot run, and that that's okay. Similar experiences have been described in many religious traditions, the hitting bottom being described as parallel to the mystic's dark night of the soul before the moment of illumination and the surrender experience.

In his writings for AA, Bill Wilson cited William James's (1902) discussion of two kinds of conversion experiences in *The Varieties of Religious Experience*: the Damascus experience, an allusion to St. Paul's sudden illumination on the road to Damascus; and the educational conversion experience. Wilson was skeptical of Damascus experiences; he had had a few of those himself and they hadn't changed him very much. So he institutionalized the educational conversion experience in the twelve steps of AA and in the AA program itself. Hitting bottom and surrendering is very much in the nature of a Damascus conversion experience. The ongoing treatment, whether in a self-help group or in professional therapy, is the educational conversion experience. "Conversion" as used here need not refer to an explicitly religious experience. One can understand it rather as a change in existential stance, or attitudinal transformation, or, in Nietzsche's words, a "transvaluation of values."

What does "mokus" mean?

Mokus is a twelve-step program word that is both a neologism and onomatopoeic. To be mokus is to suffer, one hopes transiently, cognitive disablement as a consequence of substance abuse.

Mokus refers to the state of mental confusion that people are in late in the addictive process and early in recovery. It is characterized by confusion, by mood swings, by great metastability in almost every area of being, and by what Krystal and Raskin call affect regression into an undifferentiated *Ur*-affect. It is important for the therapist to recognize that this kind of cognitive-affective confusion is characteristic of both addiction and early sobriety. None of our active or early sobriety patients is playing with a full deck, so to speak. Fortunately, much of this condition is neurochemical and reversible. All that is required is time to heal and abstinence from the addictive substance. But there are factors that make for the mokus state that are not neurochemical. On the tragic side, there may be enough alteration in brain chemistry and/or destruction of neurological tissue that such a state becomes difficult, if not impossible, to remediate. Fortunately, most patients do not experience this phenomenon, but it does occur.

On the other hand, apart from pharmacological and neurological factors, the state of being mokus is partly psychodynamic, induced by the confusion of the addictive lifestyle, its storminess, its interpersonal difficulties, and perhaps by the patient's long isolation and failure to communicate. The psychodynamic component of the mokus state is treatable psychotherapeutically.

> *How can the therapist help recovering patients deal with situations they may be exposed to in which there will be drinking or drugging?*

Particularly in early sobriety, the therapist should borrow the twelve-step slogan "First things first," and suggest that patients absent themselves from the drinking or drugging occasion. However, this is not always possible. There are some social obligations that are extremely awkward to duck. The therapist can then advise, "Go late and leave early," and can tell patients that it is crucial beforehand to give themselves permission to leave: "If I become uncomfortable, I am out of here and that's perfectly okay no matter what other people will think." Patients will then feel much calmer and much less threatened. In most cases, merely having permission to leave is enough and they will not have to do so; however, if they do begin to get strong drink signals (or drug signals) and feel uncomfortable, then they should leave.

I also tell patients that often there is a delayed reaction: "At a social occasion—wedding, dinner party, Christmas party—there are often no overt drink signals. You go through the occasion without having any desire to drink whatsoever—at least consciously. But watch out. It is my experience that many people have a slip several days after being exposed to alcohol or drugs. So be aware that your exposure may act as a delayed trigger and that you will be dangerously vulnerable to relapse in the several days after the party. That is a good time to get as much support as you can and to be careful and zealous in guarding your newly won sobriety." This is a bit preachy, but it averts many a slip. Particularly the forewarning that the days after the exposure may be the really dangerous ones is often prophylactic and prevents a relapse.

> *What is the therapist to do with religious patients who could benefit from twelve-step but feel disloyal to their religion if they go to what they perceive to be another one?*

This is a surprisingly common scenario. I have had a number of patients with strong allegiance, particularly to, but not exclusively to, fundamentalist groups, who had been loath to attend AA because they feel guilty, as their primary religious affiliation tells them that God should meet their needs and membership in their church should take care of their problems. To then go to what is perceived as a competing religion (and indeed in some ways it is) is felt to be disloyal, and evidence that the patient is not properly participating in the religious community he or she is already a part of. Under those circumstances I say, "You're trying to get your shoes fixed at the dry cleaners. Your church does a terrific job with your 'dry cleaning,' with helping you with many problems—with giving you solace, a belief system, and a guide to behavior, but its purpose is not to treat a disease, and addiction can reasonably be looked at as a disease. Therefore, just as you have to go to the shoemaker and not the dry cleaner to get your shoes fixed, you need to go to twelve-step meetings to treat your addiction—not to your primary support system, which is not specialized to do that." This or a similar homey analogy has, in my experience, made it possible for the patient with this sort of conflict to participate in twelve-step meetings and in the program.

Of course, this can be a pseudo-conflict used in defense of the addiction, when the underlying reason for not going to the twelve-step meeting is that the people there are sober and that the expectation is abstinence. If that is the case, it may or may not be wise for the therapist to comment on it. As usual, therapeutic tact and a good sense of where your patient is at are the best guides.

Do clergy become addicted?

Yes. I have treated several ministers, including a rabbi who was both an alcoholic and an opiate addict. Alcoholism is a surprisingly common problem in the Catholic clergy and religious orders. The Church is aware of this and makes strenuous efforts at prevention and rehabilitation. Most orders are quite willing to pay for treatment, so I have had the opportunity to treat many "religious" over the years. Scrupulosity, that is, obsessive guilt over "sinful"—usually inconsequentially so—thought and obsessive fear of thinking or uttering blasphemies are well-known "religious," especially but by no means exclusively Catholic, neuroses. These patients are often self-medicated with alcohol. Sister Beth Amy obsessively thought of injuring the Virgin during Mass, and Sister Judith burned with erotic desire for Jesus. Both of them got drunk as often as they could, which was nightly, and both became so ill that their superiors insisted that they seek treatment for their alcoholism. Brother Peter, less tormented by sacrilegious thoughts than by guilt over homosexual fantasies, wound up with panic attacks, disastrously self-medicated by alcohol.

Kathy, a nun, social worker, and nurse, who was clinical director of the dual-diagnosis unit of a leading rehab center, was in her seventh year of recovery when she picked up a drink. When she came to see me after going AWOL from rehab, she spent her session spewing obsessive hatred of the Pope. Daughter of a tyrannical career military officer father, she had been pushed into the cloister, although she did believe that she had a vocation. In her thirties, she had fallen madly in love with a brilliant priest who was president of the college in which she taught. They planned to leave their respective orders and marry. And he did marry—someone else. Her alcoholism followed.

In her recovery, Kathy had once again fallen in love, this time with the medical director of her unit. It was the classic doctor-nurse relationship. She wrote his professional papers for him, ran the unit to his professional benefit, and attended his kids' birthday parties. She waited for his promised leaving of his wife. He too abandoned her. It was a short distance from there to the bar. Once she picked up a drink, it took less than a week for her to escalate into around-the-clock drunkenness, a progression that eventuated in her entry into the rehabilitation unit and subsequent treatment with me.

We had barely connected when my vacation loomed. I feared that she would get drunk shortly after I left, and struggled mightily through interpretation and probing of her feelings to help her experience rather than act out her feelings of abandonment. I failed. Kathy had a spectacular and almost fatal fall—a literal one, down a flight of stairs while drunk—and entered a long-term treatment facility. I never heard from her, but years later learned that she was running her own rehab center in a distant state.

How can the therapist help patients who might benefit from twelve-step participation but who object to the "religious" aspect of AA-NA?

The therapist should recognize and acknowledge that this is a real problem (whatever its resistance side may be, which can also be commented on), and suggest that the patient approach AA as a smorgasbord where he or she can take whatever can be meaningfully used. I also tell patients that I know many agnostics and atheists who have benefited from and enjoyed AA-NA, which is true.

The therapist can also secularize the steps. For example, the third step, which states, "We have turned our will and our lives over to God as we understand him," can be rendered as "Let it happen" or "Get out of your own way," both of which address the issue of omnipotent control and its relinquishing without mentioning God or the Higher Power.

Unfortunately, the present resurgence of fundamentalist religiosity does make some of the more secularly oriented extremely uncomfortable in twelve-step programs, and the therapist should respect the patient's decision to disaffiliate.

> *In what way is AA a cognitive treatment?*

Twelve-step programs can be usefully understood as cognitive therapies that, in a very didactic way—through their slogans and their literature, as well as through their ideology embodied in the twelve steps—seek to change attitudes, beliefs, and cognitions. They do it in a rather heavy-handed, propagandistic way (no less effective for being heavy-handed and propagandistic), but this type of work on changing belief systems, for example convincing an adult that her belief that she needs to use substances in order to survive is false, can be adapted and stylistically modified by the therapist. Such cognitive work can be pursued in individual or group therapy with positive results.

> *Could you give an example of a cognitive therapy intervention in substance abuse?*

There are many cognitive interventions, one of them being a challenging of the belief that drugs will make the patient feel better. The therapist might say, "When you first started using cocaine, it alleviated your depression, but now it is only making it worse." That is perhaps more educational than cognitive. If the therapist wanted to talk more about changing an attitude, then he or she could talk about exactly the same situation slightly differently. Now the therapist says to the patient, "You believe that you can't cope with your bad feelings without short-circuiting them with drugs. That is not true; you can. As they say, 'feelings aren't facts', and feeling that you can't cope doesn't mean that you can't."

What are the clinical implications of the disease model?

Critics say that the disease model teaches addicts that they are not responsible for their disease: "Of course I get drunk, I'm an alcoholic." "What do you expect? I'm an addict, why shouldn't I be shooting up?" Although such rationalizations of drug use incorporating the disease model do occur, they are not common. This criticism of the disease concept simply doesn't hold up. It is not my experience, or that of anyone I know in the field. On the contrary, it is the case that, for the most part, people who do not believe in the disease concept are more vulnerable to slips than those who do. Why should this be so? It is because the disease concept does two vital things. One, it provides an explanation, or cognitive structure, that makes sense out of a bewildering, crippling, intensely painful experience of chaotic deterioration. "Thank God I understand now what it is. It's the cocaine and my addiction to it." The whole notion of progression and of loss of control also helps people make sense of this terribly narcissistically wounding experience of a substance taking over their lives. There is relief in that. It is no doubt an oversimplification, and there is some degree of denial in it, but it is an intellectual tool, if you will, that permits substance abusing patients to gain some distance and some perspective on what is happening and has happened to them. This is definitely therapeutic.

The other great contribution of belief in the disease concept to recovery is that it helps the patient deal with shame and guilt, particularly guilt. One would think that guilt would enable recovery. Quite the opposite is true. The guilt, including, but not limited to, the guilt about the addiction and the behaviors the patient engaged in in support of his or her addiction, can be so overwhelming that the only possible course is to use more "dope" to obliterate the guilt. Exactly the same is true for shame. The disease concept gives one a new attribution: "It wasn't me, it was my disease." This reduces guilt and shame and lessens the need to anesthetize one's mind to wipe out the guilt and the shame. It does not generally lead to a lack of responsibility. One is not responsible for having the disease, but once one knows one has it, one is responsible for doing what is necessary to recover. An analogy might be made to diabetes, a disease process for which sufferers are not reasonably held morally culpable, yet they have a responsibility to themselves, and perhaps to others, to treat that disease in as rational and effective a way as medical knowledge makes possible. The same is true of addiction. What about those who say, "I have a disease, what do you expect from me?" Obviously, they require another approach and need to be confronted.

What is the nature of addictive rage?

The rage that substance abusers and dependents feel, suppress, repress, act out, and rarely allow themselves to fully experience is complex and highly overdetermined. Part of that rage is in defense of the addiction. Try to take a bone away from a hungry Doberman or a bottle away from a hungry baby, and you will see rage in the service of defending an addiction. Another component of addictive rage is self-hatred projected outward. Addicts despise themselves and lash out at the world in an attempt to externalize that rage. Related to this is the use of rage as a defense against and avoidance of the underlying depression. This manifestation of rage is a form of manic defense.

Yet another component of addictive rage is historical, that is, long-repressed rage over childhood insult and injury. It is the unconscious acting out of rage felt toward parents and siblings many years before. This rage is almost always dynamically repressed. The last, but by no means least, component of addictive rage comes from narcissistic vulnerability, or ego weakness. Feeling extremely vulnerable, undefended, naked before the world without one's substance, suffering abysmal self-esteem and self-loathing, almost any kind of frustration, frown, or slight elicits narcissistic rage, that is, unquenchable desire for vengeance against the offending party who has threatened the very existence of the vulnerable self.

How does the therapist deal with addictive rage?

Through interpretation and pacification. The narcissistic rage in defense of the addiction can be interpreted: "You're so angry at me because you see me as taking away your marijuana." "You wanted to kill your mother because she threatened to throw you out of the house and you know you can't support your habit if you have to pay for your own apartment." The component of addictive rage, which is self-hatred projected outward, is also usefully interpretable: "You lash out at me because you can't stand yourself." "You were so angry at your wife after our talk last week about how little you like yourself because it was a way of diverting your attention away from your self-hatred." The component of addictive rage that is genetic or historical can be interpreted and worked through in the same way feelings about early childhood trauma are in any other therapy, namely through transference interpretations, genetic interpretations, and ventilation in the therapy. The component of addictive rage that comes from narcissistic vulnerability can be dealt with only by indirection. The entire therapy has as its aim strengthening of the ego and consequent lessening of narcissistic vulnerability, and this comes about as a by-product of the entire therapeutic process. Mere abstinence reduces narcissistic vulnerability as recovering patients come to experience themselves more and more as worthwhile human beings: "If I can find the strength to stay sober, I must have some good stuff inside." If addiction leads to self-hatred, recovery, not necessarily but frequently, eventuates in healthy self-love.

What is Antabuse? What is its role in treatment?

Antabuse is the trade name of the drug disulfiram. It has no effect whatsoever unless the patient drinks. (There are, however, rare individuals who have allergic responses to it.) Antabuse works by blocking the metabolic pathway of alcohol at a point at which there is an accumulation of a highly toxic substance called acetaldehyde. This makes the drinker deathly ill. Antabuse therapy can be highly effective with patients who have a strong desire to stop drinking but poor impulse control. If they wish to drink, they have to stop taking the Antabuse and wait a couple of days and usually by then the urge is long gone. It is important to note, however, that Antabuse, in itself, is not a treatment for alcoholism. It is, rather, an adjunct to therapy, and the patient's conscious and unconscious feelings about the Antabuse, which are almost always ambivalent, since the drug is simultaneously experienced as a benevolent, wise, and protective parent, and as a harsh, prohibitive, and punishing parent, need to be made conscious, verbalized, and worked through.

I once treated a Vietnam veteran who was a stably sober recovering alcoholic. (Note: this case is also discussed under posttraumatic stress disorder, in Part IV.) When the Gulf War broke out, he began to obsess about body bags. Shortly thereafter he "saw gooks" coming through the woods behind his rural home. He hid under his deck. When he emerged he drank a six-pack of beer. Thereafter as he drove home from work he thought he might be seeing Viet Cong in his peripheral vision at the edges of the highway. The closer he got to home, the more anxious he became until his car "drove itself" to the beer supplier. Each day he resolved not to drink but failed to act on his resolve. He came to hate himself for his "weakness." This self-hatred escalated, eventuating in a serious depression. His depression brought him into therapy. The only issue he was willing to work on was stopping drinking. Nothing he tried met with success and his self-hatred and loathing of his weakness deepened. Finally, I told him about Antabuse and suggested he try it. He did. This was risky since this traumatized veteran was in danger of decompensating without his medicine (Miller's High Life). He did not, in fact, decompensate. Rather, his depression lifted. For reasons that were never elicited, he needed to attribute his sobriety entirely to the medicine rather than to the therapy—me or himself. Unfortunately, he was transferred before we could work on his PTSD.

What is Naltrexone? What is its role in treatment?

Naltrexone is a drug that is an antagonist to opiates and blocks their high. It has long been used to reduce the pleasure of opiate use, and more recently the pleasure of alcohol use, so that the taking of opiates (or alcohol) is no longer reinforcing. Naltrexone's efficacy in the treatment of alcoholism is not as well established as its efficacy in treating opiate addiction.

Like Antabuse, it is an adjunctive treatment that may be highly useful, but should never be a therapy in itself. The patient's feelings, conscious and unconscious, about the Naltrexone need to be discussed and worked through.

What is horse?

Horse is street slang for heroin.

What does the horse have to do with substance abuse treatment?

In Chekhov's great short story "Heartache," a lonely cabdriver who has lost his only child goes to work at the stable and tries to talk of his loss to his boss, to his fellow cabmen, and, later on, to his passengers as he is driving through the streets of St. Petersburg. One after another, his friends, associates, business affiliates shut him up and turn him away. Finally, at the end of a long night of not being listened to, he returns to the stable and starts to unharness his horse. As he does so, he begins to tell the horse about how his child succumbed, of what the doctor said, of the downward course of the disease, of the trip to the hospital, of the child's death, of the funeral, of the funeral oration, of his feelings about the entire process of illness, loss, funeral, and aloneness. We therapists are the horse, or perhaps more accurately, "the horse of the last resort." The horse is important. Listening matters, and being heard matters. The people we treat for substance abuse are not all suffering the grievous loss of Chekhov's cabdriver, but, for the most part, they have been grievously wounded. Substance abusers often have highly traumatic backgrounds, and even if they don't, in the course of their addictions they suffer much trauma and loss. Everyone tells them that their pain is self-inflicted (which at one level is, of course, true). The corollary of being self-inflicted is being unworthy of any form of compassion. It has been a long time since anyone has been willing to listen to the substance abuser. Therefore, these patients need their therapists to be as good listeners as Chekhov's horse. We tend to forget that in treating substance abuse, which requires a very active, didactic style, active listening is no less mutative. Empathic listening and confrontation are not antithetical. To not confront someone who is engaged in a self-destructive behavior like substance abuse is not at all empathic, it is merely malpractice. So, the horse has everything to do with substance abuse treatment.

How do we deal with the self-pity of the substance abuser?

Substance abusers are frequently self-pitying; they are often confronted with that at twelve-step meetings and told, "Get off the pity pot." Therapists, of course, do not want to encourage self-pity because that goes nowhere and easily becomes an endless nursing of wounds and just as easily eventuates in an existential stance of victimization. However, there is a difference between self-pity and self-compassion. For patients who are involved in twelve-step programs, where they hear the "tough-love" line about getting off the pity pot, any form of empathy for themselves becomes problematic. Tough-love approaches, as useful as they sometimes are, can also be pernicious, and get in the way of patients' having any kind of compassion toward themselves. Therefore, I frequently tell patients, particularly substance-abusing patients, that there's a difference between self-pity and having compassion for one's self. This is an intervention intended to open up a mourning process. It allows, after a long journey through pain, the integration of the very real loss that the substance abuse, in the vast majority of cases, has entailed. Healthy relationships, careers, and emotional well-being have all been damaged. Opportunities have been lost, never to return. Recovery itself brings with it further loss. Compassion for the self enables the patient to appropriately mourn the very real losses substance abuse has inflicted and to move on into an enjoyable sobriety.

How important is transference to the substance of abuse?

Transference to the substance of abuse is critical. It needs to be understood and interpreted. In other parts of this primer, idealizing and mirror transferences to the substance are elaborated, but therapists see many other forms of transference to substances. There are negative and positive transferences to substance, leading to its idealization and demonization, both by the patient and the culture. There is a kind of contextual, or holding, transference to a substance in which it becomes the holding and soothing mother. There is more focal transference to the drug, as mother or father (or both), as loving and protective parent and as punitive parent. There is transference to the drug in terms of projection of ego ideal and of harshly critical superego. The drug may have symbolic meanings, which are a kind of transference. It may represent magic potency, blood, semen, menstrual flow, strength, comfort, the divine (as it does in many religious rituals), solidarity and communion with other human beings, and a host of other idiosyncratic things. The more the therapist explores the meaning of the drug use, rather than closing down that exploration by too didactic a stance, the better. But this takes a lot of therapeutic tact and a good sense of timing. When substance abuse is immediately injurious, then the therapist doesn't have the luxury of this kind of exploration and must take a more directive stance. But that does not preclude the later exploration of the multiple and vastly overdetermined meanings of the substance use.

What sort of transference do substance abusers have
to the therapist?

Substance abusers have all the kinds of transferences that everyone else does, plus some "stuff" that is particular to them. The transference most commonly seen in substance abuse that is rather different, though it is not unique, is the prevalence of counterdependency manifesting in the relationship with the therapist. This has to be addressed, and dependence on a person, rather than on a substance, somehow made acceptable. The therapist should interpret the reasons for the counterdependence, if they can be determined. These reasons almost always lie in two directions: (1) bad early experience with people, leaving the patient quite rationally prone to avoid close relationships; and (2) protection of the addiction. Both can be usefully interpreted. The therapist also needs to look very carefully at the contextual (or holding) transference; the focal (or object) transference; the always present, negative transference; and the various forms of selfobject transference including the mirror transference in its various manifestations as merger, as twinship, as mirror transference proper, as well as at the idealizing transference, and at the defenses against all of these transference manifestations as part of the counterdependent dynamic.

Substance abusers are said to have a very intense transference to therapists, which goes with the general intensity of their lifestyle, as well as a stormy one, so that they love us one moment and hate us the next. That, indeed, is common. It is very helpful to interpret: "You are angry at me and want to leave therapy because your substance use is threatened." This may or may not work, but at least it puts the issue on the table and patient and therapist can talk about it. Some authorities in the field recommend group rather than individual treatment because of the intensity of the transference.

Negative transference, in particular, may be unmanageable for the patient. It may induce such enormous anxiety in the patient, who becomes fearful that he or she will kill the therapist, that treatment is terminated and substance use resumed. This sort of malignant negative transference needs to be probed for, surfaced, clarified, and interpreted. The addict's hatred of the therapist is driven mostly by defense of the addiction. Particularly when the cessation of use is seen as the equivalent of death (a not uncommon occurrence), and the patient honestly and sincerely believes that he or she will not survive without the substance, and the therapist is perceived as wanting to take it away, intense hatred is to be expected. The problem is not being hated; trained therapists usually deal with that fairly well. The problem is that the hatred provokes the patient to leave treatment and provides a justification for doing so. This is best circumvented by the therapist's articulating the patient's unconscious thoughts, even if the therapist is not quite sure but has the sense that something like this is happening; the therapist will usually be on target. It is better to err on the side of interpreting the negative transference, even if the therapist occasionally looks ridiculous to the patient for whom the interpretation does not fit.

What sort of countertransference does substance abuse elicit?

Rage, frustration, and hate are common countertransferential reactions to substance abusers. They are often provocative, hostile, and devaluing, and they don't want what the therapist has to offer. Naturally, this is not the only pattern. The full range of countertransferential feelings— compassion, grief, sorrow, love, joy—is going to come up in the course of therapy with substance abusers. But the predominance of negative countertransference is reality. The therapist is dealing with primitive states, even if not with primitive personalities, in cases in which the primitivity has been induced by the substance. All of that raw emotion comes from the regressed user and is difficult to integrate, hold, process, and interpret without retaliation. The therapist's desire to retaliate may be conscious or unconscious. Conscious desires for retaliation are rationalized and justified, while the unconscious ones slip out sideways. The best safeguard against acting out retaliatory wishes is supervision (personal therapy doesn't hurt, either).

The therapist also has to look at his or her transference to the substance because therapists, too, have feelings about alcohol, marijuana, hallucinogenics, and cocaine, and our experiences, or lack of experiences, with those drugs profoundly affect our approach to our patients, as do our fantasies, conscious and unconscious, about those substances. All of this needs to be explored, perhaps in our own therapy or training analysis. Depending on our own history we may see addiction in every sip of wine, or we may utterly miss the clear diagnosis when it would be apparent to a five-year old.

In addition to transference to the patient and to the substance, therapists also have transferences to other treatment modalities. In most cases, substance abuse patients will be in more than one treatment—perhaps in a group, perhaps in the twelve-step movement, perhaps in other sorts of rehabilitative programs—and this participation can bring out very strong feelings of rivalry, of devaluation, of threat, of idealization, and of envy when the patient is having a good experience in some form of therapy that the therapist has not experienced. None of these reactions is disabling, if the therapist is aware of them. But, they will inexorably be acted out to the detriment of the treatment and the patient if they remain unconscious, repressed, or disavowed.

What is the role of dream analysis in substance abuse treatment?

Generally speaking, dream analysis is not very helpful in the treatment of active substance abusers, although there are exceptions. The therapist must be alert to the use of the dream as a diversion from talking about the substance abuse.

Rose, an English professor, referred to elsewhere in this primer, was very avid to work on dream interpretation. Her dreams, in terms of manifest or discoverable latent content, never had anything whatsoever to do with her alcoholism. But dream analysis appealed to her aesthetically and intellectually, while serving the highly salient defensive purpose of keeping the session away from her drinking problem.

On the other hand, Bill, who rarely reported dreams, and who came to treatment for depression, not for substance abuse, reported the following dream: "I was standing in front of a crowd in my underpants, which were inside out and on backwards. They had a shit stain down the middle, and I was mortified." We worked with Bill's dream, which reflected many of his concerns about exhibitionism, about anal exhibitionism, about work inhibition, about disappointment in his mother's failure to respond to his mastery of the potty, to his difficulties in being "productive"; and yet our efforts to work with the dream seemed wooden, ineffectively bland, and not very meaningful. We couldn't "do" anything with it. The session went on to seemingly unrelated topics, and for half an hour or more, there was no mention of Bill's dream. Then, suddenly, just as the session was about to end, he snapped his fingers and said, "I know what that dream was about—I got shit-faced last night." As important as the latent content—shame over getting drunk—of Bill's dream was, it is important to note that it was also a transference dream in the sense that Bill dreamt it for me in order to tell me that his problem (or at least one of his important problems) was his excessive drinking. In telling me, he told himself; and the therapy was able to move on to work with Bill's drinking problem. So dreams are occasionally useful with active substance abusers, but not usually.

This raises an important dilemma for the addictions therapist. Should the therapist risk closing down the patient by actively keeping the focus on the addiction and its impact on that patient's life, or should the therapist let the patient free associate in the hope that the repression, suppression, and denial of substance abuse will surface and be available for psychotherapeutic work? The latter course risks playing into patients' avoidance of discussing their substance abuse. In the worst-case scenario patients complete the therapeutic process without ever facing and dealing with their chemical dependency. Rose had "successfully" undergone a prolonged analysis without ever having gotten in contact with her alcoholism. Whatever the analyst's counterresistance may have been, faulty technique assuredly played a role in what, from any objective perspective, must be judged a failed analysis.

Somehow, the addictions therapist must walk a tightrope that encourages the open experience of absolutely anything that concerns the patient, while not hesitating to confront and interpret "smoke screen" defenses including using dream reporting as an avoidance. There is no magic formula for doing this. Rather, experience and clinical intuition offer the best guides.

Stacy's presenting problem was compulsive (two-plus packs per day) cigarette smoking. Unlike in Bill's treatment, we both "knew" that Stacy's problem was addiction. A social worker with a private practice, her smoking was a social and professional embarrassment. Approaching 60, she was developing serious health problems secondary to her smoking—early signs of emphysema and a cardiac arrhythmia. In addition, her cutting off conversation to "go out for a smoke," evoked angry criticism from her children and from other family members. We considered whether this was part of the "payoff" of smoking—avoiding intimacy, expressing aggression. The children were hurt by her cutting them off to smoke and Stacy was being punished for that aggression by the anger it elicited.

We worked on Stacy's addiction in every way possible—exploring its conscious and unconscious meanings, its emotional and social origins, the contingencies maintaining it, strategies for coping with and reducing or ceasing it, and we even tried psychopharmacological interventions including patch, antidepressants, and antianxiety drugs. All to no avail. In spite of Stacy's stated motivation and persistent attempts to stop smoking, she seemed emotionally insulated from the negative consequences of that smoking. In this area Stacy's denial took the form of what Freud called "isolation of affect." She was perfectly aware of those negative consequences, yet seemingly had little or no feelings about them. Of course, it was possible that Stacy wanted to kill herself (on the installment plan). She struggled with survivor guilt having lost a child—and that may have been the payoff. Then again, it may not have been. After close to a year of therapy, Stacy reported the following dream: "I was on a kibbutz—my brother's kibbutz—I looked up and saw puffs of smoke coming from the Golan Heights. People started screaming and running and then I realized that the Syrians were shelling us. Each puff of smoke was an artillery battery firing. I woke up terrified."

Stacy's associations were to a nephew who was killed in the Yom Kippur War and to her last visit with her brother, the kibbutznik, an emotionally troubled, passionate Zionist who chain smokes. Stacy mentioned neither his chain smoking nor his advanced emphysema in her associations to the dream, although we had previously discussed them. Nor did she comment on the "puffs of smoke."

I said, "Stacy do you think that there is any connection between puffs of smoke raining down death in your dream and your smoking?" She stiffened and shuddered. After a few minutes of silence, Stacy said, "Oh my God. I'm shelling myself." I said, "And other people, too." She said, "That's horrible. I've identified with the enemy. I am the enemy. I am one of the Syrians killing my fellow Jews." I said, "Including yourself." She said, "Especially myself."

Stacy's isolation of affect vis-à-vis the self-destructive and otherwise negative consequences of her smoking was at an end. In the ensuing months she became increasingly anxious. I would like to report that Stacy stopped smoking, a more satisfying conclusion, from both a human and literary standpoint, but she did not. Instead, she quit therapy, most probably because my "breakthrough" interpretation of her dream made it impossible for her to emotionally deny any longer the damage she was doing to herself, while not yet ready to stop smoking.

Stacy needed to be anxious about the negative consequences of her addiction, but not so anxious that she needed to smoke to reduce her anxiety about smoking, in order for her to stop. Unfortunately, it is difficult for therapists to titrate anxiety with any precision. Nevertheless, I believe that the piercing of Stacy's denial through dream interpretation was a constructive step toward abstinence. She would not have dreamt the dream and reported it if some part of her did not want to know the truth. I hope she stopped smoking after leaving therapy with me. This, incidentally, is a common occurrence in addiction therapy. The first, or the second, or the third therapist doesn't get to see the fruits of his or her labor. But the next therapist does. Note the transparency of the dream to the therapist and its opaqueness to the patient.

In recovery, dream analysis is as useful with substance abusers as it is with any other patient. Dreams open many doors, and, as Freud suggested, can be the royal road to the unconscious. There is absolutely no reason why dream interpretation, in its many different variations and styles, is not appropriate with recovering substance abusers—whether that interpretation occurs in group, individual, or family treatment setting.

Why should substance abusers learn to laugh like Mozart?

In Hermann Hesse's 1929 novel, *Steppenwolf*, the protagonist, Harry Haller, is an estranged, brooding, marginal, close to schizoid, alcoholic. In the novel, which has long enjoyed a vogue among college students, and speaks strongly to young people, Haller, the wolf of the Steppes—this wild, undersocialized antihero—has two tasks to perform: one, he must learn to dance; and, two, he must learn to laugh like Mozart. This laughter has something to do with self-acceptance and acceptance of life. It is detached, and perhaps has a tinge of mockery in it—yet it is life-affirming. When I think of Hesse's notion of Mozart's laughter, I think of Mozart's opera *Don Giovanni* in which, its moralizing ending notwithstanding, there is such an understanding of the seducer and the seduced and all of the other characters—Mozart is somehow laughing with all of them—that the laughter becomes a kind of acceptance of life and all of its conflict—not a bad goal for substance abusers whose lives are filled with despair and disdain and who, like Harry Haller, the Steppenwolf, are alienated, estranged, isolated, and cut off from human sympathy and togetherness. Mozart's laughter both individuates and attaches. Someone once said that in the best case, we are alone together, while in the worst case we are alone alone. Laughter moves the substance abuser from being alone alone to being alone together. Heinz Kohut (1977) tells us that humor is one of the hallmarks of mental health, and a visit to twelve-step meetings, in which there is usually much laughter, will offer evidence that indeed humor and recovery reinforce one another.

What does Roberta *have to do with substance abuse treatment?*

In Jerome Kern's operetta *Roberta*, there is the song, "Smoke Gets in Your Eyes." Therapists need to remember that substance users have quite a flame for their beloved, and when they give it up they are feeling everything the protagonist of Kern's operetta expresses in Otto Harbach's words, "When a lovely flame dies, smoke gets in your eyes." The loss is very real, and very acute, and no matter what the exhilaration at having escaped a deadly trap, there is always somewhere—conscious or unconscious—profound sadness that a lifestyle, a life stage, a big chunk of the substance abuser's journey on this earth is being relinquished and left behind. This loss must be mourned. It is vital in the therapy of substance abuse for the therapist to enable and encourage that mourning.

If the patient doesn't bring it up, the therapist should: "There must be things you really miss about getting high every night." "You lost a lot of friends when you got sober." "Sobriety, no matter how wonderful for you, leaves some real holes." This is tricky for the therapist. The last thing we want to occur in therapy is to make the substance use seem so attractive and the yearning for it so deep that the patient decides to return to the beloved. Fortunately, in my experience, that doesn't happen when the adaptive side of substance use is acknowledged, and the very real loss often of people and relationships, which is easy for the therapist to disparage as false friendships, is deeply mourned.

To tell the patient, "Well, you'll have better friends in sobriety, they were just fair-weather barfly friends anyway," is to ignore where the patient is at, and to suggest something that does not yet seem real to the newly recovering user. Far more productive is acknowledgment of the real losses sobriety brings, and encouragement of the patient to mourn those losses. The smoke does indeed get in his or her eyes.

What is satanic grandiosity and how does it relate to substance abuse?

Satanic grandiosity is the claim that "I am the worst person in the world." This is something therapists frequently hear from substance abusers in one form or another. These patients insist that they are the most evil, the most contemptible, the most disgusting human beings on earth. This kind of apparent self-hatred is often not self-hatred at all. Rather, it is a claim to specialness. There are patients who are deeply and dangerously depressed, who savage themselves from quite a different position. That sort of self-loathing is not what I am talking about here. The satanically grandiose are proud of their unique evilness. To be more evil than anyone else is something of an achievement, in fact, a very great achievement. With patients who insist that they are worse than anyone else, and that they have done worse things than anyone else (and it is often the case they have done some pretty horrible things), I have several interventions that I customarily make. One is referral to a twelve-step program in which they will quickly hear that the other people in the room have done pretty much the same things. Another is to point out the pride and the power behind such a claim to being monumentally evil. This interpretation of the power drive behind the apparent self put-down can be very effective with the right patient at the right time. I will often say, "Your nastiness and rottenness is pretty much of the garden variety type; it is not nearly as unusual or unique as you think it is. Most people who use drugs steal, cheat, and manipulate in all sorts of ways. I know that you feel guilty and are filled with shame. But ironically, your breast-beating protects you from really feeling that guilt and shame. It is coming from a different place—a prideful place. It is hard to accept that you are not the biggest badass in the room, but are just another guy who has done some things he wishes he hadn't." This is quite confrontational, although it has some humor in it. It is an intervention to be used judiciously, but it does have its uses.

> *What does John Milton tell us about substance abuse?*

Satanic grandiosity brings Milton's *Paradise Lost* to mind. In a famous quote, Milton's Satan says, "Better to reign in Hell than serve in Heaven" (*Paradise Lost* 1:213). In that line, Milton perfectly captured the defiant rage of some substance abusers who, indeed, would rather reign in Hell than serve in Heaven. This sort of Satanic grandiosity is different than the kind I was speaking of above. It is far more difficult for the therapist to deal with the patient who is deeply committed to this existential stance, and there are many of them. Pride and rage keep a substantial number of substance users, who have long since ceased to get any pleasure from their use, using. The best the therapist can do if he or she senses that the continuing use is motivated by this kind of angry defiance is to make it conscious by interpreting it: "You really don't care that much about using anymore, it hasn't given you any pleasure for years. What keeps you in there is the rebellion and defiance that you feel you need to enact—and only know how to enact—by continuing your use. You feel that as hellish as your present life is, somehow you're in control of it, while if you moved into sobriety, other people would be in control. That thought is intolerable to you, and your intolerance may cost you your life."

What is terminal uniqueness?

Terminal uniqueness is a phrase used in twelve-step programs that refers to the resistance to being a member among members of the group manifested in an exaggerated sense of individuality, difference, and separation. It is intended to be a humorous way of dealing with pathological narcissism and reactive grandiosity. It is a twelve-step term that has its uses in professional therapy. I occasionally remind patients that their terminal uniqueness is threatening their recovery.

Could you give an example of terminal uniqueness?

A vivacious, overaged counterculture-type, Lucy had gotten into serious difficulties with alcohol and marijuana in her mid-thirties. She knew she had to stop, and like so many others, she did not want to. Unable to resolve the conflict, she voluntarily came for therapy. The opening session was certainly unique. Lucy reported the following:

I've never liked to drink all that much, although I've smoked pot since I was a teenager and never had any real trouble because of my pot smoking. Then my baby was born. She was born with a tail— that's a rare occurrence, but sometimes human babies are born with a tail. It was a very small tail, to be sure, but God it was cute. I loved her tail. But the doctors immediately wanted to amputate it. I refused. They wanted to take away my daughter's uniqueness. I thought it was really cool to have a tail. I didn't want my daughter to be deprived of her tail. It made her so special. I've always wanted to feel special—in some ways I do, but not special in the way that she would be able to feel having the only tail in the whole school. They sent up the social worker. I hated her. She was one of those grim "realists." There was a sociologist—I think his name was C. Wright Mills—who talked about crackpot realists. She was a crackpot realist. She really hammered away at me about what a bad mother I was. Well, she didn't actually say that, but that's what she was trying to make me feel. And I said, "No way, I'm not gonna have her tail sacrificed." Then my husband David got in on the act. He wanted Tanya's tail amputated, too. David and I have always had a little conflict over him being more square than me. But we've been together a long time and usually it works fine. I remember our first date. We wound up in bed and I said, "Eat my pussy/Spank my tushy." He said, "I'm not into kink." I was really hurt and angry. But we worked that out. I'm not all that kinky, and he's a little bit into kink so that part of it has been just fine. But the tail business I can't forgive him for. I really wanted Tanya to have that tail and there was nothing I could do about it—the doctors, the social worker, my husband. So she had the surgery. All you can see is that there isn't much of a scar left anymore, so she lost her chance to be unique. And ever since then, I've been drinking. Drinking like a fish—I never did that before—and smoking one hell of a lot of pot. I'm so sad that my daughter will have to go through life without a tail.

I commented, "Tanya's really going to need a sober mother because she's lost her tail and won't have that advantage in life." Lucy said, "You're right, I never thought of that. Yeah, the poor kid, she's not gonna have that way of being special. I guess she does need a sober mother. David really doesn't use drugs much anymore. Neither do most of our friends. Maybe I just needed to talk about this. Nobody—but I mean nobody—has been willing to listen. I'm not sure what it was all about, maybe I was being silly, but I just felt so isolated and so alone and so unhappily unique in wanting my daughter to have . . . ah, just something a little different. What's so wrong about that?"

Lucy achieved sobriety fairly easily. She continued to occasionally smoke a joint at parties, but essentially terminated her reactive substance abuse. The therapy then focused on her need to be unique. Coming from a large family of rather simple, unintellectual, nonaesthetically oriented people who placed great value on conformity, Lucy, from an early age, had tried to carve out some sense of specialness without very much success. Even in her bohemianism, she didn't really feel inside that there was much that made her unique. When her baby was born with a rare abnormality, Lucy latched on to that in an almost psychotic manner as a way of achieving some sort of vicarious fame, a sort of uniqueness by proxy. Clearly, Lucy's substance abuse had more roots than one, and had to do with many other things than her disappointment over her daughter's loss of her tail. Nevertheless, her story is a vivid example of the role of terminal uniqueness—here once removed (or vicariously fulfilled)—in the etiology and maintenance of substance abuse.

Why do drugs not ultimately satisfy?

Freud said that great wealth rarely brings happiness, because money is not an infantile wish. Neither is alcohol, cocaine, marijuana, LSD, or amphetamine. The infantile wish is for the symbiosis, the rise in self-esteem, and the regression to primary narcissism, which are concomitant with drug use at various stages of an addictive career. However, it is the hoped for—or feared—effect of the drug, not the drug itself, that brings satisfaction. Something closer to satisfaction is perhaps derived from the drug's symbolic meaning, which can be almost anything—mother, father, magical potency, omnipotence, omniscience. But drugs, in the end, do not satisfy, just as great wealth does not. What human beings want is love and a sense of accomplishment, and neither of those is available in a bottle, in a line, or in a joint. The users of those substances often become embittered and traumatically disillusioned because the magic they sought in their transferences to, and symbolic enactments with, those drugs proved illusory, as the drugs failed them, as they always do, in the long-term.

All of this is interpretable. It is useful and helpful for the therapist to talk to substance abusing patients about their bitter disillusionment with their beloved drug. It is horrible to be failed by someone—or in this case something—one had invested such hope in. Empathic probing of these feelings opens up opportunities for mourning, for acknowledgment of unrealistic expectations, and for beginning a search for better sources of gratification.

> *What does the length of the children's legs have to do with substance abuse therapy?*

A number of years ago, I was climbing Mt. Katadin, the highest mountain in Maine and the northern terminus of the Appalachian Trail. After an extremely difficult section of trail, which climbed almost perpendicularly for a sustained distance, I came across a bunch of 8-year-olds, obviously frightened, cold, miserable, and unhappy, under the tutelage of a disgruntled and frustrating expedition leader. I inquired if anything was wrong. He replied, "The children's legs are too short!" I replied, "The children's legs are exactly the length they're supposed to be. The problem is the size of your brain! The difficulty seems to be in asking them to do something beyond their capacities." He fumed, and I moved on.

Substance abuse therapists (and other therapists as well) sometimes get themselves into the position of the disgruntled youth leader. They stew because their patients' legs are too short to accomplish the task the therapist sets for them. There is an old social work adage, "You must be where the patient is at." I would modify that slightly to say that the therapist can, and should, lead a bit, but never be too far distant from where the patient is at. Substance abusers indeed have short legs. Their addictions have been exceedingly costly to them in terms of psychological and emotional regression. To expect too much too soon is to set up a failed therapy. Therefore, remember to take the length of the patients' "legs" into account when you start climbing the mountain of sobriety with them.

What does the "dummy from questions" have to do with substance abuse treatment?

My college buddy, Bill Hill, later became chief of the Census Bureau in New York. Bill tells a story of an incident from his first years with the bureau immediately after receiving his college degree. The bureau, which used part-time, seasonal enumerators, was very concerned that the work be done properly; therefore, it sent its permanent employees out on a random basis to check on the survey work done by its seasonals. So Bill, on one of his first assignments, was sent to a poor neighborhood, the Lower East Side of Manhattan, to check that the census worker had done his job properly. Walking upstairs in a four-story tenement, he rang the doorbell of Mrs. Epstein's neat, but sparse, railroad flat. He began to ask her about the census enumerator. For a long time she shook her head in bewilderment, but finally she said, "Oh, him? I remember him! Comes by me a dummy from questions. First he asked me, 'Lady, do you have a job?' I said, 'Mister, I'm 86 years old; I can hardly get to the bathroom, so do I have a job?' And then he asked me if I had a car. So I said, 'Mister, yeah—the two Cadillacs downstairs—they're mine.' He was some dummy from questions."

It is important that the substance abuse therapist not be a "dummy from questions." The intake forms that many agencies treating substance abusers use are indeed asking 86-year-olds if they are employed, and the impoverished, if they have a car. In an agency setting, the therapist often has no choice but to follow policy; however, in the private practice situation it is not necessary to put the patient through a predetermined intake protocol that contains questions having no relevance whatsoever to this particular substance abuser. Substance abusers are looking for reasons to reject therapy and the therapist. Insofar as possible, the therapist should not give them reasons. Accordingly, we should be parsimonious in our inquiries and not ask about things we don't need to know at that particular juncture. We should try not to convince substance abusers, who are all too ready to be convinced, that we are a dummy from questions.

Are there non–twelve-step self-help groups?

Yes, there are a number of them. A movement called Sobriety Without God has a limited number of meetings, although there is an agnostics' meeting in Manhattan, and I've heard of atheists' meetings elsewhere, but the problem is that members of those groups define themselves in terms of being in opposition to something—twelve-step spirituality—rather than being for something. Nevertheless, if such groups are available, some patients might do better with them than in twelve-step programs. A referral should certainly be made. Available in far more places are meetings of Rational Recovery (RR), a self-help program associated with Albert Ellis's rational emotive therapy.

Rational Recovery disputes the twelve-step notion that recovery lies in the addicts' admitting they are powerless and can only recover by dependence on the group and on the Higher Power. On the contrary, RR teaches that addicts do indeed have control over their behavior and that there is no disease driving them to drink or to drug. However, RR does speak of the "Beast" (which seems to me not very different from the "Disease"), but the Beast is seen as tameable, while the disease is seen to exist no matter how long one remains abstinent. Rational Recovery appeals to many people. Their meetings are led by unpaid cognitive rational-emotive therapists, whose reward beyond the pleasure of helping others, I assume, is referrals from the group. Rational Recovery tends to be open on abstinence, favoring it, but not insisting on it, and tends to view treatment as time limited rather than open ended. The groups discuss such things as drink signals, coping behaviors, dealing with early sobriety, dealing with relationships, and much the same things a group leader would do in any cognitive therapy. But the emphasis is on substance abuse and on self-efficacy (on the ability of the members of the group to solve their own problems).

In a rather adolescent act of rebellion against AA, whose "bible" *Alcoholics Anonymous* is known as the "Big Book" (Alcoholics Anonymous World Services 1952), the basic text of Rational Recovery is *Rational Recovery from Alcoholism: The Small Book* (Trimpley 1989).

Another self-help group is *Women for Sobriety*, a group founded about twenty years ago by a dissonant AA member by the name of Jean Fitzpatrick. She saw much of AA as being driven by an intuitive understanding of the dynamics of male addiction (particularly grandiosity and omnipotent control), and noted that many women did not need to admit they were powerless, but on the contrary needed to find their power and begin to assert it and to use it. To talk about surrender to a gender that had long since surrendered seemed counterproductive. Fitzpatrick, however, recommends meetings of her group as a supplement to twelve-step and doesn't feel she is competing with AA but is adding something to it. That differs from RR, which is clearly opposed to twelve-step.

Albert Ellis has since distanced himself from RR, not wishing to be in conflict with the twelve-step movement, although important parts of his treatment philosophy and approach are clearly at variance, if not in flat conflict with the twelve-step approach. Rational Recovery itself is a reaction against the twelve-step movement and its teaching of reliance on a Higher Power, emphasis on surrender, and on admitting powerlessness. The entire ideology of RR teaches its members the exact opposite; and it does it in an almost adolescent, rebellious way.

Women for Sobriety does not have the same angry tone as RR. Unfortunately, there are fewer meetings of Women for Sobriety. There are many twelve-step meetings that are for women only, and there is much more awareness in the twelve-step movement now of its male bias than there used to be. And not everyone would agree with those criticisms of the twelve-step movement that suggest it suffers from implicit sexism.

Referral to Women for Sobriety meetings can be a very effective adjunctive therapy for carefully selected female substance abusers. The same is true for Rational Recovery, for selected patients, male and female.

What did my mother teach us about the treatment of substance abusers?

One non–mental health professional, my mother, was a believer in long-term treatment. When I first went into private practice she said, "Jerry, don't make 'em feel good too quick or they'll leave." There is good reason (clinical, twelve-step experiential, and research-based) to believe that longer-term treatment is more effective than shorter-term treatment, and that substance abusers need to stay in therapy for a considerable period of time—some would say indefinitely. I wouldn't go that far. But certainly there is overwhelming evidence that most serious substance abusers manifest a lot of damage. Whether this damage is a consequence or cause, or both, it takes a long time to ameliorate. Managed care notwithstanding, longer-term treatment is more effective and has a better outcome in terms of sobriety and quality of life.

Another comment from my mother comes to mind in my treating substance abuse. I had two maiden aunts who were difficult, neurotic— albeit loving—and sometimes impossible people to deal with. My mother, responding to the lack of romance in their long lives, used to say, "Jerry, you have to remember they didn't have love." I sometimes think of this in working with substance abusers who are difficult, neurotic, and sometimes seemingly impossible to deal with. Some of them, too, have not been loved in their lives, particularly in their early lives. I realize that cannot have been totally true, or they would not have survived. But relative to optimal early experience they most certainly did not have "facilitating environments," to use Winnicott's phrase. I find it helpful in dealing with countertransferential frustration and rage to recall that many substance abusers, like my often unhappy aunts, have not had enough love in their lives. And, of course, substances can readily be manipulated, at least in fantasy, into ideal parents and ideal lovers. Hunger for love in childhood and in the present, which the patient—in this case the substance-abusing patient—does not know how to obtain from people very easily, results in a delusional attempt to meet this need with chemicals and compulsive activities of all sorts.

How does the therapist integrate treatment with substance abusers who require multimodal treatment?

There are two dimensions to be considered here. The first is what the therapist does to meet the need for integration and progression from the early building of a relationship, to confrontation and education, to cognitive/behavioral/how-to/relapse-prevention interventions, and then, after perhaps six months to a year of stable sobriety, to a more historical, interpersonal, intrapsychic, and psychodynamic approach in which long-standing conflicts and deficits are dealt with. If the therapist reverses this order, he or she will almost surely lose the patient. The patient who has recently come out of detox, and is vibrating all over the place in a state of cognitive confusion, is simply not ready to deal with his lust for his mother when he was 4, let alone with her responding to that lust in inappropriate ways (unfortunately a not uncommon occurrence in substance-abusing populations). What the patient needs to know is, "How do I get past First and Main, where my favorite bar is, when I'm on my way home from work?" He will never figure out that he can walk around the block and avoid the bar because the pattern of walking by it, and in it, is so ingrained. What he needs at this early point in therapy is some advice about handling his drink signal—in this case, Fourth and Main. Only much later will he be able to usefully incorporate the knowledge that the bar represents mother's womb and that he has long been suffering from birth trauma and wishes to return to the womb. (I exaggerate to make a point, at the risk of being somewhat ridiculous, although such dynamics are not unknown.) The dynamic of returning to the womb may be extremely important for the patient to know about and to understand if he is going to have a comfortable, long-term sobriety, but he is simply not ready to deal with this early on. During the first months of sobriety he needs the kind of cognitive approach I have been suggesting.

The other dimension concerns insight and working in the transference, rather than a succession of treatment approaches on the part of the therapist, who incidentally does not disable him- or herself as an interpreter of the transference later in treatment by having been active early in the treatment. On the contrary, taking an active, cognitive approach early on seems to strengthen the therapeutic alliance and enable a rich transference. As the treatment proceeds, the therapist simply backs off and becomes less active as time goes on. This works quite well. However, working this way only usually does not work.

Substance abusers are frequently so disabled by their condition that they need to be in a group as well as in individual therapy, perhaps also in family therapy, perhaps in twelve-step therapy, perhaps in a vocational program, perhaps on psychotropic medication or Antabuse or Naltrexone, and perhaps in a residential setting or day treatment setting or halfway house setting. Whether or not all or none of this is indicated must be determined by the treatment team or the therapist, and such a determination must be based on an in-depth evaluation of where the individual patient is at. Therapists should have highly trained assessment skills and an in-depth knowledge of community resources.

As soon as the treatment moves into such multimodal therapies involving more than one therapist, coordination becomes extremely important. The primary therapist must act as a general contractor or else the result is going to be one hell of a weird-looking therapeutic house. Multimodal treatment needs an architect as well as a general contractor, both incarnated in the primary therapist, to make this type of treatment work.

Multimodal treatments inevitably induce intense, complex countertransference, as well as competitive feelings, rivalries, envy, and hatreds— in short, all kinds of feelings in the therapists on the team. None of these disables the primary and secondary therapists if they are in contact with them. However, these feelings are highly disabling, and they will be acted out in destructive and self-destructive ways if the therapists lack self-awareness. Countertransferential projection, repression, and acting out are the rule rather than the exception if the therapist lacks insight.

Professionals have particular difficulty in dealing with "peer counselors" and their feelings toward them. "Who, me? With all my years of training, feeling resentful and in competition with the peer counselor in the therapy group that my client is in? Don't be ridiculous!" The ridiculous, however, may be the truth.

Could you say more about treatment modalities and settings?

Substance abusers are treated in many different settings. The detoxification unit is essentially a medical unit, but it should include some counseling or therapeutic elements. Some withdrawals are unpleasant, frequently being aborted by return to the drugs, and some can be dangerous and even fatal. Detoxification is a necessary, if not sufficient, aspect of treatment. In most cases it can be done on an outpatient basis with the addition of support and sometimes short-term medication, but some cases need to be treated on an inpatient basis by medical personnel.

Inpatient detoxification is often followed by inpatient rehabilitation, or the patient may enter the rehabilitation unit directly. These rehabilitation units are often found in hospitals, both private and public. They also find incarnations in the form of free-standing, sometimes quite elaborate and luxurious, facilities that traditionally offered 28-day programs, which had been the length of time that most insurance plans would pay for. Such coverage is hard to find these days, so most current rehabilitation programs are much shorter—one or two weeks. It is my strong belief that this is not nearly long enough for a large number of substance abusers to achieve stable sobriety. In fact, even the 28-day program was too short for many people. Inpatient therapy often means the difference between life and death. Tragically, the economic support for this kind of "long-term" inpatient treatment is a thing of the past.

Good rehabilitation facilities work their patients very hard. They provide intensive education on substance abuse; they also confront denial and do insight-oriented work with their patients. But they can be too rigid in insisting that participation in twelve-step programs is the only possible route to recovery, and they sometimes push patients into doing psychological work—such as looking at childhood antecedents of their addiction—before the patients are ready to do so. Nevertheless, rehabs are lifesaving and the therapist's referral for such a program may be a vital intervention.

Unless people are feeling very ill, they are usually resistant to inpatient treatment and it may take quite a sales job. Thus, therapists must know about and approve of the places to which they are referring patients. Rehabs are marketed aggressively; therapists can visit them and talk to the staff. Rehabs change in quality over time, so therapists must visit periodically.

The inpatient rehabs have been largely replaced by outpatient programs, which are generally four-night-a-week didactic, confrontational groups, which can be very effective; however, they cannot do the same job that inpatient programs are able to do. Outpatient rehabilitation programs are often necessary adjuncts to individual therapy during the patient's first few months of sobriety. Individual therapy, even reinforced by twelve-step participation, is often not enough structure and support to overcome the regressive pull of drugs. The outpatient group therapy program is worth a referral for patients who are shaky. There are many such programs, and like the inpatient programs, they are aggressively marketed, so they are not very hard to find. Some outpatient programs work very well with private-practice therapists; some do not and try to steal patients. Therapists need to develop their own network in which they have a comfortable relationship with the people who manage the outpatient group therapy programs. I would not recommend that the therapist refer patients to a program—in- or outpatient—with which the therapist does not have open communication.

Halfway houses offer some degree of staffing and some programs; sober houses, which have much less structure, provide a drug-free environment, and some group activities. The cost of such facilities is usually moderate and can make all the difference between recovery and relapse.

Outpatient, individual, private psychotherapy may not be sufficient in early treatment to facilitate recovery, but it can be the key to the whole recovery process, a process in which the individual therapist acts as primary therapist, and does the assessment and necessary referral. As the process moves along and the patient stabilizes, the individual therapy often becomes the primary therapy, and the ancillary therapies drop off one by one, with the possible exception of ongoing participation in a twelve-step program.

Intensive individual psychotherapy is a unique and powerful experience, and none of the other modalities offers the same kind of experience or the same opportunities for insight and growth; therefore, the recovering person who has not had individual psychodynamic therapy after the early cognitive work is done, is, I think, missing out on an opportunity to maximize the life possibilities that have opened up in sobriety.

Could you give an example of inpatient treatment?

In the old days, alcoholics and other addicts went to what AA calls the "flight deck," that is, the closed ward. Later on, substance abuse rehabilitation units came into being and psychiatric hospitalization became rare. Currently, the ravages of managed care health plans are closing one inpatient rehab after another, so we may see a return to treatment on the flight deck.

The experience of going through a psychiatric hospitalization is traumatic. For most addicts it is a profound narcissistic wound, cutting to the core of their being. It can serve as the "ego deflation in depth" necessary to penetrate grandiosity and denial, but that doesn't always happen. The experience of hospitalization may be so upsetting that the addict drowns his or her humiliation as soon as possible. There is a bar across from the Bellevue Hospital psychiatric ward that does a booming business serving the just-discharged. Any inpatient treatment—detox, rehab, psychiatric— is a crucial event in an addictive career. It can be a fulcrum around which recovery is organized, or it can fuel the feelings of rage, shame, hopelessness, and defiance that keep people drinking.

David is a retread. He had several years of sobriety before "slipping," and precipitously deteriorating. Skid row is called skid row for a reason, and David sure skidded. His bottom was a psychiatric hospitalization. Bottom is a state of being, an inner experience, so in saying that hospitalization was David's bottom I mean that it was the occasion for that experience, not the experience itself.

I met David some years after his hospitalization. He was a social worker who used a lot of psychiatric jargon as a defense against feelings. Intellectualization is an extremely popular defense among problem drinkers. It supports denial—"I'm so smart I can't be a drunk"—and it protects against feeling too much. Patients who drink too much intellectualize too much. Smarts can work against you if you use them to fool yourself. David is an intellectualizer who learned to feel. His bottom was dramatic, but his movement from defiance and denial to acceptance and serenity is something many substance abusers identify with. This is the story he told me:

Doctor, I've come to you because I'm not enjoying my sobriety, although my present unhappiness is paradise compared to how I felt during my drinking. I've been thinking about my drinking. Four years ago I wound up on the flight deck—that's AA-ese for the psycho ward. Naturally, I didn't go to just any psycho ward, I went to the University Hospital Psychiatric Clinic. I'd been drinking since high school, except for a couple of years in AA. I didn't much like AA; I was so much smarter than most of the people there. I always thought that I would drink again, but I didn't until I broke up with my girlfriend. I used that as an excuse to pick up a drink. Doctor, I am sure you've heard that alcoholism is a progressive disease—believe me, it is. It was sheer hell once I picked up that drink. I would go on a binge, not go to work, not go home, sleep in fleabag hotels, wake up shaking in the middle of the night and reach for the bottle or run past the other bums to find an open bar. Then I would go to a few AA meetings, get sober, and go back to work. But I couldn't sustain it. Before long I would pick up another drink and be off and running again. It, or maybe I should say, I, was crazy. Since I had been in AA I knew I had to stop drinking, but I wouldn't or couldn't do it. Things got worse. My sober periods became shorter, and when I drank I drank nonstop. I couldn't get my feet on the ground. Finally, I became so ill—physically and mentally—that I went to my doctor and told him I was going mad. He suggested that I take a little rest. I got drunk and went to my job, where I resigned with a flourish. I drank some more and blacked out. The next thing I remember I was signing myself into the mental hospital. It hadn't taken me long to change from a dissatisfied, anxious, but functional human being into a stumbling zombie who couldn't even remember how he got to the funny farm.

By then I had found a new girlfriend. I had stayed away from her when I was drinking so she hadn't seen much of me. I started to call her, but two attendants interfered. I started shaking. What had I done? Signed away my freedom? I wanted a drink. I wanted a thousand drinks. I wanted to leave. Too late! The attendants led me to the elevator. I told them that I had permission to make a call. Permission to make a call? Jesus Christ, what had I gotten myself into? I called my girlfriend and told her I had signed myself into the bughouse. She said, "Good, you should have done that long ago." I gathered that she had been less than delighted with my condition and I had thought that she didn't know. In AA they say the drunk is the last to know he has a drinking problem. I found out that's true. I told Annie, "I love you," and stumbled to the elevator. The attendants looked like concentration camp guards. The clang of dungeon (elevator) doors closing resounded in my ears—You raised your eyebrows, Doctor? Think I'm overdramatizing, don't you?—Of course, I threw away my freedom myself, but it felt like it was taken away from me. By then I was quaking inside and out.

The elevator door opened and I was in the "floor." It was dark and gloomy. I was locked in. For the next month I didn't leave there without an escort. Ever been locked up, Doctor? If you're writing that the patient suffered a blow to his self-esteem, you're right. I still shudder at those locked elevators. You can put down claustrophobia, too. I felt bewildered. I couldn't remember how I had gotten there or what I did that day. Now it was night and the place was deserted. There were bars on the windows. A shiver ran down my spine. I was told to take a shower—that made me feel dirty. I wondered if I smelled. My dread of being locked in faded some, but my blood alcohol level was falling and I was feeling more and more shaky. Every nerve was screaming for a drink. I barely managed to shower and put on a hospital gown. My arms and legs were rubbery and not working very well. Two very young residents arrived to examine me. They asked an endless series of stupid questions, which I resented. These "kids" weren't exactly great at establishing rapport, and I sure needed some rapport. I put them down because I was scared. I was in such bad shape that I had a hard time answering their questions. I thought, Oh shit! I really did it this time! I'm brain damaged! Mercifully, the residents switched to a medical mode and gave me a physical. I found this reassuring.

I had been drinking two quarts of rye a day for quite a while and you might say that I was more than a little worried about my health—You had better get your eyebrows analyzed, Doctor. They're out of control. I can't be your only patient who drank two quarts a day.—The examination ended and I fell into a stupor.

I woke feeling like death. A nurse told me to come to the dayroom. All I could think of was a drink and I made my way unsteadily down a seemingly endless corridor and found the dayroom. The people there didn't look like patients—however patients are supposed to look. I found this reassuring. Maybe this wasn't such a bad funny farm. I met my regular doctor, Dr. Kruse. I perceived him to be extremely authoritarian. He told me he was detoxifying me from alcohol and that I would be given decreasing dosages of medicine for five days and then nothing. He suggested I spend a few days in bed. I found Kruse so intimidating that I forced myself to enlighten him by telling him that alcohol strips the body of B vitamins and that I wanted vitamin therapy. Kruse prescribed the vitamins and I felt more in control. Pathetic isn't it, Doctor? Still, being able to ask for something and get it helped.

Then I panicked. Five more days and then no alcohol and no medicine. I literally didn't think that I would survive. I didn't have to deal with a drugless state for five days, yet I was going up the walls. I turned to my AA experience and decided that this was going to be tough but that I could deal with it a day, an hour, a minute at a time. And I did. My years at AA were not entirely wasted. I used the program to get through the hospital experience and to get all that I could from it. I decided not to stay in bed and to participate in the hospital program from the start. My desperate attempt to retain a little dignity in front of Kruse and my decision to use AA's day-at-a-time concept to do what I had to do to face drug-freeness were important events in my recovery. I know that sounds corny, Doctor, but that was the point that I started to fight to get well and somehow, sick as I was, I knew it then. Knowing it was almost as important as doing it, because knowing it changed how I felt about myself. Nothing like an "observing ego," as you shrinks say, eh Doctor? Smiled that time didn't you? Seriously, as soon as I was capable of it, I tried to understand what was happening to me as it happened to me. Sure, this was a defense against feelings and I can intellectualize forever, but this trying to understand also helped me a great deal. If it did nothing else, even if all the insight was pseudo-insight, it increased my self-esteem.—Interesting patient, aren't I, Doctor?

These vestigial feelings of self-worth and of having a coping strategy didn't last long. As I walked back to the dayroom, my skin crawled. My breath came hard, then seemed to come not at all. I started to hyperventilate. My palms dripped sweat; my heart pounded wildly; the vessels in my temples pulsed and felt like they would pop; my legs quivered; my hands shook; my vision blurred; the lights seemed to dim. Ever have a panic attack, Doctor? Do you know Edvard Munch's painting, *The Scream*? I see you do. Well, that's what it's like. Oh, why am I explaining—you're human aren't you? Nothing human is alien to me, eh? I must stop mocking you. It's part of my cool, detached, arrogant yet proper and polite persona. In the hospital, I was super polite and very controlled—under the shaking, that is. I liked to look in control. I acted superintellectual. Technical terms poured from my lips like I had four Ph.D.'s. It was a pathetic attempt to retain some dignity.

I was given my withdrawal medicine—pentobarbital. It felt wonderful; like two triple whiskeys. Soon I felt drunk once again, and loved it. This was only a reprieve, but I didn't care. It felt good.

I was soon staggering and slurring. Pat, the big, snappish, tough black nurse who had given me the medicine, tried to talk me into going to bed. I refused. She relented and I staggered from the nursing station to the dayroom, bouncing off the walls. I'm glad the hospital let me stagger around. I needed to be allowed to fight. The will to do so made the difference. It's a mystery, isn't it, Doctor. Why did I choose life instead of death? I don't know, but I did. God? The anabolic forces of the universe? A massive psychic reorganization? Who knows, but it happened. Somehow I was able to say to myself, "I messed up but I'm going to do it differently this time. I'm going to build on bedrock instead of sand." Somehow I knew that I could do that although I would forget and return to panic and despair. I decided to use everything the hospital had to offer and to get everything I could from the experience. Kind of goody goody, eh, Doctor? Of course I was casting myself in a heroic role and I enjoyed that. But so what. Why shouldn't I have enjoyed my private version of the myth of death and rebirth?

So I staggered into the dayroom. Sitting there were an angry-looking bear of a bearded middle-aged man and a seventy-ish, stylishly-dressed woman. Bill was slapping down cards from a Tarot deck with great force and looked every bit the conjurer. I wobbled across the room, introduced myself and said, "Will you overlook my ataxia and dysarthria? They're induced by the medication that I'm taking." Sadie looked blank. Bill said, "Sure kid," and slammed down the Tarot cards harder than ever. I lunged into a jargon-filled discussion of my condition. Bill said, "Sit down and let me get a reading." I continued to play the pleasantest of gracious intellectuals who knew more or less everything, and was willing to share it with all. As they say in AA, I was being a people pleaser. Bill and Sadie took it all in stride and again invited me to join them. This time I did.

I was slurring so badly that it would have been difficult to understand me even if I was making sense—which I wasn't. That didn't bother Bill or Sadie. As we say in AA, we ran our stories. Bill, a lecturer on communications, was manic-depressive. He was in the hospital because his wife was afraid of him. Looking into the deep pools of hatred and rage that were his eyes, I understood why. Sadie was 67 and in her third hospitalization for depression. She was very much the lady, and I thought it funny that her doctor had told her to buy a set of cheap dishes and smash them. I couldn't picture that. Internalized anger doesn't do much for people, does it, Doctor? It almost killed me. Just as we were getting acquainted, a chime rang. It rang for meals, for meds, for activities, for bedtime, for everything. Structure for the structureless, I suppose. Comfort in routine. I got to hate those chimes. The dayroom filled up and we were lined up and marched to the locked elevators. The attendants were actually kind and friendly, but I experienced them as prison guards. Being escorted everywhere through locked doors was humiliating. I staggered as the others walked. We were taken up to the top floor, which had a gym, game room, and a screened-in roof garden. The younger patients played volleyball while the older patients played board games. I didn't feel capable of doing anything so I went out on the roof garden and looked down at the traffic far below through the wire mesh. At least it's not barbed, I thought, as my depression rose like waves through the waning pentobarbital.

The next four or five days I followed the hospital routine as best I could. There was individual therapy, group therapy, recreational therapy, occupational therapy, dance therapy, and community meetings. As the withdrawal medication was reduced, my anxiety returned and once again, moved toward panic proportions. The slurring and staggering gave way to a sort of spasticity. I should mention that I was withdrawing from Valium as well as alcohol. My arms and legs would jump up much as if I was a dancer in the dance of the toy soldiers. It was embarrassing, although it was hard to feel embarrassed in the totally accepting atmosphere of the floor. It was also disabling. Without warning, an arm or leg would fly up. I remember sitting, playing bridge with Bill, Sadie, and "the Princess," a wealthy, uptight woman who had gotten herself hooked on pills and had attempted suicide. I had had my last dose of pentobarbital. I could feel the drug losing its effect. I was excited about being drug-free and terrified at the same time. Suddenly, the dayroom grew bright and the objects in it sharply defined. It was as if the lights had gone on in a dark theater. I was fascinated. So this was what the world was supposed to look like. I was dealt a hand. As I picked it up my arm involuntarily snapped over my head and the cards flew across the room. The heightened illumination of the room now seemed sinister. My thoughts raced. I thought, I'm going mad. This is the madhouse. I'm losing my mind. I'll never get out of here. I felt sheer terror. Yet, I picked up those cards and bid one no-trump. Made the hand, too. I wanted to talk about what was going on inside of me but I was afraid to. My thoughts became more confused. I jumped up, ran to my room, and collapsed. Doctor, I know part of it was physiological, but I must have been close to madness that night.

I fell into a troubled sleep. After I don't know how long, I woke to one of the strangest sensations I have ever felt. Waves of force emanated from the center of my abdomen, traveled through my body, and smashed against my skin. Rhythmic and relentless, wave succeeded wave. It felt like I would shatter. The impact of the waves against the surface of my body was so strong that I feared that I would fly off the bed. I reached up, grasped the bars of the bed, and held on for dear life. Smash, smash, smash, the waves kept coming relentlessly, inexorably. I thought of screaming out, but I didn't. Suddenly a thought occurred to me. "Good God! That's my anger—my rage—my, my, my anger coming out. This is not something happening *to* me; it *is* me. It's my rage!" I held on to that thought as my last tie to reality. I repeated to myself over and over again, It's my anger and nothing else.

Doctor, it was sort of a Copernican revolution. It was my Copernican revolution. What I mean is that that thought changed the center of things for me like Copernicus changed the center of the solar system. It was I who was doing this thing, not some outside force. It took a long while for the waves of pressure to stop shattering themselves against my flesh, but the terror was gone. I fell into a deep sleep from which I awoke drained, yet somehow freer than I had been for a long time. Doctor, I suppose that you would classify what happened to me as a somatic delusion, but that doesn't matter. What does matter is that I was able to use it to "own" my anger.

The floor had two long arms connected to a body consisting of the dayroom, the nursing station, and the dining room. During the days following the anger waves, I paced those arms, the corridors, obsessively. You are probably thinking I was going in and out of Mother's arms to her breasts, the nursing station. Perhaps you're right on that, Doctor. It's probably of some significance that I forgot to mention that my mother was critically ill during my final binge.—Responded to that one, didn't you Doctor?—As it turned out, Mother survived, but her illness must have had something to do with my prolonged binge.

One of the things I am most grateful to AA for is that it taught me how to mourn. When I returned to AA, I was able to mourn my father. That was an old loss and I think that my failure to come to terms with my feelings about him and his death were connected to my slip. Gratitude for being able to mourn. That's really crazy, isn't it, Doctor? I'm embarrassed by the depth of my feelings. AA puts a lot of emphasis on gratitude—gratitude for sobriety, gratitude for the program itself. Sure, sometimes that gratitude is defensive, another form of denial; but sometimes it's genuine. At least it has been for me, and that's really important. It may sound like I'm intellectualizing again, but I'm not. On the contrary, I'm choked up thinking of all I have to be grateful for.

As the days passed, the spastic jerking of my extremities became less frequent. I still paced, but the focus of my concern had shifted. I became hypochondriacal and drove Pat, the nurse, crazy. Pat did not take kindly to my pestering and I considered her the floor ogre. During my hypochondriacal phase, I was very aware of my anger. At times it was so intense that I thought it might break me in half, but never after the anger-wave hallucination did I experience it as external. It was an objectless anger— free-floating rage.

I was so overwhelmed by the intensity of my rage and fear, that I self-consciously tried to constrict my experience to an instance at a time. My world became more and more constricted until I was living in a succession of infinitesimal discrete moments, an infinitesimal at a time so-to-speak. I did not dare look even five minutes ahead or behind. To do so engendered too much fear. I similarly constricted my spatial world. I mean this quite literally. When my anxiety was high enough I could feel my world shrinking toward an instant and a point. It was as if there was a camera in my head being focused more and more narrowly. I remember being in the gym totally overwhelmed by rage and fear and something like despair as I stared at the punching bag. Suddenly, my visual field narrowed to a patch of pebbly brown. I tried to expand my visual field, but I couldn't. I thought, You really did it this time. All you can see are spots! Then I thought, So be it, and I started pounding that patch of pebbly brown with the pent-up rage of a lifetime. When I stopped, wringing wet and exhausted, my point-world gradually expanded to encompass the gym and my fellow patients. That was scope enough for me. I knew that something important had happened, but I didn't understand what. I spent many hours punching that bag. It helped.

The hospital I was in did a terrific job of creating a sense of community. For all of the inevitable aloneness, there was a real feeling of shared adventure and of closeness on the floor. I liked the hospital's emphasis on being honest about your feelings and expressing them. It wasn't AA, but its values were similar. I know that I also have a lot of negative feelings about the hospital and the way I was treated like a prisoner. But my positive feelings aren't all phony or a form of denial either.

Paradoxically, my period of being "stimulus bound," as I thought of it, coincided with my increasing involvement in the life of the floor. The way my perception of the world would expand and contract was almost cinematic. During my expansive periods, my relationships with Bill, Sadie, and the Princess, Jan, deepened. There was a real bond around the bridge table, a bond not without its conflicts and disturbances. I became increasingly afraid of Bill. He looked like he might kill everyone on the floor. Sitting across from him at the bridge table was no easy thing. He was threatening to sign himself out because his psychiatrist was insisting that he take an antipsychotic. I told him I thought he was dangerous and that he should take the medicine. Amazingly, he agreed. After that, we became closer and I was initiated into Tarot-card mystique. When I had a good reading, I felt elated. A recovery is made of many tiny steps, like those infinitesimals I spoke of, that accrete into something substantial and solid. Telling Bill he was dangerous was such a step for me.—I'm preaching to you, aren't I, Doctor?—Sadie was a lovely person who had had a lot of loss. I wished she would break those dishes. The Princess could be arrogant, but she was bright and witty. I enjoyed her. She had been in the hospital for a long time and was scheduled for discharge. She went on pass and took an overdose. Her suicide gesture greatly upset me. I thought nobody gets out of here intact. I was surprised when the Princess was discharged anyway. She was replaced by an overtly psychotic patient. When I told him I was in for alcohol abuse, he said, "Oh, that! I stopped drinking years ago and joined AA. Look at me now!" This frightened and discouraged me more than the Princess's suicide attempt. About the same time, a late-middle-aged man was brought in on a stretcher. He was also an attempted suicide. He turned out to be a physician whose son had been killed in a South American political upheaval. He clearly did not want to live. The sadness in his eyes was as profound as the anger in Bill's. He was a charming and worldly man whose charm and worldliness were clearly automatic and emptily mechanical. He insisted on leaving the hospital. I was sure that he was going to his death.

During my "social period," I felt a great need for approbation. After I confronted Bill, I seemed to regress. He improved on his medicine and was out on pass most of the time. The Princess was gone. Sadie offered little companionship. I felt isolated and alone. I became even more of a people pleaser. I felt that I needed the approval of every single person there. My facade turned people off, particularly Pat. Every night we had a community meeting. The night Jan left and Bill's discharge date was set, I was particularly forlorn—left behind in the madhouse. At the community meeting some blowhard droned on, monopolizing the conversation. I was furious, but said nothing. I couldn't risk alienating anybody. I should tell you that a psychotic medical student had been brought in that day. Julie was a student at Einstein and kept repeating, "E equals mc squared." In the course of the day, she became more and more disorganized. They put her in the quiet room, an isolation cell used for out-of-control patients. The quiet room held a peculiar fascination for me. I was utterly and totally terrified by it. I was afraid of losing control—and I unconsciously wished to. Fear of confinement permeated every fiber of my being. The quiet room was a prison within a prison. I identified with Julie and her "E equals mc squared," and by that night all of my terrors were focused on the quiet room. At that community meeting I was not only desperately into people pleasing, I was in dread of losing control and being put in the quiet room.

So there I was, listening to a long-winded asshole ramble on. Suddenly, I knew I had to say something. I was slumped down in a couch, almost buried in it. It took every bit of my strength to force myself to sit up. Sweating and shaking, I finally managed to say, "I don't like what you're doing. You're taking over this meeting. Sit down and shut up." My body almost convulsed, but I had done it! I sank back into the couch. That was one of the hardest things I have ever done. It took more courage to say those few words than to accomplish many of the more significant things I have done. At the end of the meeting, Pat came over and put her arm around me and said, "You did good." I won't forget that.

Speaking up at the community meeting opened things up for me. Julie grew increasingly agitated. I thought that she was reacting to being locked in the quiet room. Put in the quiet room because she was agitated—agitated because she was put in the quiet room. I would look hypnotically through the window of her locked door. She became more frantic. Finally they "snowed" her—put her out with massive doses of tranquilizers. Now she lay on the floor of the quiet room, unconscious, with her arm raised and splinted as an IV dripped into it. I thought, They're killing her. I became totally absorbed in her fate. The quiet room became a symbol of all I feared and dreaded, yet perhaps secretly wanted. After all, hadn't I rendered myself unconscious with a drug—alcohol? Hadn't I sought death? That day in my session with Kruse, I said, "I'm afraid of you, you have too much power." The reference was to Julie, but I was thinking of myself. Making this comment to Dr. Kruse was difficult, but not as difficult as speaking at the community meeting. Courage is cumulative—each instance of it makes the succeeding one easier.

Another way in which I opened up was by running my story. I had learned to do this in AA. I ran my story to everybody who would listen and to some who didn't. I did it in group therapy, at community meetings, with the staff, and with my fellow patients. Each time I told my story, I learned something new.

I also opened up physically. I had been involved in recreation therapy, playing volleyball with the greatest reluctance. I played fearfully, holding my body tight and closed. I was self-protective to an extreme. Naturally, my playing was awful. A few days after the community meeting, I was cajoled into playing. This time it was different. I could feel the energy flowing through my body. I became the game. I felt myself leaping into the air. I felt myself coming down hard. I felt myself taking risks. The closeness, the tightness, the self-protectiveness fell away. It was wonderful. They say that how you play the game is a picture of yourself. It's true. I was not self-conscious while it was happening, but afterward I processed what had occurred and that helped, too.

I had a similar experience in occupational therapy. At first I was reluctant to do anything. I looked upon arts and crafts—"basket weaving"—with contempt. But I thought to myself, I'll do this garbage anyway since I've decided to work the hospital for all it's worth. Commitment won over arrogance. I struggled for weeks to make a ceramic ashtray. At first it was almost impossible because my hands shook so much. Finally I finished the damned thing. I couldn't believe my reaction. I was ecstatic! I had proved that I could function in the face of anxiety. I told Pat that the ashtray was "an external and visible sign of an internal and invisible grace." She treated this bit of pretension with the contempt it deserved, but the idea behind it is valid enough. I think of that ashtray whenever I think I can't do something.

Julie stayed "snowed out," and I kept returning to her window to stare at her prostrate body much like a child compulsively putting his tongue to a sore loose tooth. One of the staff told me, "It's okay. She needs to regress." I oscillated between thinking that this was a bullshit rationalization for what they had done to her and that it reflected really deep empathy. I guess that reflected my ambivalence toward the hospital—mistreated and understood at the same time. A few days later Julie was released from the quiet room. She and a rough street kid named Ruth immediately became friends. I remember one exchange between them. Julie asked, "How is this nuthouse different from all other nuthouses?" Ruth answered, "It's the real McCoy." For some reason I loved the medical student and the street kid for this exchange.

I was getting better. I was given a pass to leave the hospital. As I walked out of the hospital and started to walk down the street, I felt a magnetic force drawing me back to the hospital. I don't mean this metaphorically. I mean I actually felt pulled back to the hospital. Another quasi-psychotic episode, I suppose. I said, "No, this can't be happening." But it was. It felt like the force would pull me back. I fought it and succeeded in breaking loose. No doubt a projection of my desire to cling to the mother, eh, Doctor? Or was it the regressive, seductive pull of addiction? Fortunately, I had had enough regression; I feared it more than I desired it. I started to run and didn't stop until the pull was gone.

I felt a surge of joy. I was free. I bounded toward the park. I felt as if I had springs in my heels. Looking back on it, I was more than a little manicky. AA calls this the "pink cloud." I ran toward the polar bears at the zoo. They seemed glad to see me. We spoke for a while. I felt a great sense of communion with the polar bears. A psychologist wrote of the toddler's "love affair with the world." My feelings in the park were like that. Later in the day, I stubbed my toe, so to speak, and ran crying back to my mother-hospital. You know, Doctor, AA's like that—a safe home base from which you can go into the world, take your lumps, and return to be comforted. We all need that, don't we?

After a while I left the park and went to my new girlfriend's. The hospital strictly regulated phone calls and visits. When she was finally allowed to visit, Ann had been very supportive. I shared as much of my hospital experience with her as I was able to. I had an overwhelming fear of being impotent sober. If you've been to AA meetings, Doctor, you know that that's a very common fear. At her last visit, I had spent an hour explaining to Ann that we couldn't make love for at least a year. I was perfectly serious. Five minutes after I arrived in her apartment, we were in bed. Everything went fine.

Several hours later, I left Ann to go to an AA meeting. I had come down off my "pink cloud," but I was still feeling good. That wasn't to last long. I was excited about going back to my old group. I had bounced in and out of that meeting during my nine months of drinking. Now I was sober and hopeful. I walked into the meeting and immediately felt estranged. I couldn't connect with anything or anybody. It was horrible. I sat through the meeting, but I really wasn't there. I felt very far away. It was as if a viscous fluid surrounded me and isolated me. Again, I do not speak metaphorically. I could feel that viscous medium intruding between me and the people in that room. It prevented me from making human contact. It was like being under water. I must have been doing the distancing, but I sure didn't know that I was doing it. I left in a state of deep despair. Whatever my ambivalence toward the hospital, I felt warmth and concern there. I had counted on finding that at my AA meeting. I didn't, or couldn't, or didn't want to, or something; but it surely didn't work. I have never felt as alone as I did on my return to the hospital. I felt defeated and profoundly depressed. I wanted to give up. I think that was my bottom. I knew that I couldn't drink anymore. It just wasn't going to work for me, but I wasn't at all sure that I wanted to live if sobriety was going to be like that.

During the following days I went through the hospital routine mechanically. My friends had been discharged, making me feel even more forlorn and abandoned. For some reason, I didn't talk about my experience at the AA meeting. Although Julie was out of solitary, I was still obsessed with the quiet room. Although I didn't know it, I had put myself into a quiet room by emotionally detaching at that AA meeting. My discharge was approaching. I thought that I would probably kill myself. I was given another pass. I didn't want to use it, but I did. With great reluctance, I decided to try a new AA group. This one met at the Church of the Epiphany, a few blocks from the hospital. I was very shaky as I walked into that meeting. I didn't really expect anything good to happen. The meeting started. The preamble was read: "Alcoholics Anonymous is a fellowship of men and women who share their experience, strength, and hope with each other . . ." Something happened. Those words sounded like pure poetry.

The speaker was a beautiful young woman, intensely and vibrantly alive. Her vivacity and sparkle certainly facilitated what was about to happen. She spoke of her years of drugging and drinking, of her progressive spiritual and emotional death. Finally she said, "I got to the point that I couldn't feel anything. For no particular reason I went on a trip across the country with some drinking buddies. As we crossed the country, my feelings became more and more frozen. We arrived at the Grand Canyon. I looked at it and felt nothing. I knew that I should be responding with awe and wonder to the sight before me, but I couldn't. I had always loved nature, and now that love, like everything else about me, was dead. I decided to take a picture of the magnificence that spread before me so that if I ever unmelted I could look at the picture and feel what I couldn't feel then."

At that moment, something incredible happened to me. I completely identified with the speaker. I understood her frozen feelings; they were mine. I understood her wish to preserve a precious moment in the hope that someday she could adequately respond with feelings of awe and wonder to it. Something welled up in me. I began to sob—deep, strong, powerful sobs. They did not stop for the hour and a half that the meeting lasted. As the speaker told her story—how she managed to stop drugging and drinking and how her feelings had become unfrozen—my feelings became unfrozen. I was still crying when I shook her hand and thanked her. I walked out of the meeting feeling happy. *Happy*, Doctor! I couldn't even remember feeling happy.

As I walked down the street toward the hospital, the tears were still flowing. Now they were tears of happiness and gratitude. I who had been so formal and controlled and concerned to impress, walked past staring strollers with tears streaming down completely indifferent to, indeed oblivious of, their reactions. Doctor, do you know Edna St. Vincent Millay's poem '*Renascence*'? It tells of a young woman who has been buried, then the rain comes washing her grave away, returning her to life. She becomes aware of "A fragrance such as never clings/To aught save happy living things . . ." I had always loved that poem, now I truly understood it. My tears were like the rain in the poem. They, like the rain, washed me out of the grave I had dug for myself with alcohol and emotional repression. I, too, smelled the fragrance that never clings to aught save happy living things.

I walked into the floor feeling buoyant. As I joined the perpetual rap session in the dayroom, a thought came to me, God is in the quiet room. I didn't know where it came from, nor what I meant by it, but I vocalized it. I think it had something to do with feeling loved and connected and potentially capable of loving. It seemed that whatever I had experienced at that AA meeting was also present in the quiet room. That's as close as I can get to understanding what I was trying to express in that phrase. What happened at the meeting had something to do with receptivity—with being open and being able to hear. That part of it was a gift. From whom, I do not know.

Well, Doctor, I'm not much on theodicies, and I can't do much with a young girl going mad as a manifestation of divine grace. I don't know who or what, if anything, is out there and I haven't become religious in any formal sense. I don't belong to a church. So when I said, "God is in the quiet room," I must have meant it in some metaphorical sense. But I did mean it. There was certainly denial in that statement—denial of evil and pain and sorrow, denial of all I hated about the hospital, denial of my rage at the waste that my life had been. But there was something else in it too;

something that liberated me to engage in the long, slow, up-and-down struggle for health. In AA we say that sobriety is an adventure—it certainly has been for me.

What is network therapy?

Network therapy is a variant on family therapy developed by Mark Galanter (1993) at New York University Medical School. In network therapy, the patient who wishes to achieve sobriety, but has difficulty with impulse control, is asked to form a network of people to help him or her maintain sobriety. For example, Bill is trying to get off of heroin and generally does pretty well during the workweek but has an awful time on the weekends when he has had a number of slips. The therapist engages Bill about the possibility of arranging to have someone do something with him during this period of vulnerability. Alternate activities are discussed. It turns out that Bill had been a wonderful basketball player in high school, and that he still loves to play basketball, but rarely has an opportunity to do it. The therapist asks if he has any friends who don't use drugs who also like to play basketball, and he thinks of his cousin John, who, as a matter of fact, has five years in recovery and loves to play basketball. The therapist asks, "Do you think we could get John in here and see if John could take you to the gym on Friday nights, your period of greatest vulnerability? That way he could help you avoid using heroin at your Friday night weak time by playing basketball with you." John is invited to participate in the therapy. If he accepts, his going to the gym with Bill is arranged. If possible, other people are added to the network. The therapist identifies anxiety as another of Bill's triggers. In talking about how to deal with his anxiety, Bill, the identified patient, remembers that he always feels better when he is with his mother and that she is very calm and soothing, whatever the conflicts between them may be. The therapist arranges for Bill to call his mother whenever he feels anxious so that she will be able to literally, or symbolically, serve him chicken soup. And so on, until a viable network is built, a network usually consisting of two to five persons. The therapist then arranges to meet with the entire network to coordinate the treatment plan and continues to meet with the network once a month, while the patient continues to be seen on a regular basis, once or twice a week.

In network therapy there are no secrets. Whatever threats to the identified patient's sobriety come up are openly discussed. However, there is no discussion of the psychopathology of the network or the role the family may have in perpetuating the addiction. The therapist speaks to only the healthy side of the system, the part that wants Bill to recover, and not to the part of the family members or friends that may want to undermine Bill's recovery.

The psychopathology in the family, or the system, is ignored. This is common in family approaches to addiction (see Levin 1998). There are basically two approaches to family therapy of addiction. One approach shares with network therapy a strategy that ignores or even suppresses family conflict. This approach utilizes the understanding of, but does not interpret, family dynamics. Working with family pathology is held to be irrelevant to the identified patient's achieving sobriety and appeals more to the capacity of the family to work as a task (rational work) group rather than unmasking it as a basic assumption (driven by unconscious needs) group, to use Bion's (1959) distinction.

The second approach to the family therapy of addicts takes the opposite tack, believing that the identified patient cannot recover until the family stops enabling and undermining for reasons, conscious and unconscious, of its own. Therefore, it works with the family directively or interpretatively to change behavior or to increase insight.

Network therapy typically lasts six months to a year. It is seen as transitional and adjunctive to an intensive individual psychotherapy, which has both a cognitive and a dynamic dimension. There are currently outcome studies being conducted, but impressionistically, network therapy seems to be quite successful with the right patient and the right network. The "right" patient is rather similar to the ideal Antabuse patient, who is motivated to stop but has poor impulse control, and who needs help in controlling his impulses. From this point of view, network therapy is a kind of interpersonal Antabuse.

What is the role of family therapy in substance abuse?

Addiction is held to be a family disease in several senses: (1) it runs in families, for whatever reasons: genetic predisposition, modeling, self-medication of the pain of growing up in such a family, identification, identification with the aggressor, or social learning; (2) families consciously and unconsciously have been known to maintain an addiction, or to need the identified patient to be a patient; and (3) the impact of the substance abuse itself by the active user can be devastating on family members. Therefore, it is held by many in the addictions field that family therapy is a necessary modality if recovery is to occur. Necessary, I don't know about, but desirable, it often is.

All of the major schools of family therapy have had their techniques adopted to the treatment of substance abuse and those readers who are interested in the details of each of the schools and their application should consult my 1998 book, *Couple and Family Therapy of Addiction*. Many rehabilitation programs have family days, or family weeks, in which the family is admitted to inpatient treatment and has a chance to look at itself and the pain that it may have experienced in the course of the identified patient's addiction, as well as to look at its role in maintaining that addiction.

Many individual therapists will ask the family to come in for a few family sessions to help with the readjustment to sobriety. Although it is easy to commit the error of blaming the victim(s)—the spouse or other family member—of the addict's aggression and regression, thereby inflicting a grievous narcissistic wound, this need not occur. This blaming of the victim occurs when the therapist overzealously and tactlessly interprets unconscious needs to have the user use, which the family may very well have. However, even if this is true, it needs to be approached delicately. But complicity by the family has gotten to be something of a cliché. Certainly the impact of the user's use on the family members is profound, and often, at some level, wished for. This, too, must be dealt with in the family's sessions.

The usual outcome of short-term family therapy is the entering into individual therapy by the various members of the family. I believe that one of the most salient and therapeutic aspects of short-term family therapy with addictive families is precisely this process of helping people get help for themselves. In a private practice situation, of course, that can be very helpful to the therapist in terms of building practice. It is also very helpful to the family members who are inevitably affected in one way or another by the addiction, and never in positive ways.

Yet another reason for working with the family is that homeostasis—the inertia in the system—does, indeed, work toward maintenance of the status quo or reversion to the status quo ante. There is often resistance on the part of the family not so much to sobriety as to the changes that go with it.

Human beings do not relinquish power gladly, and, generally speaking, recovering people tend to want to resume their former role in their family and take back control and power. That can lead to all kinds of chaos, and not infrequently, to divorce. The recovering person is then profoundly disillusioned and deeply hurt: "Here I am trying, I'm sober and she walked out on me." Then there's bewilderment and, not infrequently, relapse. Obviously, this needs work, whether in individual or couple or family therapy.

Family therapy can also be very helpful to adolescent children of substance abusers, whether the parent or parents are active and/or in recovery. Referral to such groups as Alateen, which works with the teenage children of alcoholics and other addicts, can be transforming. Such youngsters are often confused by the change of their roles in the family and in the behavior of their parent as their parent's disease progresses. They are just as confused when roles are once more reversed in recovery. What is happening around them in the external world makes no sense, and they are confused about their feelings. The children of substance abusers need a lot of help negotiating that treacherous passage of their parent's recovery. The job for the therapist is particularly difficult in working with a recovering family because the therapist does not want to shut down family members' rage, hurt, and shame, but on the contrary allow for their open expression, yet, at the same time, the therapist may very well want to talk about the addiction as a disease (if he or she believes in the disease model) in order to reduce some of the pain and the blame. The question is how to do this without making family members feel guilty for having those feelings. This is not an easy job. The best that can be done is for the therapist to point out that cancer, which also may be partly caused by the lifestyle of the sufferer, is also a disease, yet the families of cancer patients are inevitably, albeit usually unconsciously, enraged at the patient for having it. This gives the family members permission to feel whatever they are feeling, while continuing to provide a cognitive structure for and rational explanation of a bewildering, hurtful, chaotic experience.

What is the role of group therapy in the
treatment of substance abuse?

Groups are held to be the most effective treatment modality with substance abusers—an opinion I don't share. For some patients they are, and for others they are not. Undoubtedly, they are quite effective therapeutically, as well as cost-effective. Groups are used on a daily basis in inpatient settings where they function primarily to break down denial, and to identify drink and drug signals. Group is the usual modality of aftercare and early recovery. The style of these groups is didactic. The ones run by or sponsored by rehabilitation facilities are almost inevitably twelve-step oriented; they talk a lot about the program and focus on getting people to go to twelve-step meetings. Early sobriety outpatient groups also concentrate on breaking down denial and on making drug signals (triggers) conscious. They teach coping mechanisms and try to increase "self-efficacy," the notion that the patient can get through situations and has the resources to do so without resorting to drugs. The group leader conveys this belief, and he or she and the group itself teach concrete coping skills. Aftercare groups, unfortunately, often have a high rate of recidivism, and the modeling of relapse may undo whatever good such groups do. Thus therapists who refer to, rather than lead, such a group should find one with a reasonably high rate of stable sobriety.

Middle-distance groups function somewhere between early sobriety and psychodynamic groups. They begin to look at the interaction within the group and use that as a feedback mechanism. They also begin to deal with historical issues and they begin to talk about transference. Nevertheless, they are still highly oriented to behavioral and cognitive interventions dealing with drug signals and coping with sobriety.

Third-stage groups are psychodynamic outpatient groups, except that they are homogeneous, insofar as members are substance abusers in recovery. My preference is for the patient to be in just an ordinary psycho-dynamic therapy group, which in some ways cuts down the possibility for identification because it has less homogeneity, yet it has the advantage of opening up a much broader world of experience in which the treatment is no longer focused on the use of drugs or the avoidance of the use of drugs.

Groups are powerful, and all three stages of substance abuse recovery groups have their uses. They are effective adjuncts to individual therapy, and often effective therapies in and of themselves without individual therapy. My own preference is for conjoint therapy, in which the patient is in both individual and group treatment.

For those patients who are not twelve-step oriented and for whom such a referral is not going to work because they are not comfortable with and want no part of the program's ideology, other adjunctive supports may be necessary. Whatever the resistance and denial aspect of these patient's rejection of membership in AA or NA (which needs to be interpreted), their rejection also needs to be respected. If the therapist is working with a patient who has gone through an inpatient rehab and is now in the rehab's aftercare group, in which a large part of the group's emphasis is on going to meetings, there may be a very real conflict in that patient if the AA-NA weltanschauung is unpalatable to him or her. In such a situation, the therapist must remain neutral and help the patient examine the pros and cons of going to twelve-step and his or her feelings about being pushed into the program. However, after the exploration has been completed, it is appropriate for the therapist to support the choice not to participate in twelve-step if that makes sense for that particular patient. Such an outcome makes it virtually impossible to continue in the early recovery group offered by the rehab, and some other form of group therapy should be substituted for it.

> *What is the role of neurobiofeedback in*
> *substance abuse treatment?*

Peninston and Kulkosky (1989, 1990) have used neurobiofeedback as the treatment of chronic alcoholism and drug addiction in various VA hospitals with quite good results. We don't know exactly how it works, but the idea is that therapists first give alcoholics autogenic training (a form of relaxation training developed by Jacobson [1938]), so that they can get into an alpha state (a brainwave state associated with peacefulness and serenity) and then train them to move into the alpha state using neuro-biofeedback. Presumably, this training will generalize, and alcoholics so trained will be able to induce alpha when they are feeling stressed and their thoughts would otherwise naturally go to drinking or drugging.

There have been some strange reports of unexpected side effects of this kind of treatment. For example, some who have gone through the training subsequently become ill if they drink after the neurobiofeedback experience. It is almost as if these alcoholics were taking a drug like Antabuse, though they are not. Apparently, the neurobiofeedback has done something to the brain chemistry that leads to a different reaction to the alcohol. Another totally unpredicted occurrence was the sudden derepression of traumatic memory during neurobiofeedback. This can be a devastating experience unless the therapist helps the patient process and work through the derepressed material. Although this side effect is infrequent, it is not rare. Presumably being in an alpha state relaxes psychological defenses including repression, allowing the return of the repressed. However, the phenomenon is not really understood.

In cases of chronicity that do not respond to other treatments, neurobiofeedback is worth a try. The research literature, though not extensive, is sufficient to indicate that this sometimes works when nothing else does. It is highly preferable that the patient in neurobiofeedback treatment also be in psychotherapy, particularly given the possibilities of sudden and traumatic derepression, but in practice that usually doesn't happen. Patients who go into a biofeedback program drop out of therapy.

What is the role of acupuncture in substance abuse treatment?

Acupuncture using five points in the ears is a technique pioneered by Michael Smith (1989) at Lincoln Hospital in the Bronx for treating street addicts who would not come in for any kind of regularly scheduled treatment, but would avail themselves of acupuncture on a walk-in basis. He found that many of them spontaneously gave up drugs and became engaged in more traditionally structured therapies after a period of ad hoc acupuncture.

Since then, acupuncture has become a modality used in virtually all rehabilitation facilities, including those working with middle- and upper-class patients. It is seen as adjunctive, but as something that facilitates serenity, reduces anxiety, and reduces craving. In some settings acupuncture is used as either the primary or the adjunctive detoxification technique. The reports are more mixed than on the use of acupuncture for relaxation and enhancement of alpha-wave functioning, that is, of serenity-correlated brain-wave states.

I have had a number of patients who have had acupuncture who report that it is mildly helpful but hardly transforming. Contrary to the experience of this small sample, some researchers believe that acupuncture is a very powerful modality in substance abuse treatment. Since it is one of those treatments that seems to do no harm, there is no reason not to refer substance abuse patients for acupuncture, or, if the therapist is so inclined, to receive training in performing acupuncture.

Smith argues that neither transference nor placebo effects are responsible for the positive effects of acupuncture, but others disagree.

What is the role of hypnosis in substance abuse treatment?

Hypnosis for the purpose of habit modification has been around for a long time and seems to be a good adjunct for people who are motivated to change—to give something up—but are having a hard time doing it. That is particularly true for cessation of cigarette smoking. Being hypnotized and being told that you will stop smoking, if you don't (at least ambivalently) wish to, will not do it. But the posthypnotic suggestion may be the kind of push that will get smokers and other addicts over the hump if their motivation is fairly strong but their impulse control is weak. This is strikingly similar to the use of acupuncture, neurobiofeedback, and Antabuse in the treatment of alcoholism. They seem to be good adjuncts, but not good primary treatments.

Freud saw the effect of hypnosis as being mainly modulated by a father transference. Current thinking would see it more as a mother transference—an experience like being bathed in warm water or soothed at the breast. Hypnosis, if not spectacularly successful for behavioral change, is a valuable adjunct to various types of relaxation training and can be quite effective for that purpose.

> *What are some of the behavioral techniques known to help in substance abuse treatment?*

Relaxation training is widely used in rehabilitation settings and is at least anecdotally reported to be very helpful by those who receive it. The problem for the therapist is that doing relaxation training with patients becomes boring after a while, as it is mechanical and repetitious. But relaxation training is a useful adjunctive treatment in substance abuse treatment protocols and can readily be combined with cognitive and dynamic treatment.

Assertiveness training is also incorporated into many rehabilitation programs, and it, too, is effective. Most addicts have lots of bluster and anger and rage, but they are not effectively assertive. Role playing assertiveness, usually in a group setting, can be a very helpful way of surfacing some aggression, modulating and channeling it into socially appropriate forms, and it is reported to be quite helpful by those who have had experience in assertiveness training in various treatment programs. It can be done just as well in an outpatient private practice as in a rehabilitation facility.

> *What does William James teach us about the treatment of addiction?*

William James's manifest contribution to substance abuse treatment is the incorporation of his description of conversion experiences in his 1902 classic, *The Varieties of Religious Experience*, into the twelve-step literature in which Bill Wilson speaks of Damascus and of educational conversion experiences. However, there is a passage in James that has no manifest connection with substance abuse that is nevertheless highly salient in the treatment of that abuse. Late in his life, James fell into a panic anxiety about loss of identity, in which he seemed to be mixed up in the dreams of other people, and to have dreams that did not connect with each other and seemed to be dreamt by different dreamers. He felt that he was fragmenting and falling into a dissolution of personality, possibly on an organic basis. In the midst of this terrible experience of identity diffusion and regressive fragmentation, cited by Erik Erikson (1968) in his discussion of identity, James was able to regain some perspective on his experience by becoming, once again, the psychologist observing a psychological phenomenon. In getting that distance, in regaining an observing ego, James was able to give himself a theoretical explanation of what was happening to him and, in so doing, to calm himself and quiet his anxiety. At the same time, he was able to achieve a kind of empathy for those who were suffering similar experiences. He wrote:

> At the same time, I found myself filled with a new pity for persons passing into dementia with *Verwirrheit*, or into invasions of secondary personality. We regard them as simply curious; but what they want, in the awful drift of their being out of their customary self, is any principle of steadiness to hold on to. We ought to assure them and reassure them that we will stand by them, and recognize the true self in them, to the end. We ought to let them know that we are with them and not (as so often we must seem to them) part of the world that but confirms and publishes their deliquescence. [James, quoted in Erikson 1968, p. 207]

Substance abusers are out of their customary selves. They, too, are passing into dementia with *Verwirrheit*; they, too, have a second personality; they, too, are in a panic, and suffer confusion over a loss of identity; and they, too, need to be reassured that we will stand by them rather than confirm their deliquescence. James is totally on target here. The experience of addiction is a devastating one in which not only do external blows fall one upon the other, but the inward damage is even more profound. Substance abusers need the kind of empathic support so magnificently described by James as he recounts his reassertion of his identity as healer and psychologist in the midst of his panic attack.

> *What does John Wallace teach us about working*
> *with substance abusers?*

John Wallace (1975) wrote a classic paper "Working with the Preferred Defense Structure (PDS) of the Recovering Alcoholic." Wallace's basic notion is that the therapist needs to support defenses, however pathological, in early sobriety. However, in so supporting pathological defenses, the therapist helps the patient use them in an adaptive rather than self-destructive way. The PDS is not going to go away for a long time; therefore, why not make therapeutic use of it, and Wallace does just that. For example, denial of the addiction cannot be supported; that is the route to the cemetery. But the patient's tendency to denial can be used in the service of recovery. It may be adaptive for the patient to deny his or her guilt, or at lease the depth and extent of it, during early sobriety because to fully experience that guilt too soon would be intolerable and result in relapse. Wallace recommends that the therapist not only support, but even sometimes suggest such defensive postures.

Other pathological defenses that are part of the PDS are used by Wallace in Zen paradox-like maneuvers. These defenses include projection, all-or-nothing thinking, conflict minimization and avoidance, rationalization, self-centered selective attention, preference for non-analytic modes of thinking and perceiving, passivity, and obsessional focusing.

Wallace speaks of "assimilative projection," a process somewhat like projective identification, as a mechanism that makes a healing identification with other alcoholics possible. Patients project onto their peers and then identify with them as fellow sufferers from alcoholism. There is distortion in this, yet it is adaptive and sustains sobriety. All-or-nothing thinking allows patients to attribute all of their difficulties to alcoholism, which provides cognitive structure and reduces guilt and anxiety. Similarly, the therapist can creatively use the rest of the PDS to the patient's advantage.

Eventually, these defenses need to be analyzed, but Wallace recommends postponement of this process until stable sobriety is achieved.

> *What is the role of the gestalt therapies in*
> *substance abuse treatment?*

Gestalt therapies tend to surface a great deal of affect. As Fritz Perls put it, the goal of gestalt therapy is to "lose your mind and come to your senses." Substance abusers are rationalizers and intellectualizers par excellence, and gestalt techniques are often highly efficacious in their treatment. They are particularly popular in inpatient rehabilitation settings because they are safe places in which to surface strong emotions. The usual gestalt techniques such as "empty chair" are used in that kind of work, but by far the most popular technique is the psychodrama. Psychodrama is used to reenact various aspects of the addiction, one common scenario being a funeral for John Barleycorn, or Tijuana Gold, or Snow (heroin). These funeral rituals are extremely helpful and enable mourning for the lost substance and the lost lifestyle, as well as, even if not overtly interpreted, all of the symbolic and unconscious meanings of that drug and that activity. Psychodrama is also used to enact various painful life situations. For example, the now-alcoholic daughter who remembers her father coming home and pissing in front of her teenage friends as he stumbled across the lawn, to her utter humiliation at age 14, could use psychodrama to abreact her pain, rage, and shame. The traumatic scene could usefully be enacted in a psychodrama, in which a double may assist the protagonist in accessing her feelings and finding words to express them. In some psychodramas, role reversal is used. In that case, the patient would assume the role of the father. The therapist plays the role of the director, and all the other people in the therapy group, the audience, are not there as spectators but rather to identify and, as Aristotle would have it, purge through pity and terror, their own tragic memories and internal representations.

Psychodrama is very real and loosens all kinds of feelings, so it is vital that the therapist help the group to obtain closure. That is the reason psychodrama is not widely used in outpatient settings. If a recovering addict leaves such a psychodrama too raw and open, the propensity to relapse is too strong.

Gestalt techniques are usefully integrated into a psychotherapeutic style that is able to move in an integrated manner from a cognitive to a psychodynamic stance in the treatment of substance abusers, with the gestalt techniques used at times of emotional blocking. Somewhat similar is the use of gestalt techniques in "anger work," techniques that include the pounding of pillows, the use of bats, and all of the rest of the enactment apparatus used by the active therapies.

Substance abusers, who inevitably have a huge backlog of anger (partly repressed, partly acted out, but never really experienced and integrated), often benefit greatly from this sort of anger exercise. In common with other gestalt techniques, it is very important that closure be achieved, particularly in an outpatient setting, because otherwise what is surfaced can easily lead to relapse.

What is the role of mourning in substance abuse treatment?

One cannot mourn behind an addiction, and a large number of addictions are secondary to unresolved mourning. Therefore, one of the primary tasks in the treatment of substance abusers after stable sobriety is achieved is to revisit those old losses and to help the patient mourn for what may now be quite ancient. That is essentially done by helping patients go through their photo albums and get in contact with the feelings associated with each of the photographs.

But mourning in substance abuse treatment is not only about mourning old losses antecedent to the substance use; it is also very importantly about mourning the loss of the substance. The therapist can only effectively help the patient do that mourning if the therapist is able to recognize the positive and adaptive side of the addiction for the patient—what pleasure and joy the addiction or, if not the addiction, the substance, may have given the patient at some point in his or her addictive career. Only with that empathic recognition of what was positive and of how profound the loss of the substance is can the therapist help the patient mourn the loss of the drug or the compulsive activity and help that patient *feel*, rather than act out, the huge hole abstinence leaves. Only then can the therapist assist the patient in finding adaptive alternate activities to fill that gaping hole.

Additionally, there is often a long series of terrible losses secondary to the substance use that must also be mourned. This is particularly true for IV drug users who may have lost many friends and associates to violence, to AIDS, and to overdose. So the recovering person must deal with old, historical losses, as well as those concomitant with the substance use itself, and with the loss of the substance itself. All of these losses must be mourned if a stable and enjoyable sobriety is to be achieved.

What is an intervention?

An *intervention* is a planned confrontation of an addict by members of his or her family with the goal of having that person enter into treatment, usually inpatient rehabilitation sometimes preceded by detoxification. This can be arranged by a therapist who is treating a family member, or more often by an interventionist, a person usually in recovery him- or herself, either working privately or for a rehabilitation facility, who specializes in doing interventions. Interventionists can be overzealous and uncritical in the application of their art, so therapists who enlist their services need to be wary and make sure that they can work comfortably and fruitfully with a particular interventionist. Interventions require careful rehearsal. An intervention is not the place to let it all hang out. Its purpose is to get the addict into treatment, not to express feelings. There is nothing spontaneous about an intervention; participants know exactly what they are going to say. Potential participants in an intervention who cannot control their anger should be excluded.

In the intervention, the family does not accept any answer from the addict except an agreement to go into treatment. There are two styles of interventions: one does not have consequences if the addict refuses, which I do not think works very well; the other has consequences, such as, "If you don't go to inpatient treatment, then you can't live at home any longer," or "I will not sleep with you," or "I will not give you money." The second style is generally used. Interventions are said to be motivated by love, which is always expressed, "We are all here because we love you so much, Jane, even if we want to wring your fucking neck, and you are going to go into treatment because we can't stand to sit here and see you destroy yourself." Obviously, there are feelings other than love present at the intervention, but the love is often real. Interventions are, by their very nature, coercive, and some therapists are uncomfortable with that. But interventions can be lifesaving. Therapists have to look at their own values and their own feelings about this sort of coercive treatment and decide whether or not they want to participate.

> *Could you give an example of an intervention and its aftermath?*

Tom had been intervened on by his daughters. It was an atypical intervention. The intervenors had not sought professional help nor did they read up on interventions. Theirs was a "fly by the seat of your pants" intuitive approach and it worked. It was atypical in another way: the desired outcome was cessation of drinking, but inpatient treatment was not sought. Rather, they demanded, "Quit drinking and go into therapy." It was at that point that I met the intervenee.

Tom is a retired surgeon. A brilliant man with a Yale Phi Beta Kappa key, his entire life was one of academic and professional success. A deacon of his church, commander of his yacht club, his life seemed charmed, as, indeed, outwardly it was. But not so inwardly or emotionally. Although it would not be accurate to say that he had been depressed all his life, something had been wrong. He did everything he could do not to notice it, and for the most part succeeded, but he was not happy. He compensated by drinking. Martinis gave him the love he neither felt for nor from his wife. There was a nagging regret that he should have married the Catholic girl with whom he was in love but whom he had relinquished when his strongly Protestant family disapproved. He had had a few brief liaisons and had enjoyed them, but he had enough of his father's piety not to stay with them. He had had a scare with cancer as a relatively young man and that had permanently accelerated his drinking. His wife, although better controlled, was also fond of the sauce.

He came to me shortly after his daughters "intervened." He was 67 and ambivalently retired. The intervention had caused difficulties in his stably unhappy marriage. His children, responding to his slurring and his not making sense if they called after 6 P.M., had excluded their heavy-drinking mother and confronted their father, insisting that he was alcoholic, that he had long been so, and that since his recent retirement he had accelerated his progression to the point that they felt his life was in danger, so they were intervening. They told him that they loved him too much to sit idly by and watch him kill himself, and that either he stop drinking and enter therapy or they would stop talking to him and not let him see his grandchildren. He was a dutiful, loving, if not overly involved parent, and his children's love was important to him. Further, he "knew" that they were right. Secretly greatly relieved, he took some self-prescribed Valium for a few days and stopped drinking. He couldn't get over the fact that he didn't miss drinking. There was some denial in this, yet it was substantially true. The problem was his wife. She was furious that her daughters had bypassed her. There was a family fight and the children told her that she would never have gone along with the intervention, which was true. If they had consulted a professional interventionist, he or she would almost certainly not have included the mother either. Mother and daughters were not speaking. Tom was grateful to his daughters and thought they had done the only possible thing.

When he walked into my office, he looked at my diplomas, and said, "You're so much younger than I am." This theme of aging and his fear of death was to be a central issue. In a subsequent session, he said, "Eternity is a long time," a line that reverberates in my mind on occasion, my denial of death taking the form of a philosophical quibble that eternity does not partake of time. At the end of the first session, he told me the joke of a woman who was about to be married for the third time and was still a virgin. When her friend asked her how come, she replied, "My first husband was a psychiatrist; all he wanted to do was talk about it. My second husband was a gynecologist; all he wanted to do was look at it. But this time I'm not taking any chances, I'm marrying a lawyer because I know he'll screw me." I focused on the gynecologist, and sure enough, the story was Tom's way of telling me that he had been impotent for ten years.

Tom was used to wielding power. He quickly positioned me as his buddy and advisor on alcoholism, asking me for reading recommendations and the like. At one point he said, "Therapy had reduced the entropy of my consciousness," in a self-mocking tone, pretentiousness not being one of his traits. Since I saw my task as reinforcing the intervention, I was perfectly happy to be the expert and advisor. The focus of our work was on his drinking, with occasional forays into sex and death. The turning point occurred when he conceded that he had retired earlier than he wished because of his drinking, saying, "I decided to get out before I killed somebody." After that, I wasn't much worried about his returning to drinking, and sure enough, he was soon talking about blackouts going back twenty years and a host of other symptoms. His denial first pierced in the intervention was collapsing.

Tom was perfectly intervened upon. He is undoubtedly alcoholic, the timing was right, his children were loving but firm, they marshaled evidence and they made it clear that they would not take no for an answer. Further, they had therapeutic leverage and were willing to use it, and a good-enough sense of their mother to know that she would undermine it if included. There is no doubt in my mind that his children prolonged Tom's life.

What is relapse prevention?

Relapse prevention is a term coined by Alan Marlatt (Marlatt and Gordon 1985) for an approach that is very much in the forefront of addiction treatment these days. Substance abuse counselors are discovering that they have always done relapse prevention much like the hero of the Molière play, *Le Bourgeois Gentilhomme* (1670), who discovered that he had always been speaking prose. The two essential aspects of relapse prevention are the identification of triggers, accompanied by the teaching of coping strategies for dealing with the trigger situations, internal and external; and the acquisition of self-efficacy. Teaching self-efficacy is the antithesis of the admission of powerlessness taught by the twelve-step programs. It is the inculcating of the notion that patients do have control over their lives, including their emotional states, and certainly their substance abuse. Patients learn that relapse can be prevented by learning to do other things (such as develop coping strategies for dealing with stress) than drink or drug when they are distressed or overwhelmed.

The relapse prevention approach is very much a cognitive one, and it focuses on changes in attitudes (particularly those of victimization and helplessness), and the acquisition of a "can do" attitude. I believe that the apparent conflict between the relapse prevention approach and the twelve-step notion of surrender and powerlessness is more apparent than real, because the twelve-step admission of powerlessness is a Zen maneuver that empowers as users admit that they are powerless over their drug use. The relapse prevention approach is less dialectical, and although it would agree that the patient in the DT's can't control his use, it essentially does not buy the notion of loss of control.

Although the two points of view can be reconciled, self-efficacy training as a part of relapse prevention is coming from a different place than twelve-step surrender. They both have their role in substance abuse treatment.

Relapse prevention is a cognitive therapy. The central tenet of the relapse prevention approach is teaching about what is called the abstinence violation effect (AVE). AVE is the belief patients have that if they pick up the drug, then they will lose control and proceed to use until they collapse. Marlatt and other cognitive therapists believe that twelve-step programs (and some therapists) teach their members just that. They also think that AVE becomes a self-fulfilling prophecy. Therefore, Marlatt and his followers conclude that teaching addicts that they are powerless over their addictions is highly pernicious.

In relapse prevention the opposite is taught—that relapses have a cause, that slips can be analyzed, and that once the cause is established appropriate measures can be taken to ensure that relapse does not reoccur (at least not for the same reasons). Patients are further taught that the thing to do if they slip is to stop immediately (which they know they have the power to do since that is what they have been taught in their relapse prevention class or individual therapy), and to go back and analyze the slip. Perhaps the patient was not tending to an emotional state, for example, rage. Perhaps the patient was not talking about what was bothering him or her in therapy. Perhaps the patient ignored some drink signal and failed to develop a coping strategy, an alternate behavior, in response to that drink signal. If the patient was doing some combination of relapse prevention and twelve-step work, the therapist might analyze the slip as caused by the patient's not going to enough meetings. But whatever the cause—some operant conditioning signal the patient failed to note and circumvent, or an affective problem, or a lack of assertiveness, or a failure to deal with an interpersonal conflict—something can be done so that the patient will not slip (at least on that basis) again.

However, the underlying reason for all slips from the relapse prevention point of view is that the recovering substance abuser has ceased to believe in his or her self-efficacy, and therefore has turned to a drug to do for him what he believes he cannot do for himself. So the fundamental change in the patient in relapse prevention therapy, as in all cognitive therapies, needs to be an attitudinal change, attitudinal and cognitive, for example, a change in belief from "I can't cope clean" to "I can cope without drugs."

All this is too rational for my taste. Somehow Marlatt makes recovery seem too easy. I have no doubt that relapse prevention techniques are extremely helpful to patients. What I object to is relapse prevention as ideology, which radically underestimates the sheer irrationality of addiction, the degree to which patients are driven by unconscious, often destructive and self-destructive forces.

What do you think of the use of methadone?

Methadone is a synthetic opiate used in the treatment of heroin addiction. It was developed in Germany during World War II, which leads some to doubt the wisdom of prescribing it. My own feeling is that drug-free is better, but there are some patients who are not going to be drug-free, and it is much better that they be on methadone in a well-run program, in which there is counseling and supervision, and that they be in psychotherapy, than for them to be dysfunctional street addicts.

The therapist, however, should be aware that those on methadone maintenance often supplement their methadone with various other drugs, particularly alcohol. There is a high rate of alcoholism in methadone maintenance patients. It is also vital that the therapist explore the meaning of the methadone for the patient: What kind of transference is there to the drug? What selfobject functions does it serve? With what in the internal object world does it reverberate? The therapist should follow the patients' lead and not impose his or her value of drug-freeness (if that is the therapist's value) on patients who may very well be incapable, at least at their present developmental level, of living sober without methadone. The therapist then works toward maturation and health, which may or may not lead to a drug-free lifestyle. After all, diabetics aren't drug-free and we don't consider their taking insulin as evidence of immaturity.

Admittedly, methadone is somewhat different, and its use does lead to some emotional flattening and some lack of intensity in interpersonal relations. It may, nevertheless, be a corrective to an abnormal neurochemistry, even if that neurochemistry was caused by the many years of opiate (generally heroin) use.

How would you define recovery?

For those who are addicted, recovery can be described as the sustained cessation of substance use. The reacquisition of control is a more desirable therapeutic goal for those patients who are problem users rather than addicts. However, most therapists, myself included, believe that recovery is about more than abstinence or control. It is about a transformation of the self, either a radical transformation as depicted in accounts of the twelve-step surrender, hitting-bottom experience leading to reorganization and transvaluation of values, or a more modest psychological realignment in which regression is put in the service of the ego, mourning is worked through and ended, and patients finally become capable of loving again and are then free to invest their energy in a new life of sobriety or control.

> *What is the therapist to do if the patient says, "I'm saner now as a result of therapy, but less happy"?*

The therapist should acknowledge that this may indeed be the case and invite the patient, who need not become defensive since the therapist has empathically resonated with him or her, to explore why sanity—probably meaning seeing reality more clearly in a sober state—has resulted in unhappiness. Freud's famous comment (Freud and Breuer 1895), "The purpose of analytic therapy is to replace neurotic misery with ordinary human unhappiness" (p. 305), comes to mind. The therapist need feel no guilt or responsibility for the patient's unhappiness. What may help is facilitating the patient's mourning for the losses that sobriety has brought.

> *What can the therapist say to addicts in long-term recovery who are active in twelve-step and feel guilty that they still have problems?*

This is a common snare for recovering persons with long-term sobriety who are active in the twelve-step movement and are still troubled. They believe that the ideology of the program teaches that someone with such long-term sobriety should not be troubled. This may be a misperception of the beliefs of some AA and NA members. It puts patients in the untenable position of not being able to talk about their pain in a place where they should be able to feel safe. In such a situation, the therapist can say, "All human beings have difficulties, so it is hardly surprising that the people who have had the additional burden of struggling with an addiction should continue to have problems well into sobriety. Part of this is simply the human condition, and part of it is the consequence of the losses and lost opportunities of your years of active substance use. There are parts of the program that recognize this. If you read the *Big Book*, and other AA literature, you will find that such advice as 'Keep coming back,' 'Nobody graduates,' and the tenth step—making a continuing inventory of personal defects—indicates that the program is well aware that recovery is a lifelong process and that people have trouble at all stages of sobriety. Nevertheless, there may be people in your group, particularly newcomers, who expect that the stably sober will be doing much better, which for the most part, of course, they are, as you know, so that it makes you feel bad to talk about the pain you're in because you fear you may discourage some of those newcomers and be disapproved of by some of your peers in sobriety. To some degree that is a real dilemma, but it may not be as much of one as you believe. Fortunately you have therapy and our relationship in which you can talk about absolutely anything, including your pain. You can also shop around. Some groups are more open to emotional problems than those that prefer to keep their focus narrowly on sobriety."

This intervention by the therapist will lessen patients' conflict, and perhaps permit them to talk more openly at the group meetings. It is also empathic, acknowledging the reality of the patients' social situation and encouraging their risking more openness.

How do the gender wars affect couple therapy with substance abusers?

The changing role expectations of our society engender much confusion as well as much liberation for both men and women. The best the therapist can do is to be aware that the mutual envy of the sexes enters into every relationship between men and women and becomes entangled with the substance abuse issues that have brought the couple patient to therapy. Perhaps a case illustration will help.

Mary brought Ted to therapy to complain about his drinking, his attitude, and his behavior. Ted had no desire to be there. Mary opened the session angrily berating Ted on many counts, some of which seemed only tangentially related to his drinking. Then she said to me, "He's a Neanderthal and I want a SNAG." I said, "SNAG?" "Yes," said Mary, "a sensitive new-age guy." I looked over at Ted and quickly decided that his odds of becoming a SNAG were not very high. I wondered if a compromise might be possible. I said, "Would you settle for a Cro-Magnon?" Mary was not amused. Therapy terminated after a few sessions.

Rottweilers do not become lapdogs even given the most skillful therapy. Some expectations cannot be met. I don't know to what degree Ted's incarnation of Neanderthal behavior was an artifact of his drinking and how much was baseline personality, but my experience in similar situations, not always so clearly articulated as Mary was in her request for a SNAG, is that these marriages simply do not work even if Ted gets sober. He just is not going to become a SNAG and her expectations are not going to change very much. In such cases, I try to focus on the drinking or substance abuse and see if I can help Ted and his compatriots not to continue to drink simply because they are enraged that they don't meet their partners' new expectations of them. I often interpret that and tell the drinker that there are two problems here—the drinking, and the difficulties in the marriage—and that nothing can be done about the second unless something is done about the first, although that is no guarantee that the marriage will endure. Divorce is not necessarily a bad outcome if the bond is primarily based on drinking or substance use, and the various games that are played around it. In sobriety there is often little cement to hold the couple together, and it may very well be best that each goes his or her way.

If Mary's request for a SNAG had been expressed with some humor, I would have felt far more hopeful about her marriage. When she went on the say that Ted had a "gender disability," I could only ask, again, without trying to be funny. whether she thought the disability could be treated by some sort of rehabilitation. She looked at me as though I were out of my mind. Clearly, she thought maleness was a gender disability not capable of mutation. I was tempted to ask her if SNAGs didn't suffer the same gender disability, but I decided that that was not likely to go anywhere.

I have since used the gender disability phrase with some success in working with couples—substance abusing and otherwise. Most respond favorably to the injection of a little humor into their often grim interactions, and that humor sometimes allows them to step back and take a more dispassionate look at the differences that separate them.

> *How do you do substance abuse therapy and not become a misanthrope?*

Somewhere Freud states that he has not found human beings satis-factory. He says something to the effect that he has found, with few excep-tions, that his fellow men are of little worth. That, of course, is a belief many substance abusers share, however much more it may say about Freud than it does about humanity. But that is also a frame of mind that substance abuse therapists easily fall into if they stay in the field for any length of time. Substance abuse therapists work constantly with people who lie, deceive, cheat, steal, perpetrate outrageous acts of aggression against their fellows, make no sense, believe the most outrageous irrationalities, justify their behaviors with the most transparent rationalizations, and, worst of all, value neither the therapist nor the work the therapist does.

It is hard for the substance abuse therapist not to become disillusioned and cynical. Some of that disillusionment and cynicism is self-protective and may not be a bad thing, but too much of it can interfere with the work. The therapist should remember that some patients do get well—in fact, quite a few—and that much of the obnoxious conduct therapists work with is a by-product of the addiction, not the baseline personality of the patient.

Nevertheless, negative affect is contagious and a considerable degree of projective identification goes on in substance abuse therapy; that is, the patient is somehow inducing his or her negativity and despair in the thera-pist as a form of communication and a way of getting rid of it. Although that is the case, much, if not most, of the therapist's misanthropy derives not from work with the clientele but from the therapist's own life.

It is wise for therapists to acknowledge that at times they are going to hate their work and their patients. This is inevitable. It also helps to identify and bring into consciousness those aspects of the therapist's self that reso-nate with the negative qualities and behaviors of the patient. Therapy or analysis is the best way of gaining insight into our own inner worlds, so that we do not project the unacceptable parts of ourselves onto our patients, who are often all too suitable targets for those projections. Good supervision also helps in defusing the negative emotions and the tendencies to be judgmental and devaluating. And, finally, it helps to recall Oscar Wilde's quip, "A cynic is a man who knows the price of everything and the value of nothing."

> *What do this primer's opening epigraphs have to do with substance abuse treatment?*

The epigraphs of this book are contradictory, but the reconciliation of these seeming opposites in some sort of dialectical unity is the sine qua non of effective substance abuse therapy. That is to say the ideal substance abuse therapist must somehow operate from a stance of empathic understanding and letting be so that patients may find their own way to their unique way of being, perceiving, and establishing health. The epigraph from George Eliot "It is good for me to bear with them in their ignorance . . . and not put impatient knowledge in the stead of loving wisdom," epitomizes that aspect of the effective therapist's relationship with his or her patient.

On the other hand, few substance abusing patients will arrive at abstinence or control merely through benignly being with a technically neutral therapist. Rather, the therapist must be confrontational and must have mastery of techniques of confronting that are challenging, disputing, and ego alien to the patient. It is that aspect of being an effective substance abuse therapist that is epitomized in the epigraph from Harry Tiebout. That is, the therapist must "go after" substance abusers' grandiosity, unrealistic overvaluation of themselves and ability to control, as well as the denial which that grandiosity and overvaluation of the self engenders. The reader may conclude that if such is the case, the task of substance abuse therapist is well nigh impossible. Perhaps it is. Nevertheless, useful therapy does occur with approximations to simultaneity or succession of these radically opposing existential stances on the part of the therapist. They are both useful. If the therapist does not have some sense that he or she must meet the patient where that patient is at, and is not in some real sense respectful of that "at," then nothing is going to happen. There will be no rapport and patients will correctly intuit that they are being condescended to, moralized to, or objectified. They will sense that the therapist is too invested in behavioral change—and behavioral change is the therapist's agenda, and not the patient's.

If the substance abuse therapist is only able to make contact from a George Eliot stance, by creating a bridge of empathy, of understanding, and of respect, only a small percentage of active substance abusers will move toward abstinence or control, and in any substantial way improve their lives. Technical neutrality simply will not do it in treating substance abuse.

Freud's in many ways extraordinarily sage advice to "have no therapeutic aim" is liberating for both therapist and patient, and in many therapies makes possible an openness, a nonjudgmental exploration, and a gaining of insight into defenses, drives, and irrational aspects of the self, which no other attitude uncovers. Nevertheless, the pharmacological regression in substance abuse is so powerful that whatever insight is gained is quickly swallowed up in that regression. The therapist must move into the other pole of his or her professional self, the one that Tiebout is speaking to, and become confrontational of denial and defensiveness, often manifesting itself in highly unrealistic manifestations of ego, meaning ego in the sense of "he has a big Ego." Tiebout is indeed rather punitive in tone and encapsulates an attitude the exact opposite of Eliot's, but stripped of its moralizing, judgment, and condescension, it is a necessary ingredient in substance abuse treatment.

Letting alone and not letting alone, being with and understanding and struggling with and confronting are necessary elements in the treatment. What cannot be integrated can be moved into sequentially. The trick is in the timing, in what Freud called "therapeutic tact." Although there are no hard and fast rules, in general I would recommend that "being with" precede "struggling with," that the building of rapport take precedence over using that rapport as leverage to point out to patients the self-destructiveness, the irrationality, the unreality of their perception of the world, and of their self, and of how that perception both determines and is determined by their substance abuse.

The therapist is on the side of reality. But which reality? The patient's or the therapist's? Here the therapist working with the active user must have the chutzpah, perhaps even the hubris, to assert that his or her perception of the world, at least insofar as that perception affirms that the superiority in any moral, medical, or existential sense of sobriety or control over addiction or uncontrol, is more congruent with reality than the patient's perception. So paradox must be transformed into the dialectical unity of opposites, in which utter and unconditional respect for the patient's being is somehow integrated with the therapist's certainty that he or she has something better to offer that patient.

> *Substance abuse therapy is often discouraging. In working with such disturbed and self-destructive people, I often feel that the whole weight of the world is on my shoulders. Yet I want to stay in the field. Do you have any suggestions that will help me feel less burdened?*

There is a twelve-step saying, "You can carry the message, but not the alcoholic." It is a message that applies just as well to substance abuse therapists as to twelve-steppers who are engaged in rescue work within their program. If therapists are carrying the weight of the world on their shoulders, they are doing something wrong. Unquestionably, doing substance abuse work involves coming in contact with major and profound tragedy—child abuse, wasted lives, deaths—but therapists are not responsible for those outcomes. They are only responsible for doing their best as educators, as facilitators, and as companions in the struggle for sobriety. Substance abuse is a killer and therapists are going to lose some patients. Twelve-step programs teach their members to put in the effort, but not to try to dictate the outcome. That is not a bad attitude for substance abuse therapists to assume.

It may also be helpful to think of a talmudic saying which lessens responsibility without suggesting that we need not utilize whatever power we have to enable recovery.

"It is not required of you that you complete the work, but neither are you free to desist from it."

References

Abraham, K. (1908). The psychological relation between sexuality and alcoholism. In *Selected Papers on Psychoanalysis*, pp. 80–90. New York: Brunner/Mazel, 1979.

Alcoholics Anonymous World Services (1952). *Alcoholics Anonymous*. New York: Author.

———— (1955). *Twelve Steps and Twelve Traditions*. New York: Author.

Aristotle (325 B.C.). *Nicomachean Ethics*. In *Introduction to Aristotle*, ed. R. McKeon, pp. 300–543. New York: Modern Library, 1947.

Austin, J. L. (1961). Performative utterances. In *Philosophical Papers*, ed. J. O. Urmson and G. J. Warnock, pp. 220–240. London: Oxford University Press.

Babor, T. F., Dolinsky, Z. S., Meyer, R. E., et al. (1992a). Types of alcoholics: concurrent and predictive validity of some common classification schemes. *British Journal of Addiction* 87:1415–1431.

Babor, T. F., Wolfson, A., Boivan, D., et al. (1992b). Alcoholism, culture and psychopathology. In *Alcoholism in North America, Europe and Asia*, ed. J. E. Helzer and G. J. Canino, pp. 182–195. New York: Oxford University Press.

Berglas, S. (1987). Self-handicapping model. In *Psychological Theories of Drinking and Alcoholism*, ed. H. T. Blane and K. E. Leonard, pp. 305–345. New York: Guilford.

Bion, W. (1959). *Experience in Groups*. London: Tavistock.

Blane, H. (1968). *The Personality of the Alcoholic: Guises of Dependency*. New York: Harper & Row.

Bradshaw, J. (1988). *Healing the Shame that Binds You*. Deerfield Beach, FL: Heath Communications.

Brown, S. (1985). *Treating the Alcoholic: A Developmental Model of Recovery*. New York: Wiley.

Chekhov, A. (1886). Heartache. In *The Image of Chekhov: Forty Stories by Anton Chekhov in the Order in Which They Were Written*, trans. R. Payne, pp. 99–105. New York: Knopf, 1979.

Cloninger, C. R. (1983). Genetic and environmental factors in the development of alcoholism. *Journal of Psychiatric Treatment and Evaluation* 5:487–496.

——— (1987). Neurogenetic adaptive mechanisms in alcoholism. *Science* 236: 410–416.

Cloninger, C. R., Sigvardsson, S., and Bohman, M. (1988). Childhood personality predicts alcohol abuse in young adults. *Alcoholism: Clinical and Experimental Research* 12:494–505.

Conger, J. J. (1956). Reinforcement and the dynamics of alcoholism. *Quarterly Journal of Studies on Alcohol* 13:296–305.

Conners, R. (1962). The self-concepts of alcoholics. In *Society, Culture, and Drinking Patterns*, ed. D. Pittman and C. Snyder, pp. 455–467. Carbondale, IL: Southern Illinois University Press.

Cox, W. M. (1987). Personality theory and research. In *Psychological Theories of Drinking and Alcoholism*, ed. H. T. Blane and K. E. Leonard, pp. 55–89. New York: Guilford.

Dostoyevsky, F. (1880). *The Brothers Karamazov*, trans. C. Garnett. New York: Modern Library, 1950.

Durkheim, E. (1897). *Suicide*. Glencoe, IL: The Free Press, 1951.

Erikson, E. (1968). *Identity, Youth and Crisis*. New York: Norton.

Fairbairn, W. R. D. (1940). Schizoid factors in personality. In *Psychoanalytic Studies of the Personality*, pp. 3–27. London: Routledge and Kegan Paul, 1952.

Fenichel, O. (1945). *The Psychoanalytic Theory of Neurosis*. New York: Norton.

Festinger, L. (1957). *A Theory of Cognitive Dissonance*. Evanston, IL: Row, Peterson.

Freud, S. (1897). *The Complete Letters of Sigmund Freud to Wilhelm Fliess*, trans. and ed. J. M. Masson. Cambridge, MA: Harvard University Press, 1985.

——— (1900). The interpretation of dreams. *Standard Edition* 4/5:1–626.

——— (1905). Three essays on sexuality. *Standard Edition* 7:123–243.

——— (1914). On narcissism: an introduction. *Standard Edition* 14:67–104.

——— (1920). Beyond the pleasure principle. *Standard Edition* 18:1–64.

—— (1921). Group psychology and the analysis of the ego. *Standard Edition* 18:65–144.

—— (1928). Dostoyevsky and parricide. *Standard Edition* 21:173–196.

—— (1930). Civilization and its discontents. *Standard Edition* 21:64–148.

—— (1937). Analysis terminable and interminable. *Standard Edition* 23: 209–254.

Freud, S., and Breuer, J. (1895). Studies on hysteria. *Standard Edition* 2:1–313.

Fromm, E. (1941). *Escape from Freedom*. New York: Rinehart.

Galanter, M. (1993). *Network Therapy for Alcohol and Drug Abuse: A New Approach in Practice*. New York: Basic Books.

Gedo, J. (1997). *Spleen and Nostalgia: A Life and Work in Psychoanalysis*. Northvale, NJ: Jason Aronson.

Gedo, J., and Goldberg, A. (1973). *Models of the Mind: A Psychoanalytic Theory*. Chicago, IL: University of Chicago Press.

Glover, E. (1928). The etiology of alcoholism. *Proceedings of the Royal Society of Medicine* 21:1351–1355.

Goldstein, K. (1939). *The Organism*. New York: Schocken.

—— (1940). *Human Nature in the Light of Psychopathology*. Cambridge, MA: Harvard University Press.

—— (1952). Functional disturbances in brain damage. In *American Handbook of Psychiatry*, ed. S. Arieti, pp. 770–785. New York: Basic Books.

Hartocollis, P. (1968). A dynamic view of alcoholism: drinking in the service of denial. *Dynamic Psychiatry* 2:173–182.

Heath, D. B. (1958). Drinking patterns of the Bolivian Camba. *Quarterly Journal of Studies on Alcohol* 19:491–508.

Hesse, H. (1929). *Steppenwolf*, trans. B. Creighton. New York: Fredrick Ungar.

Horney, K. (1942). *Self-Analysis*. New York: Norton.

—— (1945). *Our Inner Conflicts*. New York: Norton.

Hull, J. G. (1981). A self-awareness model of the causes and effects of alcohol consumption. *Journal of Abnormal Psychology* 90:586–600.

Jacobson, E. (1938). *Progressive Relaxation*. Chicago: University of Chicago Press.

James, W. (1902). *The Varieties of Religious Experience*. New York: Longmans.

Jellinek, E. M. (1943). Heredity and premature weaning: a discussion of the work of Thomas Trotter, British Naval Physician. In *The Dynamics and Treatment of Alcoholism: Essential Papers*, ed. J. Levin and R. Weiss, pp. 28–34. Northvale, NJ: Jason Aronson, 1994.

—— (1960). *The Disease Concept of Alcoholism*. New Haven, CT: College and University Press.

Jones, M. C. (1968). Personality antecedents and correlatives of drinking patterns in adult males. *Journal of Consulting and Clinical Psychology* 32:2–12.

——— (1971). Personality antecedents and correlatives of drinking patterns in women. *Journal of Consulting and Clinical Psychology* 36:61–69.

Jung, C. G. (1961). *C. G. Jung: Letters*, vol. 2, 1951–1961. Princeton, NJ: Princeton University Press, 1973.

Kaminer, Y. (1994). *Adolescent Substance Abuse: A Comprehensive Guide to Theory and Practice.* New York: Plenum.

Kandel, D. B. (1975). Stages in adolescent involvement in drug use. *Science* 190:912–914.

Kandel, D. B., Yamaguchi, K., and Chen, K. (1992). Stages of progression in drug involvement from adolescence to adulthood: further evidence for the gateway theory. *Journal of Studies on Alcohol* 53:447–457.

Kernberg, O. (1975). *Borderline Conditions and Pathological Narcissism.* New York: Jason Aronson.

Khantzian, E. J. (1981). Some treatment implications of ego and self-disturbances in alcoholism. In *Dynamic Approaches to the Understanding and Treatment of Alcoholism*, ed. M. H. Bean and N. E. Zinberg, pp. 163–188. New York: The Free Press.

——— (1999). *Treating Addiction as a Human Process.* Northvale, NJ: Jason Aronson.

Khantzian, E. J., and Mack, J. E. (1989). Alcoholics Anonymous and contemporary psychodynamic theory. In *Recent Advances in Alcoholism*, ed. M. Galanter, pp. 67–89. New York: Plenum.

Kierkegaard, S. (1849). *The Concept of Dread*, trans. W. Lowrie. Princeton, NJ: Princeton University Press, 1944.

Klein, M. (1975a). *Love, Guilt, and Reparation and Other Works 1921–1945.* New York: Dell.

——— (1975b). *Envy and Gratitude and Other Works 1946–1963.* New York: Dell.

Knight, R. P. (1937). The dynamics and treatment of chronic alcohol addiction. *Bulletin of the Menninger Clinic* 1:233–250.

——— (1938). The psychoanalytic treatment in a sanitorium of chronic addiction to alcohol. *Journal of the American Medical Association* 111:1443–1448.

Kohut, H. (1971). *The Analysis of the Self: A Systematic Approach to the Psychoanalytic Treatment of Narcissistic Personality Disorders.* New York: International Universities Press.

——— (1972). Thoughts on narcissism and narcissistic rage. In *The Search for the Self*, ed. P. H. Ornstein, pp. 615–658. New York: International Universities Press, 1978.

―――― (1977a). *The Restoration of the Self.* New York: International Universities Press.

―――― (1977b). Preface. In *Psychodynamics of Drug Dependence*, ed. J. D. Blaine and D. A. Julius, pp. vii–ix. Northvale, NJ: Jason Aronson, 1993.

Kramer, P. D. (1993). *Listening to Prozac: A Psychiatrist Explores Anti-depressant Drugs and the Remaking of the Self.* New York: Penguin.

Krystal, H., and Raskin, H. (1970). *Drug Dependence: Aspects of Ego Function.* Northvale, NJ: Jason Aronson, 1993.

Lassek, A. M. (1970). *The Unique Legacy of Doctor Hughlings Jackson.* Springfield, IL: Charles C Thomas.

Levin, J. D. (1981). *A study of social role in chronic alcoholic men affiliated with Alcoholics Anonymous.* Ph.D. dissertation, New York University. Ann Arbor, MI: University Microfilms International 8210924.

―――― (1987). *Treatment of Alcoholism and Other Addictions: A Self-Psychology Approach.* Northvale, NJ: Jason Aronson.

―――― (1993). *Slings and Arrows: Narcissistic Injury and Its Treatment.* Northvale, NJ: Jason Aronson.

―――― (1995). *Introduction to Alcoholism Counseling: A Bio-Psycho-Social Approach*, 2nd ed. Washington, DC: Taylor and Francis.

―――― (1998). *Couple and Family Therapy of Addiction.* Northvale, NJ: Jason Aronson.

Loper, R. G., Kammeier, M. L., and Hoffman, H. (1973). MMPI characteristics of college freshman males who later became alcoholics. *Journal of Abnormal Psychology* 82:159–162.

MacAndrew, C. (1965). The differentiation of male alcoholic outpatients from non-alcoholic psychiatric outpatients by means of the MMPI. *Quarterly Journal of Studies on Alcohol* 26:238–246.

Mack, J. G. (1981). Alcoholism, A. A. and the governance of the self. In *Dynamic Approaches to the Understanding and Treatment of Alcoholism*, ed. M. H. Bean and N. E. Zinberg, pp. 128–162. New York: The Free Press.

Mahler, M., Pine, F., and Bergman, A. (1975). *The Psychological Birth of the Human Infant: Symbiosis and Individuation.* New York: Basic Books.

Marlatt, G. A., and Gordon, J. R. (1985). *Relapse Prevention: Maintenance Strategies in the Treatment of Addictive Behaviors.* New York: Guilford.

Masters, W. H., and Johnson, V. E. (1970). *Human Sexual Inadequacy.* Boston: Little, Brown.

Masterson, J. F. (1976). *Psychotherapy of the Borderline Adult: A Developmental Approach.* New York: Brunner/Mazel.

McClelland, D. C., Davis, W., Kalin, R., and Wanner, E. (1972). *The Drinking Man: Alcohol and Human Motivation.* New York: The Free Press.

Menninger, K. (1938). *Man Against Himself.* New York: Harcourt Brace.

Millay, E. S. (1917). Renascence. In *Collected Poems*, ed. N. Millay, pp. 3–13. New York: Harper & Row, 1956.

Milton, J. (1674). *Paradise Lost*, revised edition. In *The Portable Milton*, ed. D. Bush, pp. 231–548. New York: Penguin, 1949.

Molière, J. B. P. (1670). *Le Bourgeois Gentilhomme.* In *Eight Plays by Moliere*, trans. M. Bishop. New York: Random House Modern Library, 1957.

Nesse, R. M., and Berridge, K. C. (1997). Psychoactive drug use in evolutionary perspective. *Science* 278:63–66.

Ogden, T. (1986). *The Matrix of the Mind.* Northvale, NJ: Jason Aronson.

O'Neill, E. (1946). *The Iceman Cometh.* New York: Random House.

Parsons, T. (1954). *Essays in Sociological Theory.* Glencoe, IL: The Free Press.

Pascal, B. (1670). *Pensées*, trans. A. J. Krailsheiner. London: Penguin, 1966.

Peninston, E. G., and Kulkosky, P. J. (1989). Brainwave training and beta-endorphin levels in alcoholics. *Alcoholism: Clinical and Experimental Research* 13:271–279.

———— (1990). Alcoholic personality and alpha-theta brainwave training. *Medical Psychotherapy* 3:37–55.

Pittman, D., and White, H. R., eds. (1991). *Society, Culture, and Drinking Patterns Re-examined.* New Brunswick, NJ: Rutgers Center of Alcohol Studies.

Prochaska, J. V., DiClemente, C. C., and Norcoss, J. C. (1992). In search of how people change: applications to addictive behaviors. *American Psychologist* 47:1102–1114.

Rado, S. (1933). The psychoanalysis of pharmacothymia. *Psychoanalytic Quarterly* 2:2–23.

Richards, H. J. (1993). *Therapy of the Substance Abuse Syndromes.* Northvale, NJ: Jason Aronson.

Rush, B. (1785). An inquiry into the effects of ardent spirits upon the human body and mind. In *The Dynamics and Treatment of Alcoholism: Essential Papers*, ed. J. Levin and R. Weiss, pp. 11–27. Northvale, NJ: Jason Aronson, 1994.

Schachter, S., and Singer, J. (1962). Cognitive, social and physiological determinants of emotional state. *Psychological Review* 69:379–399.

Scharff, D. E. (1992). *Refinding the Object and Reclaiming the Self.* Northvale, NJ: Jason Aronson.

Scharff, D. E., and Scharff, J. S. (1991). *Object Relations Family Therapy*. North-vale, NJ: Jason Aronson.

Schopenhauer, A. (1851). *Parerga and Paralipomena*, trans. T. Bailey. Saunders, NY: Wiley, 1942.

Schuckit, M. A., and Gold, F. O. (1988). A simultaneous evaluation of multiple markers of ethanol/placebo challenges in sons of alcoholics and controls. *Archives of General Psychiatry* 45:211–216.

Seligman, M. E. P. (1975). *Helplessness: On Depression, Development and Death*. San Francisco: Freeman.

Seligman, M. E. P., and Maier, S. F. (1967). Failure to escape traumatic shock. *Journal of Experimental Psychology* 74:1–9.

Sher, K. J. (1987). Stress response dampening. In *Psychological Theories of Drinking and Alcoholism*, ed. H. T. Blane and K. E. Leonard, pp. 227–271. New York: Guilford.

Simmel, E. (1948). Alcoholism and addiction. *Psychoanalytic Quarterly* 17: 6–31.

Smith, M. O. (1989). *The Lincoln Hospital Accupuncture Drug Treatment Program*. Testimony presented to the Select Committee on Narcotics of the U. S. House of Representatives, July 25.

Solomon, R. L. (1977). An opponent process theory of acquired motivation: the affective dynamics of addiction. In *Psychopathology: Experimental Models*, ed. J. D. Maser and M. E. P. Seligman, pp. 66–103. San Francisco: Freeman.

Stern, D. N. (1985). *The Interpersonal World of the Infant: A View from Psychoanalysis and Developmental Psychology*. New York: Basic Books.

Szasz, T. (1958). The role of the counterphobic mechanism in addiction. *Journal of the American Psychoanalytic Association* 6:309–325.

Tarter, R. E. (1991). Developmental behavior genetic perspective of alcoholism etiology. In *Recent Development in Alcoholism*, vol. 9, ed. M. Galanter. New York: Plenum.

Tarter, R. E., and Alterman, A. I. (1989). Neurobehavioral theory of alcoholism etiology. In *Theories of Alcoholism*, ed. C. D. Choudran and D. A. Wilkinson, pp. 29–102. Toronto: Addiction Research Foundation.

Tiebout, H. M. (1949). The act of surrender in the therapeutic process. *Quarterly Journal of Studies on Alcohol* 10:48–58.

——— (1957). The ego factor in surrender to alcoholism. *Quarterly Journal of Studies on Alcohol* 15:610–621.

Toennies, F. (1887). *Gemeinschaft und Gesellschaft*. Berlin: Curtius, 1926.

Trimpley, J. (1989). *Rational Recovery from Alcoholism: The Small Book*, 3rd ed. Lotus, CA: Lotus.

van der Kolk, B. A., McFarlane, A. C., and Weisaeth, L., eds. (1996). T*raumatic Stress: The Effects of Overwhelming Experience on Mind, Body, and Society*. New York: Guilford.

Wallace, J. (1975). Working with the preferred defense structure of the recovering alcoholic. In *The Dynamics and Treatment of Alcoholism: Essential Papers*, ed. J. D. Levin and R. Weiss, pp. 222–232. Northvale, NJ: Jason Aronson, 1994.

Wilsnack, S. C. (1973). Sex role identity in female alcoholism. *Journal of Abnormal Psychology* 82:253–261.

——— (1974). The effects of social drinking on women's fantasy. *Journal of Personality* 42:43–61.

Winnicott, D. W. (1958). The capacity to be alone. In *The Maturational Processes and the Facilitating Environment*, pp. 29–36. New York: International Universities Press, 1965.

——— (1960). Ego distortion in terms of the true and false self. In *The Maturational Process and the Facilitating Environment*, pp. 140–152. New York: International Universities Press, 1965.

——— (1963). The development of the capacity for concern. In *The Maturational Processes and the Facilitating Environment*, pp. 73–83. New York: International Universities Press, 1965.

Winokur, G., Rimmer, J., and Reich, T. (1971). Alcoholism IV: Is there more than one type of alcoholism? *British Journal of Psychiatry* 18:525–531.

Witkin, H. A., Karp, S. A., and Goodenough, D. R. (1959). Dependence in alcoholics. *Quarterly Journal of Studies on Alcohol* 20:493–504.

Witkin, H. A., and Oltman, P. K. (1967). Cognitive style. *International Journal of Neurology* 6:119–137.

Wurmser, L. (1978). *The Hidden Dimension: Psychodynamics in Compulsive Drug Use*. New York: Jason Aronson.

——— (1981). *The Mask of Shame*. Baltimore, MD: Johns Hopkins University Press.

Zuckerman, M. (1979). *Sensation Seeking: Beyond the Optimal Level of Arousal*. New York: Wiley.

Index

Tiebout, H., 77, 89–90, 277
Toennies, F., 164, 165
Tolerance, described, 40
Toxic shame, 157–158
Transference, 215–217
Treatment
  abstinence, 197–199
  acupuncture, 258–259
  addictive rage, 210–211
  Antabuse, 211–212
  behavioral techniques, 260
  burdens of, 278
  cognitive techniques, 192–193,
    208–209
  confrontation
    of denial, 193–194
    timing of, 195–197
  countertransference, 217–218
  couple therapy, 273–275
  denial, example of, 194–195
  disillusionment and, 275–276
  dream analysis, 218–222
  dynamic techniques in, 191–192
  expectations, 228–229
  family therapy, 253–256
  gestalt therapy, 263–264
  group therapy, 256–257
  hypnosis, 259–260
  inpatient treatment, 236–252
  intervention, 265–268
  least-harm approach, 199
  length of, 232
  methadone, 270–271
  mourning and, 264–265
  multimodal treatment, 232–234
  network therapy, 252–253
  neurobiofeedback, 257–258
  questioning, 229–230
  relapse prevention, 268–270
  settings and modalities, 234–236
  situational factors, 204–205
  sponsors, 201–202

  surrender experience, 202–203
  transference, 215–217
  twelve-step program alternatives,
    230–231
  twelve-step programs, 199–201
Tri-dimensional personality theory,
  addiction, 154–156
Triggers, described, 151–152
Trimpley, J., 231
Trotter, T., 10, 77
True self, 175
Twelve-step programs
  alternatives to, 230–231
  cognitive treatment, 208
  described, 32–34
  Klein and, 132–134
  mokus, 203–204
  religion, 205–208
  sponsors, 201–202
  working with, 199–201

Uniqueness, terminal, 225–227
Ur-affect, 60

van der Kolk, B. A., 176, 177

Wallace, J., 262–263
White, H. R., 53
Wilsnack, S., 153
Wilson, B., 10, 89, 126, 127, 128,
  163, 203, 261
Winnicott, D. W., 73, 105, 114, 116–
  117, 175, 232
Winokur, G., 23, 26
Withdrawal
  described, 37–38
  irrational behavior and, 39–40
Witkin, H. A., 45, 46
Wurmser, L., 31, 64, 77, 92–94, 158,
  175, 193

Zuckerman, M., 23, 28